IanHay

6⁄6 2 50

THE SECOND ADVENT

THE ORIGIN OF
THE NEW TESTAMENT DOCTRINE

BY THE SAME AUTHOR

Thomas Glasson: Lay Preacher

(Wayside Book No. 12: Epworth Press)

TO

LAWRANCE O. BROOKER

THE SECOND ADVENT

The Origin of the New Testament Doctrine

BY

T. FRANCIS GLASSON

Bachelor of Divinity
Master of Arts in Classics (Ancient Philosophy)
1st Class Theology Honours in Greek Testament and Apocrypha
Doctor of Divinity
(*University of London*)

THE EPWORTH PRESS
(EDGAR C. BARTON)
25–35 City Road, London, E.C.1

BOOK
PRODUCTION
WAR ECONOMY
STANDARD

*This book is published in complete conformity
with the authorized economy standards*

Made in Great Britain

PREFACE TO SECOND EDITION

THIS edition does not differ from the first except for a few minor corrections and some short additions at the end of the Epilogue and elsewhere. A few further points suggested by reviews and correspondence may be mentioned here briefly.

1. It has been suggested that too prominent a place is given to the Caligula affair. As the Thessalonian correspondence receives special attention, it was inevitable that this episode should be referred to in connection with 2 Thessalonians ii. In the chapter on 'The Note of Imminence', however, it will be observed that half a dozen factors are mentioned of which the Caligula affair is but one. The factor to which I should assign most importance on this particular point is the one mentioned on p. 194—that the spirit of intense expectancy which existed in Judaism at this period, as evidenced, for instance, by John the Baptist, was carried over into the Church, naturally taking on in the process a Christian colouring.

2. Something should perhaps have been said about the use of symbolic language in Scripture. Difficulties have often been needlessly created by taking as literal what was originally spoken in the poetic style characteristic of Semitic speech.

3. A suggestion has been made (by Dr. E. L. Allen in a private communication) that our Lord's predictions of triumph beyond the Cross, which were actually fulfilled in the Resurrection, may have been of so vague a kind that some further fulfilment was looked for. The main framework of the thesis would, I think, leave room for suggestions of this kind.

While one cannot hope to carry every reader with him in all the details of every passage, differences on isolated points obviously need not imperil the main lines of the case propounded.

34 CLARENCE ROAD   T. F. G.
   WINDSOR

PREFACE TO FIRST EDITION

THE writing of this treatise was completed in the summer of 1943, but mainly owing to war conditions it is only now making its appearance. I should like to express my thanks to my former tutor, Professor F. B. Clogg, M.A., B.D., and to Professor W. F. Howard, M.A., D.D., for their counsel and encouragement. I am also deeply indebted to the Dr. Williams' Library. My wife has given valuable help at every stage, including the proof-reading.

The University of London has accepted the work as an approved thesis for the degree of Doctor of Divinity, and its production has been aided by a grant from the Publication Fund of the University.

T. F. G.

34 CLARENCE ROAD
WINDSOR

ABBREVIATIONS

E.B.   Encyclopaedia Biblica.

H.D.B.   Hastings' Dictionary of the Bible.

LXX.   Septuagint; the Greek Version of the Old Testament.

N.T.   New Testament.

O.T.   Old Testament.

S.B.E.   Sacred Books of the East.

Where foreign works are cited by English titles, quotations and page references are from the English translations.

CONTENTS

Part Three

The Parousia in the Early Church

Part Four

The Parousia in Jewish Writings of the Christian Era

INTRODUCTION

In his *Collected Essays*, T. H. Huxley refers to the view that Jesus foretold His speedy return to the earth in glory, and makes the comment: 'If he believed and taught that, then assuredly he was under an illusion, and he is responsible for that which the mere effluxion of time has demonstrated to be a prodigious error.'

Every New Testament writer refers to the doctrine of the Second Advent, or the Parousia, to give it its technical name, but a fixed point in our inquiry is provided by the letters of St. Paul to the Thessalonians. These are held to be the earliest of the New Testament writings (though some adherents of the South Galatian theory would place Galatians earlier), and since there was on this subject no division of opinion between the Apostle and his fellow-Christians they demonstrate that at the middle of the first century the Christian Church held definite beliefs concerning Christ's return, an event which in their view lay in the near future. These two letters also provide us with the fullest description of the Parousia to be found in the New Testament:

> For this we say unto you by the word of the Lord, that we that are alive, that are left unto the coming of the Lord, shall in no wise precede them that are fallen asleep. For the Lord himself shall descend from heaven, with a shout, with the voice of the archangel, and with the trump of God: and the dead in Christ shall rise first: then we that are alive, that are left, shall together with them be caught up in the clouds, to meet the Lord in the air: and so shall we ever be with the Lord. Wherefore comfort one another with these words (1 Thessalonians iv. 15–18).

This is what the Church believed about the year A.D. 50. We are to inquire into the question: How did this belief arise? Did the Church derive it from the teaching of Jesus? If so, how did He in turn arrive at this conviction?

The usual answer is that Jesus Himself taught the doctrine of His return in glory, and while some maintain that He set no time for this event, others ascribe to Him the view which Huxley found so erroneous.

Many scholars take the line that we must in honesty admit that Jesus was mistaken; He expected the end of the world to take place in a short time and it did not occur. This, however, does not impair (it is said) the greatness of His teaching, nor need it imperil the Catholic doctrine of His Person. References to the Davidic authorship of Psalm cx or the Mosaic authorship of the Pentateuch are similarly explained; indeed, Jesus would not have lived a truly human life unless He had accepted certain limitations in knowledge.

One cannot help feeling, however, that the doctrine of the Parousia carries with it certain conceptions of the divine character, and has far more serious results than mere acceptance of the authorship of a psalm. Nevertheless, one respects the honesty of scholars who loyally accept uncongenial results because their devotion to truth demands it.

While it is generally admitted that some of the Gospel references to the subject are due to the writers rather than the Master Himself, two considerations strengthen the view that it formed part of the genuine teaching of Jesus:

1. It is said that the doctrine was taught by contemporary Judaism, and that Jesus took over a ready-made thought-form and applied it to Himself, regarding Himself as the Messiah.

2. Stronger still is the argument that we cannot account for the vivid hope of the early Church on any other supposition than that it was based upon the Master's own promise.

In the present work the pre-supposition that the

Parousia was a popular dogma of Jesus' time is first examined. A discussion of the teaching of Jesus on the subject follows. Then comes an examination of the beliefs of the early Church, and an answer to the original question is submitted. Part Four, on later Jewish teaching, is added to round off the main argument.

Part One

The Parousia in Jewish Literature Extant in the Time of Jesus

CHAPTER I

THE OLD TESTAMENT

IF Jesus took over the conception of a Parousia from current Jewish teaching, we must inquire where exactly this doctrine is to be found in pre-Christian literature. It is certainly absent from the Old Testament, the most important source for the teaching of Jesus.

The Old Testament prophecies make frequent mention of a Messianic Age, a golden time of righteousness and prosperity when the knowledge of God is to cover the earth and even the animals are at peace. In some passages a personal Messiah is referred to, e.g. Isaiah xi. 1–9. Whenever this Messianic king is mentioned he is described in human terms and is envisaged as a son of David's house, born of the tribe of Judah. Nowhere is it suggested that he will come in visible glory from the sky.

Even the book of *Daniel* is no exception; indeed, while the kingdom is prominent here, no Messiah is mentioned. In the great vision of chapter vii four beasts represent four empires: the lion=Babylon, the bear=Media, the leopard =Persia, the ten-horned monster=Greece. They are succeeded by 'one like unto a son of man' who comes with the clouds to the Ancient of Days. The interpretation given in the same chapter shows that this human figure represents 'the people of the saints of the Most High'

(v. 27). The beast-like kingdoms give place to the more humane kingdom of God. 'Humanity is contrasted with animality; and the human form, as opposed to the bestial, teaches that the last kingdom will be, not like the Gentile kingdoms, a supremacy of brute force, but a supremacy ostensibly humane and spiritual' (Driver).

It should be noted that even if the figure in v. 13 be taken mistakenly to represent the Messiah, there is still no descent from heaven, for the same verse continues: 'and he came even to the Ancient of Days, and they brought him near before him. 14. And there was given him dominion and glory etc.' Montgomery (in the *International Critical Commentary*) translates:

I was seeing in the night visions,
And behold with the clouds of heaven: one like a man was coming,
And to the Ancient he came: and before him he was presented.

He adds: 'The idea is that of a royal audience. . . . There follows in v. 14 the description of the viceregal investiture of the humanlike being.'

The passage, it is clear, speaks neither of a Messiah nor of a descent from heaven. If Daniel was written, as is usually maintained, about the year 165 B.C., this figure appears to have been taken from Enoch xiv, a chapter which belongs to the pre-Maccabean section of that book. Enoch himself is described as ascending to heaven and being brought into the divine presence. If we place the two passages side by side the dependence of Daniel vii on Enoch xiv is obvious.

R. H. Charles in his editions of Enoch gives good reasons for assigning a pre-Maccabean date to vi-xxxvi. This section of Enoch is an important source of the Book of Daniel which came later, a source which some commentators ignore, or alternatively they imply that the dependence was in the other direction. The Watchers of

Daniel come from Enoch vi–xxxvi; the names of the angels Michael and Gabriel which are found in Daniel appear earlier in this section, where they are mentioned for the first time in Jewish literature. Even a phrase like the 'dissolving of doubts' (Daniel v. 12) may come from Enoch (see viii. 3).

But our present concern is with Enoch xiv and its connection with Daniel vii. The same scene is found in both; God is enthroned and surrounded by angels; a man is borne on the clouds and approaches the divine presence. In the former passage the human figure is Enoch himself, who is also the speaker.

Enoch xiv

8. And the vision was shown to me thus: Behold, in the vision clouds invited me . . . and the winds in the vision caused me to fly and lifted me upward, and bore me into heaven. (verses 9–17 describe the crystal walls and the divine dwelling-place).

18. And I looked and saw therein a lofty throne: its appearance was as crystal, and the wheels thereof as the shining sun, and there was the vision of cherubim.

19. And from underneath the throne came streams of flaming fire so that I could not look thereon.

20. And the Great Glory sat thereon, and His raiment shone more brightly than the sun and was whiter than any snow.

22. The flaming fire was round about Him, and a great fire stood before Him, and none around could draw nigh Him: ten thousand times ten thousand (stood) before Him, yet He needed no counsellor.

24. . . . and the Lord called me with His own mouth, and said to me: 'Come hither, Enoch, and hear my word.'

Daniel vii. 9–13 (omitting 11–12, which are concerned with the 'beasts')

9. I beheld till thrones were placed, and one that was ancient of days did sit: his raiment was white as snow, and the

hair of his head like pure wool; his throne was fiery flames, and the wheels thereof flaming fire.

10. A fiery stream issued and came forth from before him: thousand thousands ministered unto him, and ten thousand times ten thousand stood before him: the judgement was set, and the books were opened.

13. I saw in the night visions, and, behold, there came with the clouds of heaven one like unto a son of man, and he came even to the ancient of days, and they brought him near before him.

The literary connection between these two passages is unmistakable. The same scene is represented and there are many points of identity. Both accounts were originally written in Aramaic and the original resemblance was probably even closer. Among the more striking coincidences the following may be noted:

Daniel vii. 9: throne . . . and the wheels thereof.

Enoch xiv. 18: throne . . . and the wheels thereof.

Daniel vii. 10: fiery stream . . . ten thousand times ten thousand stood before him.

Enoch xiv. 19: streams of flaming fire; v. 22: ten thousand times ten thousand (stood) before him.

Daniel vii. 9: His raiment was white as snow.

Enoch xiv. 20: His raiment . . . whiter than any snow.

Daniel vii. 13: I saw in the night visions, and, behold, there came with the clouds of heaven one like unto a son of man.

Enoch xiv. 8: . . . Behold, in the vision clouds invited me.

Daniel vii. 13 thus corresponds to Enoch xiv. 8. In addition to (*a*), the general point that both occur in similar contexts and describe a human figure approaching the divine presence, there are close verbal resemblances: (*b*) one has 'in the night visions', the other 'in the vision'; (*c*) both have the word 'behold'; (*d*) both speak of 'clouds'.

It does not follow from this that the writer of Daniel vii identified the one like unto a son of man with Enoch; he merely drew upon the imagery of the earlier work in depicting this symbolic figure, which in his vision represents 'the people of the saints of the Most High'. We may compare Slavonic Enoch iii. 1 where in another account of Enoch's ascent to the throne of God he is again associated with clouds: 'It came to pass, when Enoch had told his sons, that the angels took him on to their wings and bore him up on to the first heaven and placed him on the clouds.'

Comparison of the two visions given above shows that the 'original' of the one like unto a son of man was Enoch himself. There is therefore no need to delve into primeval chaos to find the source of this conception, or to introduce the Babylonian 'Urmensch', as some have suggested. The answer lies closer at hand. It is not surprising that in Enoch lxxi the identification, son of Man=Enoch, reappears. It may be pointed out here that in that chapter we have a third account of the royal audience scene, which is plainly based upon the two we have considered (Enoch xiv and Daniel vii); and while the words 'came with the clouds of heaven' are not quoted there or anywhere else in Enoch they appear to have been interpreted as referring to a coming into the divine presence. But this will need attention later.

Our main concern at the moment is with the correct interpretation of Daniel vii. The use made of it in later times will come up at various points in the discussion. While it is true that verse 13 was later misunderstood and taken to refer to a personal Messiah and to his visible descent in glory, one would hardly expect that the passage by itself could give rise to the Parousia conception; for even those who individualized the one like unto a son of man would presumably read the whole sentence, and the remainder of the verse says explicitly 'and he came even to the ancient of days, and they brought him near before him'.

B

It may be noted that the Book of Common Prayer appropriately appoints Daniel vii. 9–15 to be read on Ascension Day, associating with it the story of Elijah's ascent to heaven. Similarly, in Cyprian's *Testimonies against the Jews*, Daniel vii. 13–14 is quoted under the heading, 'That after He had risen again He should receive from His Father all power, and His power should be everlasting.'

CHAPTER 2

NON-BIBLICAL LITERATURE

WE have seen that the Old Testament teaching concerning the Messiah makes no mention of a Parousia, a glorious descent from heaven. But there are other important writings outside the canon which must be taken into account.

The Apocrypha has nothing which calls for consideration, traces of Messianism being rare and these in line with the Old Testament. The Apocrypha is, roughly speaking, the excess of the Alexandrian Jews' Greek 'canon' over the Hebrew, and 2 Esdras (sometimes known as 4 Ezra) did not belong to either collection. It is absent from all copies of the Septuagint, it is not included among the apocryphal books in Luther's Bible, in the Roman Catholic Bible it is relegated to the appendix, and it belongs to the period following the fall of Jerusalem in A.D. 70. In all these matters it differs from Wisdom, Ecclesiasticus, Judith, etc.; and though usually included in English editions of the Apocrypha it belongs rather to the apocalyptic writings (see below).

In the Apocrypha proper there is no mention of the Messiah at all, but there are a few traces here and there of the Messianic era. One example may be quoted from the song of praise in Tobit xiii. 1–18 concerning Jerusalem:

That thy tabernacle may be builded in thee again with joy,
And that he may make glad in thee all that are captives,
And love in thee all that are miserable and all the generations
    of eternity.
A bright light shall shine unto all the ends of the earth;
Many nations shall come from afar,

And the inhabitants of the utmost ends of the earth unto thy
  holy name.
With their gifts also in their hands unto the King of heaven,
Generations of generations utter rejoicing in thee,
And thy name that is elect unto the generations of eternity.

(Verses 10–11).

The apocalyptic writings are of more importance for our
subject as they have numerous references to a personal
Messiah. One would gather from some writers that while
the Old Testament gives a human Messiah, the apocalyptic writings generally present a superhuman figure who
descends from heaven and breaks into human history in
a catastrophic fashion. E. F. Scott, in *The Kingdom and
the Messiah*, which may be taken as representative, several
times distinguishes the Old Testament hope of a prince
from the apocalyptic vision of an angelic being. Similarly
A. Schweitzer writes in his *Quest of the Historical Jesus*:

. . . if the eschatological hope was generally current, was it
the prophetic or the apocalyptic form of that hope? We know
the Messianic expectations of the prophets; we know the
apocalyptic picture as drawn by Daniel, and following him,
by Enoch and the Psalms of Solomon before the coming of
Jesus, and by the Apocalypses of Ezra and Baruch about the
time of the destruction of Jerusalem.

One would gather from this that the prophets of the
Old Testament stood on one side with a human king as
Messiah and the apocalyptic writings stood on the other
with a supernatural figure who should come from heaven
in glory. When we examine the apocalyptic writings,
however, we find in most of them the Old Testament
conception of an earthly king. 2 Esdras and 2 Baruch
must be left out of account as they belong to the latter
part of the first century A.D.—indeed, the apocalypse
contained in 2 Esdras was probably put forward in its
complete form about A.D. 120. They will be considered

in Part Four together with various Sibylline Oracles[1] dated considerably later than the ministry of Jesus; but they cannot rightly be adduced in a study of Christian origins.

In the apocalyptic writings which are usually held to have been extant in the time of Jesus, we find the Messiah presented as a rule in the familiar colours of Old Testament prophecy. The Psalms of Solomon which are specifically cited by Schweitzer as giving the 'apocalyptic' view prove on examination to do nothing of the kind; instead there is the familiar picture of a warrior king, a son of David. Even in the book of Enoch four out of the five parts are either silent on the subject of the Messiah or else speak of him as a human king. The sole exception in this literature is the part of Enoch known as the Similitudes (xxxvii-lxxi); this demands closer consideration and will occupy us in the succeeding chapters. But the fact is noteworthy that the pre-Christian apocalypses generally do not describe the Messiah as descending in glory from heaven.

In these writings, which may be found in Vol. 2 of Charles's *Apocrypha and Pseudepigrapha of the Old Testament*, there is a certain amount of variety; indeed, the 'fixed

---

[1] *Sib. Or.*, iii. 652 should be mentioned here, since it is usually dated in the B.C. period:

'And then from the sun God will send a king.'

(a) 'From the sun,' ἀπ' ἠελίοιο, may mean from the east; cf. Revelation vii. 2, xvi. 12, and Isaiah xli. 25, LXX. In Charles's *Apocrypha and Pseudepigrapha* it is translated 'from the sunrise'.

(b) Alternatively, it may be an example of the exalted language used of kings at that period (Hofstil) and which became attached to the Jewish Messianic teaching. Bousset in *Die Religion des Judentums* (1926), p. 486, quotes an Egyptian oracle which has the same phrase; a king who comes from the sun (ἀπο ἠλιου) reigns for fifty-five years. Reitzenstein identifies the king as Euergetes II.

In a similar way, the *Sib. Or.* speak of Cyrus as from heaven, οὐρανοθεν (iii. 286).

In neither case is a literal descent from the sky implied.

Lanchester (in Charles) includes the following in his note on *Sib. Or.*, iii. 652: 'Holtzmann thinks of Simon Maccabeus as the heaven-sent king.'

eschatological programme' often spoken of is a figment of the imagination. Sometimes an eternal kingdom on the present earth is envisaged; sometimes a new heaven and earth follow the judgement and the destruction of the old universe; elsewhere the kingdom on earth is a temporary one. Then again, the eternal kingdom on earth was sometimes associated with a Messiah (as apparently in Enoch lxxxiii-xc), sometimes there was an eternal kingdom on earth without a Messiah (Enoch vi-xxxvi).

Usually the Messiah comes from the tribe of Judah, as in the Book of Jubilees:

And to Judah he said:
May the Lord give thee strength and power
To tread down all that hate thee;
A prince shalt thou be, thou and one of thy sons, over the sons of Jacob;
May thy name and the name of thy sons go forth and traverse every land and region.
Then shall the Gentiles fear before thy face,
And all the nations shall quake.

(xxxi. 18.)

In the Testaments of the Twelve Patriarchs, the Messiah comes from Judah in the Testament of Judah xxiv (Judah is addressing his sons):

Then shall the sceptre of my kingdom shine forth;
And from your root shall arise a stem;
And from it shall grow a rod of righteousness to the Gentiles,
To judge and to save all that call upon the Lord.

But elsewhere in the Testaments he is from the tribe of Levi; see Testament of Levi xviii: 'Then shall the Lord raise up a new priest', etc. Other passages held to refer to Messiah's Levitic lineage are not conclusive (Testament of Reuben vi. 7–12; Testament of Levi viii. 14; Testament of Dan. v. 10–11, 'the tribe of Judah and of Levi'; Testament of Joseph xix. 5–9).

In the Zadokite Fragment yet another conception of the Messiah's genealogy emerges, e.g. ix. 29: 'until there shall arise the Messiah from Aaron and from Israel'.

The Assumption of Moses and Slavonic Enoch are probably to be dated in the former half of the first century A.D., and neither of them mentions the Messiah.

It is unnecessary for us to distinguish further the wide variety of conceptions connected with the future, which this apocalyptic and pseudepigraphic literature represents. We are concerned with the sole point of the Parousia, the descent of the Messiah in visible glory from heaven; we are trying to find on what basis the common view rests which finds a heavenly Messiah as a main thought of the pre-Christian literature concerned. And it is sufficient for our present purpose to indicate that the great bulk of this literature is either silent concerning the Messiah or else speaks of him as a human king born in the community. The words of Psalms of Solomon xvii are typical:

Behold, O Lord, and raise up unto them their king, the son of David,

At the time in the which Thou seest, O God, that he may reign over Israel Thy servant.

And gird him with strength, that he may shatter unrighteous rulers,

And that he may purge Jerusalem from nations that trample her down to destruction.

Wisely, righteously, he shall thrust out sinners from the inheritance,

He shall destroy the pride of the sinner as a potter's vessel.

With a rod of iron he shall break in pieces all their substance,

He shall destroy the godless nations with the word of his mouth.

(For the imagery see Isaiah xi. 4 and Psalm ii. 9.)

In the Gospels, such passages as throw light on current

Jewish hopes point in the direction of a human Messiah born on earth. Thus it was mooted that John the Baptist might be the Messiah, Luke iii. 15. Such suggestions would have been impossible had the current belief been that Messiah would come from heaven in visible splendour.

CHAPTER 3

THE BOOK OF ENOCH

In 1770 the great Scottish traveller Bruce reached Abyssinia in the course of his African journeys. After rediscovering the source of the Blue Nile, he left the country for the north, bringing away with him two copies of the Book of Enoch in the Ethiopic language. Up to that time only fragments of the book were known, and even to-day the only ancient version of the entire work is the Ethiopic,[1] though we have important parts in Greek. Unfortunately, the Greek does not include any part of the Similitudes.

There are five main sections, belonging to different dates and giving widely different teaching:

1. i-xxxvi, of which i-v was probably added latest of all as an introduction to the whole collection.
2. xxxvii-lxxi, the Similitudes.
3. lxxii-lxxxii, the Book of Heavenly Luminaries.
4. lxxxiii-xc, the Dream Visions.
5. xci-civ, including the Apocalypse of Weeks.

They are held together by their association with the patriarch Enoch and by certain themes which run through all of them: (a) all speak of the coming judgement, and the O.T. passages which refer to God's advent to judge the world are amplified; (b) another prominent theme is the angels who led mankind astray; the relevant passages are influenced by Genesis vi, and there is

[1] In the Abyssinian Bible it comes before Job. The Imperial Ethiopian Legation, London, kindly informs me that 'the Book of Enoch is admitted into the Old Testament Canon by the Ethiopian Christian Church as well as the Israelites (Felasha), who have the same Old Testament Bible as that of their Christian brothers'.

considerable development of angelology; (c) a third theme which runs through practically every part is concerned with the 'geography' of the next world; whole chapters are given up to descriptions of the unseen realm, the places of punishment or bliss. It was believed that Enoch was during his lifetime allowed to see the secrets of the unknown and after writing them down was later translated to heaven without dying.[1]

Four of the five sections are fairly easy to understand, and though there is much which is bizarre and startling the development is orderly and straightforward. Chapters vi-xxxvi describe Enoch's journeys in heaven and Hades, his introduction to the divine presence; God's coming to the earth for judgement is followed by the eternal kingdom on the present earth. The ideas of this section are particularly crude; it is said that God will sit on a mountain 'when He shall come down to visit the earth with goodness' (xxv. 3), and in the new age the earth will be very fruitful and men will have thousands of children. No Messiah is mentioned. Chapters lxxii-lxxxii are concerned with astronomical secrets, but here again God's coming for judgement is mentioned. The Dream Visions, lxxxiii-xc, give a résumé of the history of the world up to the time of the writer (about 160 B.C.) and then go on to describe God's descent to the earth. He takes His place in Palestine and, accompanied by an angel, judges the world. Later comes the Messianic Age, when the people of God are ruled by a Messiah who is born from their own community. In xci-civ there is no Messiah, but a temporary kingdom on the earth. The final judgement, the destruction of heaven and earth, and the creation of a new heaven also appear in this section.

[1] (a) cf. xxv. 3, xxxviii, xlv-xlviii, lx, lxi. 8, lxii-lxiii, lxxvii. i, lxxx. 8, lxxxi. 4, lxxxiv. 4, xc, xci. 7, xciv-xcvii, xcviii. 7-c, cii *ff.* (b) vi-xi, xii-xvi, lv. 4-lvi. 4, lxiv, lxv, lxvii-lxix, lxxxiv. 4, lxxxvi-lxxxviii, xc. 21-27; c. 4. (c) xiv, xvii-xxxvi, xxxix-xli, xliii-xliv, xlviii, lii-liv, lix, lx, lxxii-lxxx may be included here, though they are mostly astronomical, ciii. 7-8.

When we turn, however, to the remaining section, the *Similitudes*, xxxvii-lxxi, it is obvious that the work is not in an orderly sequence and it is most difficult to find uniformity in the teaching. There are three distinct 'parables', as they are sometimes called, xxxvii-xliv, xlv-lvii and lviii-lxxi (strictly lviii-lxix), and the work has a superficial appearance of order; but it is as though a pile of disjointed fragments have been tied into three bundles. The usual theme of judgement is prominent throughout, and the most remarkable feature is the place given to the Messiah, who is not born on the earth, but is in heaven under the wings of the Lord of Spirits. (In lxxi. 14 he is described as 'born unto righteousness'.) He is known by various names, the most usual being 'the Elect One', a title found in all three similitudes. Another name of great importance is 'the Son of man', evidently taken from Daniel vii; this title is not found in the first Similitude, but it occurs in xlvi, xlviii, lxii, lxix, lxx-lxxi (lxiii. 11 is probably an interpolation).

It has been suggested that there were two main sources behind the Similitudes, one of which spoke of the Son of man and the other of the Elect One. In addition there are several passages which originally belonged to a distinct work, the Book of Noah; lvi. 5-lvii. 3*a* probably comes from a fourth source, and lxxi, or lxx-lxxi, from yet another. It is therefore probable that five different writers had a hand in the Similitudes of Enoch and the result is great confusion. It is impossible to get a clear idea of the teaching because inconsistent elements are present. R. H. Charles says that this section 'is in a fragmentary condition'; according to his analysis[1] the 'Elect One' source differs from the 'Son of man' source in recognizing 'the judgement of the sword xxxviii. 5, xlviii. 8-10, and the attack of the hostile Gentiles on Jerusalem, lvi, the progressive conversion of the Gentiles who had

[1] cf. p. 65 in his 1912 edition of Enoch.

no part in oppressing Israel, l. 2–4, and the triumphant return of the Dispersion, lvii. . . . There is no hint of the judgement of the sword in the ("Son of man") source.'

However, in spite of these inconsistencies, we can clearly trace the three main themes mentioned earlier, (*a*) the judgement, (*b*) the angels who led mankind astray, and (*c*) descriptions of the unseen world. Judgement is sometimes said to be carried through by God Himself,[1] sometimes by the Messiah.[2] Again, it is variously a judgement of angels, of the kings of the earth, or of mankind.

The distinctive feature of the Similitudes as compared with the other sections is that when God appears for the judgement the Messiah appears too, and the latter takes part both in the judgement and the reign which follows.[3] We can trace here the influence of Daniel vii. 13, whence the term 'Son of man' has been derived. The Dream Visions (lxxxiii–xc) had also been influenced by this chapter of Daniel; and, as we have already seen, when the judgement was set God was assisted by an angel, who is probably to be identified with Michael (xc. 20). This writer evidently thought that the phrase in Daniel vii. 13 stood for Michael; several modern scholars have taken the same view. The Messiah of the Dream Visions, the 'white bull' of xc. 37, does not appear until the kingdom is set up after the close of the judgement, and he is born from the community. Thus in lxxxiii–xc God is assisted

[1] xlvii. 3: 'In those days I saw the Head of Days when He seated himself upon the throne of His glory, and the books of the living were opened before Him. . . .'

l. 4: 'And He [i.e. the Lord of Spirits] is righteous also in His judgement. . . . At His judgement the unrepentant shall perish before Him.' cf. liii. 2.

[2] lxii: the judgement of kings (2: 'And the Lord of Spirits seated him on the throne of His glory', etc. The MSS. have 'sat' and not 'seated him', but in verse 5 'that Son of man' is described as sitting on the throne of his glory); xlix. 4, lxix. 27; he judges Azazel in lv. 4, and angels in lxi. 8 (xlv. 3 is probably 'choose', not 'try').

[3] Heaven and earth are transformed, xlv. 4–5, not destroyed and replaced by a new creation. li. 5: 'the earth shall rejoice'. cf. with verse 1.

by Michael in the judgement, and in the reign by the human Messiah.

In xxxvii-lxxi these two offices have been combined, and the Messiah not only assists at the judgement, but he is also king in the new age which follows. Thus while God still judges and reigns, the Messiah is also described as fulfilling these functions.

This conception of the Messiah is different from anything we have previously found. Instead of a Son of David Messiah who is a human king born on the earth, the Messiah now appears as an angelic being who is pre-existent, living in heaven under the wings of the Head of Days,[1] until the time comes when both appear for the great judgement, he himself having part in the judgement and sitting on a throne of glory. But while this conception presents a marked contrast with that found in the O.T. and in those non-canonical works which refer to a Messiah, it presents also marked differences when compared with the N.T. teaching concerning the Parousia. Let us consider the following contrasts:

A. God is still present even when the Elect One is acting; the latter is throughout kept in close association with the Lord of Spirits, and the two appear together. In lxii the Son of man is seen on the throne of glory by the kings and mighty, and as part of the same picture 'the Lord of Spirits will so press them that they shall hastily go forth from his presence' (10). As for the righteous and elect, 'the Lord of Spirits will abide over them, and with that Son of man shall they eat and lie down and rise up for ever and ever' (14); cf. xlix.

This is a very different conception from the N.T. Parousia which is nowhere expounded in this fashion. In the N.T. the Lord Jesus Christ is described as descending

---

[1] xxxix. 6-7. But, according to MSS. variations, 'the Elect One' may be 'the place of the elect'; and 'his' and 'his days' should perhaps be 'their' and 'their days'.

from heaven in glory; the Parousia passages are unanimous on this point, none of them speaking of God accompanied by Christ.

How the Similitudes envisage the appearing of the Messiah together with God is doubtful. The N.T. gives a detailed picture in which the Messiah descends in glory and fire with his angels, and we are apt to read Enoch in the light of our Christian preconceptions. Nowhere in Enoch is the Messiah said to descend from heaven, or to come with clouds, or even to come. His pre-existence with God is described, and his later session on the judgement throne, but no account is given of the mode of transition from one state to the other. As inconsistent elements are placed together, it is impossible to work out a harmonious picture which will find room for all the facts. At times the Messiah is in heaven judging the angels (lxi. 8: 'And the Lord of Spirits placed the Elect One on the throne of glory. And he shall judge all the works of the holy above in the heaven'); at other times the judgement appears to be taking place on earth (e.g. liii). A reader of the times when this literature was produced would presumably interpret the Similitudes in the light of the other sections, and would conclude that when God descended in glory for the judgement, He would be accompanied by the Messiah. Just as in lxxxiii-xc, when God descends to judge and sits on a throne in Palestine, He is assisted by Michael, so here He is assisted by the Elect One or Son of man.

And unrighteousness shall disappear as a shadow,
And have no continuance;
Because the Elect One standeth before the Lord of Spirits . . .
And he shall judge the secret things,
And none shall be able to utter a lying word before him;
For he is the Elect One before the Lord of Spirits according
   to His good pleasure.

(xlix. 2, 4.)

Charles rightly summarizes the great advent in the words: 'Suddenly the Head of Days will appear, and with Him the Son of man.'[1]

B. Other characteristic features are different in the two cases. For instance, in the N.T. the Messiah is to be accompanied at His coming by angels (Mark viii. 38, xiii. 27; 2 Thessalonians i. 7; 1 Thessalonians iii. 13); nowhere is there any hint in Enoch of the Messiah having an angelic retinue.[2]

Again, the trumpet, connected with the Parousia in 1 Corinthians xv. 52, 1 Thessalonians iv. 16, Matthew xxiv. 31, is absent from Enoch, as are the fire (2 Thessalonians i. 8) and shout (1 Thessalonians iv. 16). Closer study of the N.T. phraseology will come later; but at this point we note that the N.T. conception is not explained by Enoch and there are fundamental differences. Whether we call the Messiah's appearance in the Similitudes a Parousia is a matter of personal choice; the word itself is not applied to the Messiah by Jewish writers, and it is wise to reserve it for the Christian doctrine, in view of the numerous distinctive features.

It is sometimes carelessly said that the Similitudes describe the Son of man as coming with the clouds of heaven. This is not correct; nowhere in Enoch does this phrase occur. It may be said that since Daniel vii is being drawn upon, we must interpret the 'appearing' in the light of the Son of man's coming with clouds in Daniel vii. 13. But this is not so; Daniel vii. 13 describes the approach of the Son of man to God and is apparently

---

[1] *Eschatology* (2nd ed.), p. 265.

[2] Some have attempted to find the Messiah's angelic retinue in lxi. 10. It will be sufficient to quote the passage: 'And He [the Lord of Spirits] will summon all the host of the heavens, and all the holy ones above, and the host of God, the Cherubin, Seraphin, and Ophannin, and all the angels of power, and all the angels of principalities, and the Elect One, and the other powers on the earth [and] over the water. 11. On that day shall they raise one voice . . . and shall all say with one voice: "Blessed is He, and may the name of the Lord of Spirits be blessed for ever and ever." '

so understood in Enoch lxxi where the same scene is repeated.

C. The chapter just referred to (lxxi) is of some importance, and the language shows that the writer has drawn upon and combined Daniel vii and Enoch xiv; some phrases come from one, and some from the other source. Phrases like Head of Days and Son of man are found in Daniel and not in Enoch xiv; while others like the 'structure built of crystal' and 'that house' go back to Enoch xiv, not to Daniel. We saw earlier that in Enoch xiv it was Enoch himself who entered the divine presence; this teaching reappears in Enoch lxxi, and the Son of man is explicitly identified with Enoch who is told: 'Thou art the Son of man who art born unto righteousness' (14); cf. also the following verses, which are also in the second person.

We saw earlier that the writer of Daniel vii drew upon the imagery of Enoch xiv, and the human figure became in Daniel a symbol of the saints of the Most High. The exaltation (vii. 14) of this human figure was added to the original picture. In Enoch lxxi, the individual conception has reasserted itself and the original identification with Enoch reappears; in addition Enoch is exalted to Messianic dignity, a feature apparently suggested by the language of Daniel vii. 14. The writer would perhaps find some confirmation for this bold step in the consideration that Enoch and Elijah were the only two men who did not die; Elijah was already designated as the forerunner (Malachi iv); Enoch remained to fulfil the work of Messiah.

Whether this identification was due to the combination of the two earlier passages or not, the fact remains that Enoch is in lxxi designated Son of Man and Messiah.[1]

The question now arises: Is Enoch lxxi in agreement

---

[1] In rabbinic literature Enoch is identified with Metatron, i.e. the highest ministering spirit, who stands next to God and represents His rulership over the universe (*Jewish Encyclopaedia*, I, 676); cf. Jubilees iv. 23.

with the rest of the Similitudes on this point, or was it added by a different writer? There are parts where the seer seems to be distinguished from the Messiah. Further, xlviii. 6 speaks of Messiah's existence before the creation; could this have been written of Enoch?

It is probable that this chapter has been added by a later writer or editor, who has not brought the earlier chapters into harmony with his interpretation. If this were the case, it would explain the inconsistent features in this matter: in some places Enoch speaks of the Son of man as a different person from himself, while in lxxi he is told that he is himself the Son of man. Charles has got round the difficulty by altering the text to 'This is the Son of man . . .' instead of 'Thou art the Son of man', and making similar alterations which have no MS. support whatever, and by inserting a 'lost' passage between verses 13 and 14. This drastic method, however, is really cutting the knot.

We have here, however, another feature which, like those previously mentioned, differentiates the teaching of Enoch from that of the N.T.

Thus, while Enoch xxxvii *ff.* is unique in Jewish writings, it presents marked differences from the eschatology of the N.T., and we may conclude this section with the summary statement that in the Similitudes:

1. The Messiah appears simultaneously with God at the judgement.

2. We look in vain for such characteristic N.T. features as the Messiah's coming with angels, fire, trumpet, etc.; and

3. The identification of the Son of man with Enoch makes any connection even more remote and unlikely. The conception is in many important respects different from the Parousia found in the N.T., and it is difficult to believe that the latter grew from roots found in this striking pseudepigraph.

C

Additional Note

Several theories have been put forward concerning the origin of the Messianic conception of the Similitudes. Of one source we can be sure—the Old Testament; and much is explained by the consideration that the Son of man of Daniel vii has been individualized and combined with other conceptions drawn from Isaiah xi; Psalm ii; Psalm lxxii, etc.[1]

It has been suggested that the Zoroastrian Messiah, Saoshyant, lies behind Enoch xxxvii *ff*.[2] But this theory, even if correct, does not throw any further light on the mode of Messiah's appearance, for Saoshyant is born of a human mother on the earth. He is the third of three Messiahs who are separated by 1000 years in their advents. All are born of virgins who conceive through bathing in the Lake Kansu and drinking of the waters, for in this lake the seed of Zoroaster has been miraculously preserved. The fully developed story is found in the Pahlavi literature, but its beginnings can be traced back to the later Avestan period. In the Gathas, the earliest Zoroastrian sources, Saoshyant is not a proper name, but a generic term for Zoroaster and his helpers. It is in the latter part of the Avestan period that we first become acquainted with a person bearing this name.[3]

---

[1] e.g. Enoch xlix. 3:

> 'And in him dwells the spirit of wisdom,
> And the spirit which gives insight,
> And the spirit of understanding and of might . . .'

with Isaiah xi. 2:

> 'And the spirit of the Lord shall rest upon him,
> The Spirit of wisdom and understanding,
> The spirit of counsel and might. . . .'

Again, Enoch xlviii. 4: 'And he shall be the light of the Gentiles'; cf. Isaiah xlix. 6.

[2] cf. Oesterley and Robinson, *Hebrew Religion*, p. 351 *f*.

[3] Dhalla gives the following dates: Gathic period, *c*. 1000; Avestan period, 800 B.C.–A.D. 200; Pahlavi period, third to ninth century A.D.

The following references may be given:

Avestan Sources
Vendidad xix. 5:
Zoroaster: I will smite the Pairika Knathaiti till the fiend-smiter Saoshyant come up to life out of the lake Kansu, from the region of the dawn, from the regions of the dawn (*S.B.E.*, iv. 205).

Yasht xix. 88–90:
We sacrifice unto the awful kingly Glory, made by Mazda . . . that will cleave unto the victorious Saoshyant and his helpers, when he shall restore the world, which will (thenceforth) never grow old and never die, never decaying and never rotting, ever living and ever increasing, and master of its wish, when the dead will rise, when life and immortality will come, and the world will be restored at its wish; when the creation will grow deathless—the prosperous creation of the Good Spirit—and the Druj shall perish, though she may rush on every side to kill the holy beings; she and her hundred-fold brood shall perish, as it is the will of the Lord (*S.B.E.*, xxiii. 306).

Yasht xix. 92:
When Astvat-ereta [=Saoshyant] shall rise up from Lake Kansu, a friend of Ahura Mazda, a son of Vispataurvairi, knowing the victorious knowledge (*S.B.E.*, xxiii. 307).

Yasht xiii. 142:
Vispataurvairi the holy maid who brings forth the deliverer.

Pahlavi Period
Dinkard VII. x. 17
Then she (Gobak-abu) sits in that water, when she is fifteen years old and it introduces into the girl him whose name is the Triumphant Benefiter. . . . 18. not before that has she associated with men. . . . 19. When that man becomes thirty years old the sun stands still thirty days and nights.

In xi. 1 it is said that Saoshyant's work lasts fifty-seven years. In xi. 8 he 'marches forward from the water Kanyisa' (the name is variously given) (*S.B.E.*, xlvii. 115) cf. also Bundahish xxxii. 8 (*S.B.E.*, v. 144).

Nowhere is Saoshyant described as judge. It is doubtful

if Enoch owes much to Zoroastrian sources as far as its conception of the Messiah is concerned.[1]

Another theory traces the origin of the 'Son of man' to Babylonian mythology. Hommel,[2] who is thinking mainly of the phrase in Daniel vii. 13, finds that Adapa, the son of Ea, bears in one fragment the epithet '*zir-amiluti*' (literally, 'seed of mankind'), 'that is to say, he from whose seed the whole of mankind is sprung'. Further, Adapa is at times identified with Marduk, the sun-god, who is also 'son of Ea'. Since the sun reappears after its setting, it is argued that Adapa, a kind of primal man, was expected to reappear too—though this part of the 'legend' is missing.

This theory must be pronounced very unlikely, and it should be noted that the essential part of the Marduk myth is the struggle with Tiamat and her horde. In Daniel vii, the Son of man does not engage in any battle, for the enemies are destroyed before his appearance.

Others have turned to the Iranian redemption mystery to find the origin of the Son of man. In this the human soul is regarded as a divine element sunk in the material world and forgetful of its true origin. A message comes from the realm of light to awaken the soul and to lead it home. It is important to notice that in some of the numerous forms which this myth takes, it is not a deliverer who comes to the soul; for example, in the Hymn of the Soul in the 'Acts of Thomas'[3] (a hymn which is older than its context and has ancient roots), the prince is aroused from his stupor by a letter.

But in some versions, the messenger or deliverer is the Primal Man; and the individual soul is regarded at times as a fragment of the great soul (the Primal Man).

[1] cf. J. H. Moulton in *H.D.B.*, iv. 988 *ff.*

[2] Fritz Hommel, 'The Apocalyptic Origin of the Expression "Son of Man" ', *Expository Times*, vol. xi (1899–1900), 341 *ff.*

[3] cf. M. R. James, *Apocryphal N.T.*, pp. 411 *ff.*

These ideas reappear in Gnosticism, Manichæism, Mandaism etc.[1] But they have little if anything to do with Jewish Messianism. It is not a legitimate argument to say that because (1) the Primal Man appeared in Iranian myths and (2) the Son of man, or the Man, is prominent in Enoch, therefore the Son of man in Enoch was derived from Iranian sources. The two things belong to different realms of thought.

The Iranian myth has obvious affinities with Hinduism, which also regards the soul as a divine element enmeshed in the world of matter. Again, the identity of the soul with the Primal Man is related to the Hindu doctrine of the identity of the human soul with Brahma, the doctrine associated with the words, *Tat tvam asi*—Thou art that. There is even a closer parallel than this, for the Hindu Purusha is the Primal Man from whom humanity was derived, and *purusha* is the individual soul.

This circle of ideas has nothing or little to do with the Messiah of the Similitudes, and it has no light to throw on the question of the Parousia. It is significant that (a) when the Gnostics connected their system with the Gospel or found room in it for Christ, they related the coming of the Deliverer, the Aeon Christ, with the earthly life and ministry of Jesus—His birth or baptism—not with the Second Advent; and (b) the more orthodox doctrine of the Harrowing of Hell is probably connected with the

[1] It is possible to show that a prominent element in Gnosticism concerning the Primal Man has contacts with the Iranian redemption mystery. (For an example of Primal Man cf. the Ophites: 'Others, again, portentously declare that there exists, in the power of Bythus, a certain primary light, blessed, incorruptible, and infinite; this is the Father of all, and is styled the first man. They also maintain that his Ennoia, going forth from him produced a son, and that this is the Son of man—the second man.' Irenaeus i. 30.) But many elements in Gnosticism came direct from pagan sources without passing through either Judaism or Christianity. While the Iranian teaching concerning the Man is of great importance for the study of Gnosticism, there is little evidence that it had any influence upon Jewish Messianic teaching, whose origins lay elsewhere.

redemption myth of which we have been speaking—a heavenly being descending into the realm of darkness; cf. 1 Peter iii. 19-20, iv. 6; Ephesians iv. 9 (?); and James, *Apocryphal N.T.*, *passim*. In neither case is there any connection with the Parousia.

The Son of man in the Similitudes is from Daniel vii, as Enoch xlvi shows beyond a doubt; and in Daniel vii the phrase is not a title, but simply means that after the beasts (representing the pagan empires) there appeared 'a man', or one like 'a man' (representing Israel). There is not the slightest need to invoke foreign mythologies to explain this. The general idea may have been suggested by Psalm lxxx, where a similar contrast occurs between the 'boar . . . and the wild beast' of 13 (the heathen oppressors) and 'the son of man whom thou hast made strong for thyself' of 17 (Israel). See Curtis in *H.D.B.*, i. 556*a*. see also Psalm viii where man, 'the son of man', has dominion over the beasts. The pictorial details (in Daniel vii) of the enthroned Deity and the man's approach probably came, as suggested earlier, from the pre-Maccabean portion of Enoch.

Reitzenstein in a brief reference in *Das iranische Erlösungsmysterium* (p. 123) compares a few passages in Enoch, including one chapter from the Similitudes—xlviii—with Mandaean and similar extracts which are alleged to be evidence for the old Iranian myth. Apart from the uncertainty which the relation of dates involves, we know that the writers of Enoch were well acquainted with the O.T., and the references from Enoch xlviii may have been inspired by Psalm lxxii. Thus Enoch xlviii. 5, which he cites, is reminiscent of 9 and 11 in the psalm; Enoch xlviii. 3 and 5 may depend on 17 in the psalm (where 'before the sun' [Hebrew] was sometimes taken temporally instead of spatially); this is supported by the fact that 4 in the same chapter of Enoch ('the hope of those who are troubled in heart') may be inspired by 12-14 in the same psalm. It is quite likely that some elements of Enoch are Iranian, and the imprisoned angels of the earlier chapters may well be connected with such sources, but the specifically Messianic teaching owes most to the O.T.

Otto says roundly that if the Primal Man of Iranian religion lies behind the Enochic Son of man, all essential traits have been assiduously suppressed, for the figure of the Son of man in Enoch has not a single trait specific to primordial humanity.[1]

Other theories are bewildering in their variety; in addition to those already mentioned (Saoshyant, Adapa, Marduk, the Iranian Urmensch), Hsathra vairiya—one of the Amesha Spentas, Mithras, Yima, the angel Sraosha, Gayomart, Horus, and others have all been put forward; and Iranian, Babylonian, Egyptian, and Hellenistic mythologies have all been alleged as the source. If Daniel, Enoch, and 2 Esdras (with all their differences) are joined together on one hand, and several myths combined on the other, as is sometimes done, it is difficult to avoid striking coincidences, but these prove nothing. We must beware of what Moulton calls 'parallels made plausible by selective description'. The wide variety of these suggestions shows that none of them is convincing enough to drive the others from the field. As contended above, they are all for the most part unnecessary, since the roots in the O.T. are unmistakable.

Apart from that, it is wrong to seek a foreign origin for everything in Judaism. The Jews were great creators as well as borrowers. Not all the plants which grew on their soil were exotic.

[1] R. Otto, *Kingdom of God and Son of Man*, Appendix IV.

CHAPTER 4

ENOCH AND THE NEW TESTAMENT

In the previous chapter we have examined the Messianic teaching developed in the Book of Enoch and have discovered marked differences from anything found in the N.T. Some scholars, however, have built up an impressive case to prove that the teaching of Jesus was directly inspired by the Similitudes, and we must now examine their arguments more closely.

It must be stated at the outset that the Book of Enoch has many features which to a Christian mind are repulsive, features which seem quite out of harmony with the ruling ideas of the Gospels; and we shall require very cogent proofs to convince us that Jesus accepted it as authoritative —especially as it at no time formed a part of the Jewish canon. We have evidence that Jesus objected to scribal additions to the scriptures, and called them human traditions (Mark vii). It would be surprising if He accepted, and even modelled His life upon, a non-canonical production. Further, the conception of God developed in Enoch is vastly inferior to that of the prophets and to the rabbinic teaching of the time of Jesus. Orthodox Judaism regarded God with such reverence that all anthropomorphic expressions were modified; and in the later Targums we have the kind of Aramaic paraphrases which Jesus would hear in the synagogues.[1]

As Dalman has shown, Jesus was fully in sympathy with this reverential way of speaking of God; and he gives

[1] e.g. Exodus xx. 18: 'Moses drew near unto the thick darkness where God was.' Onkelos has 'where the Glory of God was'. Exodus xxiv. 10: 'and they saw the God of Israel', etc. Onkelos: 'And they beheld the majesty of the God of Israel, and beneath His majestic throne [instead of "under His feet"] was work of precious stones.'

numerous instances in his book, *The Words of Jesus*. Now, the tendency in Enoch is the other way; and many passages are crude and retrograde in their descriptions of God sitting on a mountain or in Palestine, and words of the prophets which were originally intended as symbolic are here pressed in a starkly literal manner. Again, such conceptions as grinding to powder the teeth of the sinners, or stars whose privy members are like those of horses, do not figure prominently in the teaching of our Lord.

Nevertheless, we are told by scholars of great ability that Jesus drew many important parts of His message from the Book of Enoch. Charles and, more recently, Otto have both given detailed attention to this thesis, the former relying mainly on linguistic evidence, and the latter on fundamental ideas. We will consider Charles first.[1]

A. *Charles's Parallels*

R. H. Charles, in his three commentaries on the book, gives impressive lists to show that again and again words, phrases, and ideas found in the N.T. were derived from it. He maintains that the influence of Enoch on the N.T. has been greater than that of all the other apocryphal and pseudepigraphical books taken together, and that 'all the writers of the N.T. were familiar with it'. He supports this by referring to over one hundred parallels, a very imposing list. About sixty of these are to be found in the *Apocrypha and Pseudepigrapha of the O.T.* (ed. Charles), but others not included there are in his separate editions of Enoch (1893 and 1912).

[1] All students of the apocryphal and pseudepigraphical literature are indebted to the researches and voluminous writings of the late Dr. R. H. Charles. It is a matter of regret that in the following pages attention has to be drawn mainly to those points in which disagreement is expressed. I wish to place on record my admiration for his vast erudition and industry, and my acknowledgement that without the help of his writings the present studies would have been practically impossible.

One striking fact, however, needs to be pointed out immediately. In all these passages, only *one* is a direct quotation (in Jude, one of the latest books of the N.T.; quotation from Enoch i-v). All the others are parallels in thought or phraseology. This is a very different matter from the dependence of the N.T. upon the O.T. books; whole passages from Isaiah and the Psalms are quoted verbally and cited by name, e.g. Luke iii. 4-6: 'As it is written in the book of the words of Isaiah the prophet'; Romans ix. 25-26: 'As he saith also in Hosea.' In the case of Enoch, there is only one citation of this kind in the whole of the N.T. and it is in a book which many critics place in the second century and which had a struggle to get into the N.T. at all.

Further, when we examine these alleged parallels some are seen at a glance to be very inconclusive. For instance, *Romans ix. 5* ('God blessed for ever') is set by the side of *Enoch lxxvii. 1* ('He that is blessed for ever'). Now, there are numerous passages in the O.T. which might have suggested to Paul this phrase—closer parallels too, since they have 'the Lord' and 'God', while Enoch has merely 'He'. Four of the five sections of the Book of Psalms close with a phrase of this kind, and in the LXX there is close verbal agreement with Paul's language; cf. Psalm lxxxix (LXX lxxxviii) 52.

The verse from Enoch is as follows:

And the first quarter is called the east, because it is the first; and the second, the south, because the Most High will descend there, yea, there in quite a special sense will He who is blessed for ever descend.

Is it credible that this obscure passage from the Book of Heavenly Luminaries (lxxii-lxxxii) was in the Apostle's mind when he wrote Romans ix. 5? Yet this is one of the examples quoted to prove that Paul 'was well acquainted with and used the Book of Enoch'. We know that he was well acquainted with the O.T., and it is surely a sound principle that where his language can be explained by the O.T. all the probabilities lie in that direction.

The great majority of these one hundred parallels are very unconvincing. But there are a few which appear at first sight to establish Enoch as the source. Let us examine two of the most plausible examples:

Matthew xxvi. 24=Enoch xxxviii. 2
Matthew: It had been good for that man if he had not been born.
Enoch: It had been good for them if they had not been born.

In his article on Apocalyptic Literature in *E.B.*, 221, Charles classes this among the 'indubitable instances' of dependence on Enoch. But in his 1893 commentary reference is made to Edersheim, who 'points out that this was a well-known rabbinic expression'. In his commentary on 2 Baruch,[1] Charles describes this sentence as 'a Jewish commonplace'.

Luke i. 52=Enoch xlvi. 5
Luke: He hath put down princes from their thrones.
Enoch: He will put down the kings from their thrones.

Charles writes: 'Luke i. 52 seems to depend directly on this verse in Enoch in phrasing and thought.' Here three observations may be made:

(*a*) It is generally recognized that the Magnificat is saturated with LXX phraseology and almost every line has a parallel in the O.T. It is especially reminiscent of the song of Hannah. Luke was probably well acquainted too with Ecclesiasticus (cf. Moffatt, *Introduction to Literature of the N.T.*, p. 26) and there is a much closer parallel to his words in Ecclesiasticus x. 14: 'The Lord hath cast down the thrones of proud princes, and set up the meek in their stead.'

[1] *Apoc. and Pseud.*, II, 479.

(*b*) One of the main points in Luke i. 52 is the contrast: 'He hath put down princes from their thrones, and hath exalted them of low degree.' This contrast is absent from the Enoch passage: 'And he will put down the kings from their thrones and kingdoms because they do not extol and praise him, nor thankfully acknowledge whence the kingdom was bestowed upon them.' The contrast is present in Ecclesiasticus x. 14 and in the song of Hannah. The past tense is also common in Luke, Ecclesiasticus, and 1 Samuel ii, while in Enoch the tense is future.

(*c*) The critical note, however, shows that the MSS. designated GM have 'put down the kings, throne upon throne of them'. As Charles points out in the Introduction, G is superior to all other MSS. M too is rather better than the others. A combination of G and M certainly outweighs the rest, and in the table which deals with his departures from Dillmann, Charles shows that 102 times he has followed G alone (counting this sufficient warrant for rejecting the other authorities) and 126 times he has followed GM. The reading given here by GM is even more remote from Luke i. 52.[1]

It thus appears that on closer scrutiny some of the most striking parallels adduced by Charles simply evaporate. It seems clear that he has over-estimated the influence of Enoch on the N.T. and much of the evidence brought forward is by no means cogent. The writers of Jude, 2 Peter and Revelation drew upon it, but in the N.T. generally its influence is slight. Such books as show traces of its influence belong to the later section of N.T. writings, as does the Fourth Gospel, in which v. 22

[1] Perhaps the most striking parallel claimed in the 1893 edition is Luke xvi. 9=Enoch lxiii. 10 ('Mammon of unrighteousness'). It is, however, disclosed in Appendix D that Enoch really has not 'Mammon of unrighteousness', but 'riches of unrighteousness'. In the 1912 edition 'Mammon' is accordingly altered to 'riches'. In *Apoc. and Pseud.* (1913) the parallel is dropped altogether.

may be a reminiscence of Enoch lxix. 27. Of the one hundred parallels listed, very few are convincing or even probable.

B. *Jesus and the Similitudes*

Our main concern is with the Similitudes, for only in these chapters does Enoch speak of a supernatural Messiah, the other sections being either silent on the subject of the Messiah or speaking of him as a human king in the style of the O.T. We must therefore give closer attention to the influence of the Similitudes upon the teaching of Jesus.

Luke xviii. 7=Enoch xlvii. 1–2

Luke: And shall not God avenge His elect, which cry to Him day and night, and He is longsuffering over them? (or 'He deferreth His anger on their behalf').

Enoch: And in those days shall have ascended the prayer of the righteous . . . that judgement may be done unto them and that they may not have to suffer for ever.

It will be noticed that the wording is entirely different, only the ideas being similar. There is a much closer parallel in Ecclesiasticus xxxii, where 'judge' and 'widow' are mentioned in the context:

The Lord is judge and with him is no respect of persons. He . . . will hear the prayer of the oppressed. He will not despise the supplication of the fatherless; nor the widow when she poureth out her complaint. Do not the tears run down the widow's cheeks? and is not her cry against him that causeth them to fall? . . . The prayer of the humble pierceth the clouds; and till it come nigh he will not be comforted; and will not depart till the Most High shall behold to judge righteously, and execute judgement. For the Lord will not be slack, neither will the Mighty be longsuffering towards them, till he have smitten in sunder the loins of the unmerciful, and repayed vengeance to the nations . . . till he have judged the cause of his people, and made them to rejoice in his mercy.

It is of course possible that Luke xviii. 7, which is not a part of the parable itself, has been added by the Evangelist and that the genuine words of Jesus cease with verse 6; words of interpretation added to parables often arouse suspicion, and even Augustine[1] saw that Luke xviii. 7 seemed to be out of harmony with the main trend of Jesus' teaching. But our immediate point is that *if* the words are derived from some literary source, that source is not Enoch xlvii, but Ecclesiasticus xxxii. We have already seen that Luke's language may at times have been influenced by Ecclesiasticus, and in this particular case there are striking coincidences in the Greek.

Enoch lxii. 5
When they see that Son of man sitting on the throne of His glory.

A similar phrase occurs twice in Matthew's Gospel and nowhere else in the N.T. Matthew xix. 28 has, 'When the Son of man shall sit on the throne of His glory'. The parallel in Luke, however (xxii. 29–30), omits this phrase and we have 'in my kingdom', which is likely to be nearer the actual words used by Jesus. Evidence will later be given to show that Matthew has a tendency to enhance the apocalyptic element, and this is generally agreed by N.T. scholars. It is fairly evident that in xix. 28 the words from Enoch, like the expression, 'in the regeneration', are a typical Matthean addition. This makes it likely that Matthew has done the same in xxv. 31, where the same reference is found, 'then shall He [the Son of man] sit on the throne of His glory'.

It may be mentioned at this point that Charles couples *Matthew xxv. 41* with *Enoch liv. 4–5*. The whole framework of Matthew xxv. 31 *ff.* is suspect for many reasons, but, apart from that, '*fire* prepared for the *devil* and his *angels*'

---

[1] 'How is this saying of Christ to be reconciled with His precept to pray for our enemies?' (He, of course, finds an answer to his question.)

is not the same as '*chains* prepared for the *hosts* of *Azazel*'.

The remaining cases adduced of Jesus' dependence on the Similitudes are as follows and do not demand detailed consideration:

Luke xxi. 28=Enoch li. 2
  Luke: Your redemption draweth nigh.
  Enoch: The day has drawn nigh that they should be saved.

The only verbal parallel is 'draw nigh' and several O.T. parallels to the thought can be found. Further, this chapter contains Luke's alteration and expansion of the Little Apocalypse, a subject which will arise later.

Matthew xix. 29=Enoch xl. 9
  Inherit eternal life.

'Eternal life' occurs in Daniel xii. 2; the word 'inherit' is by no means confined to Enoch, e.g. Psalm xxxvii. 18, 34, etc.; cf. also the Marcan wording, which is different (x. 30).

See further on the expression, Dalman, *The Words of Jesus*, pp. 125 *ff.* and 156 *ff.*

The expression, the Elect or Chosen One, probably came to the N.T. from Isaiah xlii, where it is used of the Servant of God. It was apparently not used by our Lord. The title 'Son of man' will be dealt with after Otto's theory has been considered.

So far we have found nothing to prove that Jesus drew upon the Similitudes. Some reference should, however, be made to other parts of Enoch, for although their teaching differs in various ways from that of the Similitudes it may be said that if Jesus quoted from the other parts the Similitudes must have been known to Him. (This, of course, assumes that the five sections were all written and assembled before the ministry of Jesus.

Something will be said concerning the dates of the various
parts in the next chapter. Charles and Otto both assume
pre-Christian dates for all five parts, and we must consider
their case first of all on their own ground.) The remaining
parallels given by Charles from the teaching of Jesus are
as follows (all apply to sections other than Enoch xxxvii-
lxxi):

> Matthew xix. 28: Ye also shall sit on twelve thrones.
> Enoch cviii. 12: I will seat each on the throne of his honour.
> Matthew v. 22, 29, 30; x. 28: Gehenna.
> Enoch xxvii. 2: Then Uriel, one of the holy angels who was
> with me, answered and said, This accursed valley is for those
> who are accursed for ever, etc.
> Matthew xiii. 42: The furnace of fire.
> Enoch xcviii. 3: Their spirits shall be cast into the furnace
> of fire.
> Matthew xxiii. 38, Luke xiii. 35, and Enoch lxxxix. 54–6.
> The point here is that the temple of God becomes 'your
> house'—'their house', God's no longer.
> Luke xvi. 8: Sons of light.
> Enoch cviii. 11: The generation of light.

None of these is any more satisfactory than those discussed earlier from the Similitudes, and it cannot be
admitted that the dependence of Jesus upon any part of
Enoch is established.

C. *Otto's Theory*

We turn now to the important work of R. Otto, *The
Kingdom of God and the Son of Man* (German edition, 1934).
The revision of this work for the English edition of 1938,
from which quotations are taken, was one of the last tasks
of this versatile scholar.

He maintains that 'Jesus lived in the ideas of Enoch's
apocalyptic tradition', and speaks of 'the Messianic
tradition which Jesus himself clearly followed, viz. that
of Enoch's apocalyptic' (p. 175). Jesus belonged, it is

said, to circles in which a certain idea was fully developed:

The idea was that a powerful preacher alike of righteousness, the coming judgement, and the blessed new age, a prophet of the eschatological Son of man, would be transported at the end of his earthly career to God; that he would be exalted to become the one whom he had proclaimed, in the literal sense that he himself would become the very one whom he had proclaimed. But that also meant that his activity during his earthly life was nothing else than the proleptic activity of this very redeemer.

We must notice the point that in this summary, instead of Enoch's name an impersonal phrase is substituted: 'a powerful preacher'. If we are to attach such enormous importance to Enoch lxxi (where alone the identification is made), we must insist that the chapter speaks of Enoch, not of some anonymous figure, not of some role which any candidate might fill. It is illegitimate to summarize the teaching of the book as referring to 'a powerful preacher' who would be transported at the end of his earthly career to God. If Jesus accepted lxxi literally, He must have accepted the identification of the Messiah with Enoch. If the work were wrong in this matter, why should He accept the rest of it as authoritative? The idea that Jesus, having read a book in which certain things were said about Enoch, decided to play the part Himself surely cannot be the key to the understanding of His mind!

While recognizing a basic document to which later passages were added, Otto speaks as though the Book of Enoch were a consistent whole. Indeed, he includes Slavonic Enoch in the general heading of Enoch literature, and holds that this too influenced Jesus.

Slavonic Enoch is dated by some scholars (Charles, etc.) in the first half of the first century A.D.; and in any case it says nothing about the Messiah at all—neither the transcendent nor the human Messiah. It is mainly concerned

D

with Enoch's journey to heaven; he passes through the ten heavens and finally reaches God Himself, a God whose face is 'very, very terrible', emitting sparks like heated metal, so terrible that Enoch's face is frozen that he may gaze upon it.

We have seen earlier that the three main themes of Ethiopic Enoch are the descent of God for judgement, the angels who led mankind astray, and the 'geography' of Hades—three subjects on which Jesus was silent.

Otto fails to distinguish the five parts of Ethiopic Enoch which are distinct in teaching and date. It is misleading to speak of an 'Enoch tradition', for the five sections differ considerably in their teaching on the future, and Slavonic Enoch is different again. If Jesus accepted the teaching of lxxxiii-xc, He believed that the Messiah would be born from the community in the new age after the judgement, a judgement carried out by God sitting upon a throne in Palestine and assisted by Michael. If He accepted the teaching of xci-civ, then He did not believe in the Messiah at all. There is no Messiah in vi-xxxvi, but the kingdom is upon the present earth and is conceived in a grossly material fashion (a conception which Jesus explicitly rebuked, e.g. in Mark xii. 25). Again, there is no Messiah in lxxii-lxxxii. The Son of man is found only in the Similitudes, and the teaching of these chapters is unique. The identification of Enoch with the Son of man is found only in lxxi, where it is probably due to the final editor. This identification was apparently quite absent from the mind of the main writers of the Parables.

Otto's treatment of the difficulty that in the main part Enoch appears to be distinct from the Son of man is most ingenious. In Appendix IV ('Son of Man and Primordial Man') he suggests, as a conjecture only, that the heavenly Son of man is not a primordial man but the 'fravashi' of Enoch. He maintains that the book is based upon Iranian conceptions, and refers to the well-known

Zoroastrian idea that every one has a heavenly counterpart, a *fravashi*. The counterpart of Enoch was the Son of man, and on his translation Enoch was 'united with his *fravashi*', thus becoming the Son of man. He quotes J. H. Moulton's words, 'The soul at death becomes immortal by union with the *fravashi*.' This, of course, would make the parallel with the N.T. even more unlikely.

In another appendix there is given a 'Literary comparison between the preaching of Jesus and the Book of Enoch'. Most of the illustrations are taken from Slavonic Enoch, and are concerned mainly with the Woe and Blessed sayings. Beatitudes and woes, however, occur in the O.T. Among the illustrations taken from Ethiopic Enoch, it is significant that only *one* comes from the Similitudes, and this is the colourless saying: 'Blessed are ye, ye righteous and elect, for glorious shall be your lot', lviii. 4, compared with Matthew v. 4.

R. Bultmann, in a searching review of Otto's book in the *Theologische Rundschau* (1937), appears to regard the section relating to Enoch as the weakest of all. Otto's reconstruction of the 'Enoch tradition' he calls a complete illusion. In dealing with the argument about Enoch's exaltation to Messianic dignity and its importance for understanding the mind of Jesus, the contention that there are four stages of exaltation in lxx-lxxi and that later the title 'Son of God' is given (cv), Bultmann points out that:

1. lxxi is probably a later addition, and lxx, lxxi, are not a unity.

2. cv, to which Otto appeals on account of the title Son of God, has nothing to do with the Similitudes.

3. Enoch was not represented as a powerful preacher of righteousness. The revelations are thought of as secret revelations written for the godly of the last time—they are not Enoch's sermons to his contemporaries.

4. The decisive lxxi. 14 is doubtful. Reference is made

to Charles's suggestion that the original read, 'This is the Son of man'. Bultmann himself regards the verse as an interpolation. Presumably he also holds that the following verses were brought into agreement by the alteration of the third to the second person.

Otto's attempt to find in the Synoptic words of Jesus the controlling influence of the so-called Enoch tradition is described by Bultmann as fantastic.[1]

D. *The Son of Man*

Otto and Charles both maintain that Jesus took the title 'Son of man' from the Similitudes.

The 'Son of man' passages in the Gospels have been set out and classified so often that it is unnecessary to repeat the process here. It appears that in Aramaic *Bar-nasha* means 'the man'. In some passages of the Gospels it seems likely that Jesus was referring to man in general and not to Himself, e.g. Mark ii. 27–8. At other times it may have been a periphrasis for 'I', just as somewhat similarly Job is speaking of himself when he says: 'Why is light given to a man whose way is hid, and whom God hath hedged in?' (Job iii. 23). Again, allowance must be made for cases where the words have been introduced by the Evangelist (cf. Matthew xvi. 13 with Mark viii. 27).

Some have denied that Jesus ever used this designation as a Messianic title[2] and attribute it (in this sense) to the primitive community. But its absence from the Epistles, and its presence in all the sources we can trace behind the

---

[1] It has been suggested that Otto's work marks a turning-point in the life of Jesus research. Nevertheless, the main contention, that the Enoch literature is the key to the life of Jesus, must be pronounced a failure. The view that Jesus combined the Enochic Son of man with the Servant of Isaiah is not new—it was put forward by R. H. Charles towards the end of last century. And, as Bultmann has pointed out, there is nothing particularly fresh in the conception of the powers of the impending Kingdom operating in the present. The exegesis of separate passages is valuable and stimulating, but even here the basis is a dubious Synoptic theory.

[2] cf. G. Dupont, *Le Fils de l'Homme* (1924).

Gospels, strongly confirm the evidence that He did use it in this sense.

But whence did He derive it? Since the Similitudes[1] took it from *Daniel*, surely Jesus could have done the same. This view is confirmed by the fact that several reminiscences of Daniel are found in the teaching of Jesus. The Kingdom of God, a very rare phrase in apocalyptic writings, was probably taken by our Lord from Daniel (cf. vii. 27, 'His kingdom', and ii. 44). Again the description of the tree into which the mustard-seed grew reflects Daniel iv:

'. . . putteth out great branches; so that the birds of the heaven can lodge under the shadow thereof' (Mark iv. 32).

'. . . the tree grew . . . the beasts of the field had shadow under it, and the fowls of the heaven dwelt in the branches thereof' (Daniel iv. 11–12).

Similarly, the stone which grinds to powder that on which it falls is from Daniel ii. 34 (cf. Luke xx. 18). Luke xii. 32 again—'Fear not, little flock, it is your Father's good pleasure to give you the kingdom'—seems inspired by Daniel vii. 27, where 'the kingdom' is 'given to the people of the saints of the Most High'; there are several points of similarity: (*a*) in both cases we have 'the kingdom' absolute, (*b*) in both the kingdom is 'given', (*c*) the people to whom the kingdom is given are mentioned—Jesus is in effect identifying them with His disciples.

All these come from the Aramaic section of Daniel (ii–vii),

[1] In Enoch it is not quite certain that the phrase is used as a title; in every case but one the demonstrative is joined with it, and it is possible that in the original the meaning was 'that man', etc., so that xlvi may have meant originally: 'And there I saw One, who had a head of days, and His head was white like wool, and with Him was another being whose countenance had the appearance of a man . . . and I asked the angel . . . concerning that man, who he was, and whence he was, and why he went with the Head of Days? And he answered and said unto me: This is the man who hath righteousness, etc. . . . . 4. And this man whom thou hast seen shall raise up the kings and the mighty from their seats.'

and these chapters may have had a special appeal for Jesus. We shall see later that He interpreted His Messiahship along lines suggested by the Servant of Deutero-Isaiah, but apart from the phrase 'sitting on the throne of his glory'—which is peculiar to 'Matthew', who apparently took it from Enoch—the Son of man in the Gospels takes us back to Isaiah or to Daniel. If we examine the words of Jesus' claim to be the Son of man in His utterance at His trial, we are led back not to Enoch, but to Daniel. 'Ye shall see the Son of man . . . coming with the clouds of heaven' (Mark xiv. 62). Nowhere in Enoch is this phraseology used; nowhere is the Son of man said to come with the clouds of heaven, or even to come; he appears. The phrase is from Daniel vii, and we conclude that it was from that chapter that Jesus took the designation 'Son of man'.

One difficulty which the title involves is that in Daniel it stands for a community, not an individual. Just as the four beasts represent four empires, the beasts having no more existence than the figures in a cartoon, so the human figure represents 'the people of the saints, etc.' T. W. Manson, in a very suggestive argument in his *Teaching of Jesus*, maintains that 'Son of man' is virtually equivalent to 'the Remnant' and that Jesus originally used it of a community. He sought in His ministry to gather this community of the saving Remnant, but finally had to fulfil the role Himself. While there seems something strained about this interpretation and one cannot accept it in its present form, it nevertheless contains a valuable clue. Jesus conceived of His work in relation to a community, and His Messianic teaching involves a body of followers. To Him the Messiah was not a figure of isolated glory, or a king remote from his subjects, but one indissolubly linked with a community. Even to-day scholars are divided about Isaiah xlii, liii; Daniel vii. 13—do they refer to an individual or a society? This suggests that our

Lord intentionally chose a designation which was wrapped up with the conception of a community. Again, the contrast between the beast-like empires and the humane kingdom of the saints would have an obvious appeal to His mind; it was in harmony with His own teaching about the future belonging not to the masterful but to the meek.

F. Kattenbusch in his essay, '*Der Quellort der Kirchenidee*'[1], remarks that while 'Jesus' in Christian writings always stands for an individual, 'Christ' is a wider term which at times suggests a sphere or community. He finds the root of this distinction in Daniel vii. Jesus, he says, must have read the whole passage and have noticed that the individual of verse 13 was a symbolic figure standing for 'the people of the saints of the Most High'. He turned the vision into a reality. He regarded Himself as the Son of man; but this involved not only His own Messiahship, but also that He was the representative of a community, which it was His task to create. Hence Jesus called together His band of disciples. Kattenbusch finds here the source of the Church-idea. Jesus combined this conception of the Son of man with the Suffering Servant of Deutero-Isaiah. The main trend of this interesting argument is confirmed by the parallel noted above between Luke xii. 32 and Daniel vii. 27.

Something will be said in Part Two concerning Jesus' conception of Messiahship. It is sufficient at this point to note that in order to explain His use of 'Son of man' it is by no means necessary to call in the Similitudes of Enoch.

It is interesting to notice that N.T. scholars are more and more turning away from Enoch in their treatment of the sources of our Lord's teaching:

T. W. Manson: 'When Jesus quotes he quotes from Daniel, not Enoch.'[2]

Vincent Taylor: 'In all His references to the Son of man

---

[1] Contributed to *Festgabe für A. Harnack* (1921).
[2] *Teaching of Jesus*, p. 229.

there is no certain trace of dependence upon the ideas of Enoch.'[1]

This is also the conclusion of C. J. Cadoux (*Historic Mission of Jesus*, p. 99) and C. H. Dodd (*Parables of the Kingdom*, pp. 92–3).

[1] *Jesus and His Sacrifice*, p. 26.

CHAPTER 5

THE DATE OF THE SIMILITUDES

We have failed to trace the influence of the Similitudes in the teaching of Jesus, and the question suggests itself: Were they even in existence at that time? In the foregoing chapters it has been assumed that all the parts of Enoch were written before the time of Jesus; but there is considerable doubt in the case of the Similitudes.

Charles's dating of the various parts of the whole book is as follows:

i-v: The latest of all; no particular date is assigned. The chapters may be by the final editor.

vi-xxxvi: Pre-Maccabean and before 170 B.C.

xxxvii-lxxi: Either 95–79, or 70–64 B.C.

lxxii-lxxxii: Before 110 B.C.

lxxxiii-xc: Period of Judas Maccabaeus, who died 161 B.C.

xci-civ: Either 95–79, or 70–64 B.C.

There is also the Book of Noah, interpolated in various places, which is dated before 161 B.C.

The Similitudes are dated thus for the following reasons:

1. There is no reference to Rome, and therefore the book is before Pompey's invasion.

2. The recurring phrase, 'the kings and the mighty', must refer to the later Maccabean rulers and their Sadducean supporters. As the writer was a Pharisee, the period must be later than the split between the Pharisaic party and the Maccabean rulers, and later than the time when 'the blood of the righteous was shed' (xlvii. 1 *ff.*); therefore, later than 95 B.C. The years 79–70 are ruled out, since the Pharisees were then in power.

Reason 1 is a precarious argument from silence. Since the work purports to be by an antediluvian patriarch, a reference to Rome would be difficult to contrive, and the terms are for the most part left in an appropriate vagueness. Occasionally in works of this kind a detailed prophecy of the 'future' is given (as in Daniel xi) and the date of writing can be fixed by tracing the point where the alleged prophecy ends; something of the sort is done in lxxxiii-xc, but not in the Similitudes.

Let us examine reason 2. 'The Kings and the mighty' is a general expression which may have been taken from Psalm ii. 2, where 'the kings of the earth' and 'the rulers' are mentioned. If we trace the phraseology indicated, we cannot find that two clearly defined parties emerge:

xxxviii. 4: From that time those that possess the earth shall no longer be powerful and exalted.

5: Then shall the kings and the mighty perish
And be given into the hands of the righteous and holy.

xlvi. 4: Shall raise up the kings and the mighty from their seats
And the strong from their thrones.

5: He shall put down the kings from their thrones and kingdoms.

xlviii. 10: The kings of the earth and the strong who possess the land.

In the passage lvi. 5 *ff.*; Parthians and Medes and kings invade the holy land.

lxii. 1: The kings and the mighty and the exalted, and those who dwell on the earth.

3: The kings and the mighty, and the exalted and those who hold the earth

6: The kings and the mighty and all who possess the earth.

9: All the kings and the mighty and the exalted and those who rule the earth.

lxiii. 1: The mighty and the kings who possess the earth.

12: The mighty and the kings and the exalted and those who possess the earth.

lxvii. 8: The kings and the mighty and the exalted, and those who dwell on the earth.

12: The kings and the mighty who possess the earth.

Charles points out that lvi. 5 *ff.* seems out of place in the Similitudes. If we therefore consider the remaining passages it is difficult to discover in them the Maccabean princes and their Sadducean supporters. At times more than two classes are mentioned, and xlvi. 7 suggests heathen rulers ('their trust is in their gods'). The reference is rather to the kings of the earth generally. Is it credible that the writer is referring to Jewish kings (who reigned one at a time) and Sadducees, in such words as 'all the kings and the mighty and the exalted and those who hold the earth'? The thrones and kingdoms of xlvi can hardly refer to the Maccabean state; and the shedding of the blood of the righteous in xlvii must be interpreted in the light of xlvi. It seems much more likely that the Roman period is indicated, and not the persecution of the Pharisees by Alexander Jannaeus. The time of Pilate or Caligula would be appropriate. Charles himself writes in his comment on lvi. 5 *f.*: 'the Parables deal only in general terms and avoid names and clear indications of date'.

The dating of any literary work depends on the following factors:

1. The book's own claim as to authorship and date.

2. Internal evidence such as allusions to contemporary events.

3. Its place in doctrinal development.

4. References made to it in other writings.

In the present case the book claims to be by Enoch the patriarch, and this does not provide any help, as all agree that the work is a pseudepigraph. The internal evidence as we have seen is inconclusive (1 and 2).

3. The doctrinal position shows an advance in development on the other parts of Enoch. References to the Messiah are rare in the Maccabean period, and he is absent from most of the remaining parts of Enoch. The Similitudes speak of a pre-existent and superhuman Messiah, as does the apocalypse of 2 Esdras, which comes from the latter half of the first century A.D.

4. With regard to quotation; traces of Enoch are suspected in a few later books of the N.T., but it will be noticed that these are mainly from other sections of Enoch (thus Jude 14–15 is from Enoch i. 9). The influence of the Similitudes is probable in a few touches in Matthew (*c.* 80–5 A.D.) and in John v. 22 (*c.* 100). Citations in non-Biblical writings do not bring us any earlier,[1] and this roughly indicates the terminus *ad quem*.

Most English authorities in recent years have been content to repeat Charles's dates for the Similitudes, but these have not been universally accepted by any means. A date in the Roman period is preferred by Bousset, Gressmann, Schmidt, and others, and this is far more likely.

Dalman refers to the Similitudes as coming 'from the first Christian century' (*The Words of Jesus*, p. 242; see also 243: 'it cannot be proved that they originate from a pre-Christian period').

Bousset, in his book *Jesus*, places them in the middle of the first Christian century.[2]

[1] Most of the parallels with Jewish writings given by Charles are concerned with the other sections of Enoch, and they are mainly of the indefinite type found earlier, e.g. 'sirens' in 2 Baruch x. 8 have several points of contact with the sirens of Isaiah xxxiv. 14; Micah i. 8, LXX, the reference in Enoch xix. 2 being quite different; 2 Baruch xxxv. 2 and liv. 2 are probably drawn from the O.T., Jeremiah ix. 1, xxxii. 17. One parallel from the Similitudes is claimed with Testaments of the Twelve Patriarchs; but since Charles himself dates the Testaments 109–5 (i.e. earlier than his own dating of the Similitudes) the literary dependence can only be in the other direction.

[2] '. . . *Bilderreden des Henochbuches, einer entschieden jüdischen Schrift aus der Mitte des ersten christlichen Jahrhunderts*', p. 85 in *Jesus*, 3rd ed., 1907.

The American scholar, *N. Schmidt*, writes as follows:

'. . . The kings and the mighty', who are often mentioned as persecutors, are supposed to be Alexander Jannaeus and the Sadducees. It is difficult, however, to see how they could be charged with putting their 'faith in the gods they have made with their own hands' (xlvi. 7); and many scholars have considered it more natural to understand the phrase as referring to pagan rulers. If Roman emperors and governors are meant, the time of Gaius Caligula (A.D. 37–41) is more likely than that of Herod the Great. A Jewish expansion in the time of Domitian is not improbable.[1]

Schmidt suspects successive expansion, first by Jewish, and then by Christian hands.

V. H. Stanton[2] throws out the valuable suggestion that the conception of the Messiah found in the Similitudes—a conception which is unique in Jewish writings—may be due to Christian influence upon Jewish thought. (He adds that even if it is a mistake to trace the peculiarities of the Similitudes to Christian influence, it may still be post-Christian.)

If the Enochic Messiah is a kind of rival view produced under Christian stimulus, this would explain why the Messiah is depicted as judge—an idea which only occurs here in Jewish teaching and for which we have so far failed to account. There is therefore a good deal to be said for the date proposed by Bousset.

However, whatever date is preferred for the Similitudes, the evidence submitted in the foregoing chapters remains, and it is this rather than the date of Enoch which has an important bearing on the theory that the N.T. Parousia is to be traced to Jesus and that He in turn derived it from the Similitudes. Even if these chapters were in existence

---

[1] *Encyclopaedia Americana* (1937), article 'Enoch'. This is evidently the reprint of an article written for the 1918 ed.

[2] *H.D.B.*, III, 356.

before the birth of Jesus, it is still true that His teaching does not reveal their influence, and it is still true that their basic conceptions are different from His, and their eschatology is different from the Parousia teaching of the N.T. generally. Thus, the first link in the chain has snapped.

Part Two

The Parousia in the Teaching of Jesus

CHAPTER 6

THE REPLY TO CAIAPHAS

In the six chapters which now follow, the references to the Parousia in the Synoptic Gospels will be examined. We shall then turn to considerations of a wider nature in connection with the teaching of Jesus. It will be as well to begin with the reply of Jesus to the High Priest at His trial since this is sometimes regarded as the clearest reference to the Parousia in the words of Jesus. Some have gone so far as to say that it is doubtful whether the earlier Gospel tradition contained explicit predictions of the Second Advent apart from this saying.[1]

The High Priest had asked, 'Art thou the Christ, the son of the Blessed?' and Jesus replied, 'I am: and ye shall see the Son of man sitting at the right hand of power, and coming with the clouds of heaven.' (Mark xiv. 62.)

Otto, in his *Kingdom of God*, writes: 'We must clearly distinguish those passages which give full expression to Jesus' claim to the status of the Son of man.' He accordingly fastens upon Mark xiv. 62 and adds: 'The meaning is that the judges themselves will be the witness of the truth of His Messianic claim. They themselves will live to see and know Him as the exalted Son of man, and they themselves must then concede that Christ spoke the truth when He confessed, I am. Such words could not be

[1] C. H. Dodd, *Parables of the Kingdom*, p. 96.

invented from the standpoint of a later community'
(p. 277). Otto maintains that the words were not fulfilled,
that the judges did not see His coming. But is this what
the words really mean? It is important to notice that in
the parallel passages Matthew xxvi. 64 has, '*From now* ye
shall see the Son of man, etc.' (ἀπ' ἄρτι), and Luke
xxii. 69 has, '*From now* shall the Son of man be seated at
the right hand of the power of God' (ἀπὸ τοῦ νῦν).

Before discussing this additional phrase, it will be best
to consider the Marcan form of the words. The saying
combines two Old Testament quotations: Psalm cx. 1
and Daniel vii. 13. These may be described as two
'coronation' passages. The former is the passage quoted
by Jesus in Mark xii. 36: 'The Lord said unto my Lord,
Sit thou on my right hand, Till I make thine enemies the
footstool of thy feet'. The latter describes one like unto a
son of man coming with clouds to the Ancient of Days and
receiving a kingdom. It is unwarranted to assume that
Jesus would quote an Old Testament saying without
knowing the remaining half of the sentence; and Daniel
vii. 13 says explicitly that the one like unto a son of man
came to the Ancient of Days and was brought near unto
him; he thereupon received authority. The coming with
clouds is not a descent from heaven in glory, though the
Church later, in defiance of the original context, took it in
that sense. It is unquestionable, as we have seen earlier,
that the reference is to Daniel and not to the Similitudes
of Enoch; the phrase 'coming with the clouds of heaven'
does not occur in the Similitudes, but is taken from Daniel.

The meaning of Jesus' reply would therefore seem to be
that although He was about to be put to a shameful death
He was really entering upon His reign. The idea is
brought out by Philippians ii. 8–11, where the supremacy
of Jesus springs from His humiliation: 'He became obedi-
ent even unto death, yea, the death of the Cross; where-
fore also God highly exalted Him.' The teaching and

ministry of Jesus confirm the view that He faced the
Cross with the conviction that it was not defeat, but the
gateway to His glory. He was, of course, not thinking of
personal exaltation so much as the results for mankind
which would follow from the Cross. He regarded it as a
necessary part of His service for men (Mark x. 45). It is
probable that Jesus identified Himself with the Suffering
Servant of Second Isaiah, who was exalted and lifted up
because he had first poured out his soul unto death and
was numbered with the transgressors. As the triumph of
the Servant startled the nations, so the suffering of Jesus
would be followed by His vindication. His triumph
would be evident even to His judges. If we may press
the words, 'Ye shall see', they may be compared with
John viii. 28, which gives the main thought in Johannine
language, 'When ye have lifted up the Son of man, then
shall ye know that I am he'; cf. Hebrews ii. 9: 'we
behold . . . Jesus because of the suffering of death crowned
with glory and honour'. History has vindicated the claim
which Jesus made.

Let us now consider the phrase found in Matthew and
Luke in their versions of this saying—'From now'. The
fact that the Greek words are different rules out the
suggestion that one of them is a harmonistic gloss. The
agreement of meaning is very striking, and the fact that
Matthew and Luke were written independently of one
another supports the view that the words 'from now'
belonged to the genuine utterance of Jesus on this occasion. We have already seen the sense which the Marcan
form yields; the addition of this phrase would put the
matter beyond dispute. (Dr. W. Temple, the late Arch-
bishop of Canterbury, in his essay on the Divinity of
Christ in *Foundations* (1912), stressed this remarkable
agreement, p. 262. Again, in his more recent *Readings in
St. John's Gospel*, he wrote: 'The different expression for
the same substance makes strong evidence' (vol. 2. xxx).

E

But how are we to account for this agreement in the light of Synoptic criticism? 'Matthew' (using the name as a convenience for 'the writer of the First Gospel') and Luke both made use of Mark's Gospel; were they here making use of a complementary tradition concerning Jesus' statement at the trial? It is very probable that Luke had a source of the Passion story independent of Mark, and he may have taken from this his version of the saying (as Dr. V. Taylor holds): 'From now shall the Son of man be seated at the right hand of the power of God.' But it is usually held that Matthew's Passion story is based upon Mark, and the presence of ἀπ' ἄρτι needs some explanation. To say that Matthew is heightening the eschatology is absurd; for if he took the words eschatologically as a reference to the Parousia the insertion of 'from now' would only create a difficulty by introducing a statement which history had already falsified. Sir J. Hawkins some years ago suggested that the expression 'from now' may have stood originally in Mark. B. H. Streeter, in a foot-note to his final essay in *Oxford Studies in the Synoptic Problem* (1911, ed. W. Sanday) wrote: 'Sir J. Hawkins suggests to me that ἀπ' ἄρτι Matthew=ἀπὸ τοῦ νῦν Luke perhaps points to some such expression having dropped out of the text of Mark.' They apparently did not know at that time that in one important authority the phrase 'from now' occurs in Mark. In the Sinaitic Syriac, discovered by Mrs. Lewis in 1892, the equivalent of ἀπ' ἄρτι stands in Mark; and, to quote Streeter's later words, 'this reading cannot be dismissed forthwith as an assimilation, for in both Matthew and Luke the Syriac reading is the equivalent of ἀπὸ τοῦ νῦν, i.e. the Syriac assimilation has worked in the reverse direction' (*Four Gospels*, p. 321 in the 1930 edition). The phrase therefore may have stood originally in Mark; it is easier to understand its omission than its insertion.

Streeter holds that the words did not stand in Mark,

and that Matthew and Luke inserted them independently. He gives four reasons:

1. Precisely the same addition (ἀπ' ἄρτι Matthew = ἀπὸ τοῦ νῦν Luke) is made in the parallel, Mark xiv. 25 = Matthew xxvi. 29 = Luke xxii. 18. 2. The word ἄρτι is used seven times by Matthew (ἀπ' ἄρτι three times), never by Mark or Luke. 3. The phrase ἀπὸ τοῦ νῦν is used five times in Luke and once in Acts, never by Mark or Matthew. 4. Origen (*Commentary on Matthew*) explicitly contrasts the absence of the words from Mark with their presence in Matthew. This shows that the words were absent from the old Caesarean text as well as from the Alexandrian and Western texts.

It may be pointed out, however, that:

1. It is not the case that the same addition is made in the parallel cited. In Mark xiv. 25 we have οὐκέτι οὐ μὴ πίω. Matthew alters this to οὐ μὴ πίω ἀπ' ἄρτι, while Luke has οὐ μὴ πίω ἀπὸ τοῦ νῦν. Thus Mark has a word which he uses more frequently than Matthew or Luke, οὐκέτι; Luke employs his favourite ἀπὸ τοῦ νῦν and Matthew his characteristic ἀπ' ἄρτι. (In DΘ Mark has οὐ μὴ προσθῶ πεῖν; if this was the original, Matthew and Luke may have intentionally avoided a Semitism.) The meaning in all three Gospels is the same. We have here not an addition but a substitution. This instance therefore does not support Streeter's view.

2 and 3. It is true that ἀπ' ἄρτι and ἀπὸ τοῦ νῦν are confined to Matthew and Luke respectively in all our Greek MSS.; but this does not by any means rule out the possibility that ἀπ' ἄρτι was used in this one place by Mark. There would be nothing unusual in finding a word used once in Mark and several times in Matthew or Luke; in fact, several examples could easily be culled from Hawkins's *Horae Synopticae*, pp. 4–23 (e.g. 'Father in heaven' is absent from Luke, occurs thirteen times in Matthew and once in Mark).

4 is not an important point since admittedly the

Sinaitic Syriac is the only documentary authority we have.[1] There are cases where an apparently true reading has been preserved in only one source.

If we assume that the words originally stood in Mark we can explain their presence in the Sinaitic Syriac, their presence in Matthew is accounted for, and we can understand their subsequent omission. And if Luke xxii. 69 is drawn from Mark we can understand also the presence of 'from now' in that verse, the alteration to Luke's favourite expression, ἀπὸ τοῦ νῦν, being also quite explicable.

But even as they now stand, the meaning of all three versions is the same; the seeming defeat of Jesus is the beginning of His real triumph. He 'for the joy that was set before Him endured the cross, despising shame, and hath sat down at the right hand of the throne of God' (Hebrews xii. 2). One is reminded of the early Church's inspired misquotation of Psalm xcvi: 'God hath reigned from the tree'; Tertullian, for example, after referring to this Psalm, speaks of 'Christ who has reigned from that time onward when He overcame the death which ensued from His passion of the tree' (*Answer to the Jews*, x).

It is interesting to find that Father M.-J. Lagrange, the French Roman Catholic scholar, declares most emphatically that there is no reference to the Second Advent in Jesus' reply to Caiaphas, and he gives an almost identical interpretation with that adopted in this chapter.[2]

[1] Apart from one MS of the Sahidic version—see the Oxford edition of Mark with critical apparatus (S. C. E. Legg).

[2] '*C'était un texte de Daniel* (vii. 13) *combiné avec le texte d'un psaume* (cx. 1), *tous deux parlant très expressément de l'intronisation du Roi ou du Fils de l'homme. Cette venue n'est pas celle de la consommation, mais de l'inauguration, on ne saurait élever là-dessus le moindre doute*' (*Evangile selon S. Matthieu*, clxv).

CHAPTER 7

FACTORS DUE TO THE EVANGELISTS

ONE consideration to be borne in mind in discussing the eschatological sayings reported in the Gospels is that the original words of Jesus may have been coloured by the beliefs of the early Church.

In recent years 'Form Criticism' has insisted that in the Gospels we have traditions strongly influenced if not created by the Christian community. The more extreme adherents of this school maintain that the life and teaching of the historical Jesus are largely veiled from us. They thus join forces with sceptics in doubting the reliability of the Gospels. But these documents are self-evidencing, and many writers guilty of no leanings towards orthodoxy have been forced to admit that they bear the stamp of reality. Thus John Stuart Mill, the Victorian rationalist, once wrote:

It is of no use to say that Christ, as exhibited in the Gospels, is not historical, and that we know not how much of what is admirable has been superadded by the tradition of His followers. Who among His disciples, or among the proselytes, was capable of inventing the sayings described as those of Jesus, or of imagining the life and character revealed in the Gospels? Certainly not the fishermen of Galilee, still less the early Christian writers.

In more recent times H. G. Wells has affirmed:

'Our only direct sources of information about the life and teaching of Jesus are the four Gospels. All four agree in giving us a picture of a very definite personality. One is obliged to say: "Here was a man. This could not have been invented." '[1]

[1] *Short History of the World*, ch. xxxvii.

The Gospels nowhere claim to be inspired or infallible, but if we may judge by Luke's preface they set out to record genuine reminiscences and this claim cannot be invalidated. Though they had dogmatic as well as historical aims they cannot be explained as the 'unconscious secretion of a community of believers'.

But this does not mean that we may accept everything reported in the Gospels as the actual words of Jesus. The Fourth Gospel is in a class apart and in our discussion of the teaching of Jesus it will only be referred to incidentally; the view has long been recognized that it includes in its pages devotional paraphrases and expansions of the Master's words. Even in the Synoptics we must be prepared to find at times the later thoughts and interests of the Church, which the Evangelists shared. This, however, does not open the door to uncontrolled subjectivity and no qualifications must be made on this score without definite reasons.

One early Christian writer born in the first century, Papias, ascribed to Jesus a strange apocalyptic saying concerning the miraculous fruitfulness of vines and wheat in the New Age; this saying has been traced to its real origin in a Jewish pseudepigraph written in the latter part of the first century A.D. There is no reason to think that the Evangelists were as careless or as misinformed as Papias, but as Sanday and Headlam[1] point out after citing this instance the possibility must be borne in mind that 'even in the N.T. our Lord's words may have been defined in a sense which was not exactly that originally intended. . . .'

We have only translations of the words of Jesus and every translation is bound to contain an element of paraphrase;[2] it is almost impossible to make sense by transliterating from any language into another. Every

[1] *Romans*, p. 211.
[2] 'He who translates quite literally is a liar' (*The Tosefta*).

translator has to form his own opinion of the meaning of the words, and his interpretation (which may be faulty) colours his translation.

To give a modern illustration. If an American fundamentalist read the hymn, 'Sing we the King who is coming to reign', he would heartily approve of every word; if asked to give a paraphrase in prose he would bring out the idea that the world will only find peace and prosperity in the millennial reign of Jesus which is to follow His return in glory. A non-fundamentalist could sing the same hymn with equal sincerity and in his paraphrase he would bring out the conception of the spiritual supremacy of Jesus and His increasing control of men's lives; the idea of a visible return and reign would not occur to him. I imagine the second interpretation would be nearer to the original thought of the writer. In a similar way there may have been sayings of Jesus which could be taken in two senses or more, and if a translator took a strongly apocalyptic line the original meaning of the saying might be obscured.

Comparison of the Gospels shows clearly that this has happened. We are fortunate in having several versions of many of Jesus' sayings, and it is easy to see that an apocalyptic element has crept into some of them. Especially is this the case with *Matthew*. Synoptic study has shown that Matthew made use of Mark, and he did not scruple to make slight alterations and modifications.

The reasons for these are often obvious. He alters anything which seems to disparage the divine dignity of the Master: e.g. instead of 'Why callest thou Me good?' he substitutes 'Why askest thou Me concerning that which is good?' (Mark x. 18; Matthew xix. 17). It is incredible that Jesus asked both questions, one after the other, and that the accounts are complementary. But Matthew, feeling that the question had been inaccurately rendered by Mark, since it might be taken to impugn the sinlessness of Jesus, altered the words, thinking that this must really be what Jesus actually asked. Again, Mark vi. 3; Matthew xiii. 55, 'carpenter' becomes 'carpenter's son'.

Passages which show up the disciples in a bad light are similarly altered. Again, the narrative is occasionally modified to bring it more into line with O.T. prophecy.

It is thus established from such instances that Matthew did not hesitate to alter Mark, no doubt from a pious motive. When we find other passages in which an eschatological element has been imported or enhanced, the conclusion is inescapable that the writer has coloured the original saying of Jesus:

Mark ix. 1=Matthew xvi. 28

Mark: Verily I say unto you, There be some here of them that stand by, which shall in no wise taste of death, till they see the kingdom of God come with power.

Matthew: Verily I say unto you, There be some of them that stand here, which shall in no wise taste of death, till they see the Son of man coming in his kingdom.

The Parousia has here been introduced into a saying of Jesus which originally did not mention it. We may compare the question of the disciples in the two Gospels:

Mark xiii. 4=Matthew xxiv. 3

Mark: Tell us, when shall these things be? and what shall be the sign when these things are all about to be accomplished?

Matthew: Tell us, when shall these things be? and what shall be the sign of Thy coming [Greek: *Parousia*], and of the end of the world?

The words *Parousia* and 'End of the world' (strictly 'consummation of the age') are peculiar to Matthew among the Evangelists. *Parousia* occurs only in this chapter in all the four Gospels. Comparison of Matthew xxiv with Mark xiii shows that the former has added several apocalyptic touches, e.g. the great trumpet.

All this throws suspicion upon other eschatological sayings in Matthew which cannot be checked by reference to other Gospels. A few other points may be mentioned in connection with Matthew:

(*a*) Dr. P. Dearmer, in his *Legend of Hell* (p. 163), gives a remarkable table of eight phrases relating to future punishment and eschatology and their occurrences in the Synoptic Gospels. The figures are as follows: Mark, five; Luke, five; Matthew, forty-four. Though the numbers perhaps need some slight amendment, they are nevertheless very striking and significant.

(*b*) Many scholars maintain that in Matthew xiii the explanations of the parables are not genuine words of Jesus, but are due to the Evangelist. The description in that chapter of the Son of man sending forth His angels at the consummation of the age is thus due to the writer and does not belong to the Master's teaching. F. C. Burkitt, in *The Gospel History and its Transmission*, calls attention to the circumstantial nature of the interpretation of the Tares parable:

Indeed, it is too correct: the Field is the world, the Enemy is the devil, this figure in the scene means this, and that means that, until the whole picture of the Harvest of men has melted away, and the just are represented as shining like the sun, instead of lying stored like wheat in a barn. I can well believe that the Explanation is altogether the handiwork of the Evangelist or of his contemporaries, but the original picture of the good and the bad, growing together unhindered until the harvest is ripe, seems to me to come from another and a more creative mind. And I know of no one else to whom to ascribe this picture save our Lord, who taught His disciples to imitate their Father in Heaven whose sun shines alike on bad and good . . . (p. 196).

Matthew's interest in the Drag Net and the Tares is significant—he adds no interpretation to the Leaven and

Mustard Seed or the Pearl and Treasure which do not lend themselves to eschatological treatment.

(*c*) It may be pointed out as further evidence of Matthew's tendencies that he in a few places puts upon the lips of Jesus words which are first ascribed to John the Baptist. 'Every tree therefore that bringeth not forth good fruit is hewn down, and cast into the fire'; this is an utterance of John in Matthew iii. 10=Luke iii. 9 (Q). The same words occur again in the teaching of Jesus in the Sermon on the Mount (Matthew vii. 19), where comparison with Luke vi. 43–44 suggests that they have been added by Matthew to another Q saying. Again, John's words: 'Ye offspring of vipers, who warned you to flee from the wrath to come?' (Matthew iii. 7=Luke iii. 7), reappear in Matthew's version of the teaching of Jesus in the form: 'Ye serpents, ye offspring of vipers, how shall ye escape the judgement of hell?' (xxiii. 33). This makes it very doubtful, on literary grounds alone, whether Jesus ever uttered this saying, especially when we notice that the phrase 'offspring of vipers' occurs in only one other place in the N.T., Matthew xii. 34; in this instance also they are absent from the Lucan parallel (vi. 35).

To return to the Parousia; it is likely that in *the other Gospels* there are similar instances to those cited from Matthew. As a result of Synoptic criticism we can not only compare Mark with those who drew upon him, we can also compare the different sources for the teaching of Jesus which apparently lay behind the Gospels—Mark, Q (roughly the non-Marcan matter common to Matthew and Luke), and the material peculiar to Matthew and Luke respectively; and though the limits of some of these are uncertain it is clear that in some cases we have the same saying of Jesus reported in two or more versions. Let us, for example, consider Mark viii. 38:

For whosoever shall be ashamed of Me and of My words in this adulterous and sinful generation, the Son of man also shall be ashamed of him, when He cometh in the glory of His Father with the holy angels.

(Matthew in xvi. 27 and Luke in ix. 26 take over this saying from Mark. Matthew makes a characteristic addition: 'and then shall He render unto every man according to his deeds.') But it appears that the saying also occurred in Q—Matthew x. 32 *f.*:

Everyone therefore who shall confess me before men, him will I also confess before my Father which is in heaven. But whosoever shall deny me before men, him will I also deny before my Father which is in heaven.

Luke's version of this Q passage is as follows, xii. 8–9:

Everyone who shall confess me before men, him shall the Son of man also confess before the angels of God; but he that denieth me in the presence of men shall be denied in the presence of the angels of God.

Thus these five passages are derived from two sources, Mark and Q, and it will be observed that in the Q form of the saying there is no mention of the Parousia, and hardly anything that could be described as apocalyptic. It may be said that the Marcan form has as much right as the Q form to be considered as the original version uttered by Jesus. But the following consideration tips the scale in the direction of Q. We can well understand the form of words given in Q gradually changing into the Marcan and Matthean forms—it is a process we have traced in cases where no doubt exists. But we cannot understand how an original in the form of Mark viii. 38 could be reduced by the community into the other form.[1]

---

[1] Luke xxiii. 42 *may* be an instance of the same tendency in the textual development. (*a*) BL Old Latin, Vulgate, have: 'Jesus, remember me when Thou comest into Thy kingdom.' (*b*) Other MSS., however, alter (if we may assume that the above was original) 'into' to 'in'—'When Thou comest in Thy kingdom'. (*c*) D completes the process: 'Remember me in the day of Thy coming.'

CHAPTER 8

THE LITTLE APOCALYPSE (A)

It is widely held that in Chapter XIII Mark incorporated a 'fly-sheet' which formerly had a separate existence. It probably contained some genuine words of Jesus, but much of it consisted of Old Testament phrases and teaching of an apocalyptic nature, the whole being arranged in a conventional sequence. Some suggest that it was a product of the sixth decade, when the trouble between the Jews and Rome was about to flare up; others maintain that it appeared soon after the year 40, the reference to the abomination of desolation being suggested by Caligula's attempt to erect his statue in the temple at Jerusalem.

The chapter opens as follows:

1. And as He went forth out of the temple, one of His disciples saith unto Him, Master, behold, what manner of stones and what manner of buildings!

2. And Jesus said unto him, Seest thou these great buildings? there shall not be left here one stone upon another, which shall not be thrown down.

3. And as He sat on the mount of Olives over against the temple, Peter and James and John and Andrew asked Him privately,

4. Tell us, when shall these things be? and what shall be the sign when these things are all about to be accomplished?

The usual view is that 1–2 are historical and that Jesus did foretell the destruction of the temple at Jerusalem. The long apocalyptic speech, 5–37, is based upon the composite document referred to above, and 3–4 provides a connection with the former narrative. The Apocalypse,

however, is awkwardly joined to the opening verses about
the destruction of the temple and deals with a different
topic; as one of the Fathers noticed, they asked one question and He answered another.[1] The subject is the end
of the world and the events leading up to it; these include
the desecration of the Temple, but no mention is made of
its destruction. A great tribulation is described, at the
close of which the Son of man comes with great glory and
sends forth His angels to gather His elect from the uttermost parts. All is to be fulfilled before the contemporary
generation passes away. Needless to say, this prophecy
was not fulfilled. There was indeed great distress at the
time of the fall of Jerusalem in A.D. 70, but it was not
followed by the Parousia and the gathering of the saints.
In Mark's version (on which both Matthew and Luke
probably based theirs, though the dependence of the
former is more obvious than in the case of Luke) there is
no room for any interval of time between the tribulation
and the Parousia; nor is it possible to affirm with the old
commentators that the tribulation of A.D. 66–70 was a
type or foretaste of another tribulation at the end of the
age. Verse 19 describes in language as definite as can be
conceived a tribulation which is unique; it is impossible
that this language can refer to two events. It is not,
however, this non-fulfilment which has led scholars to
dispute the genuineness of this passage; indeed, some of
those who hold the theory of the Little Apocalypse believe
that Jesus elsewhere prophesied a return which would be
very soon after His death and which, in contrast with the
teaching of this chapter, would give no signs of its
approach.

Matthew xxiv and probably Luke xxi also are based
upon Mark xiii, further details and passages being added.
It is likely that Matthew and Luke both wrote after A.D. 70
and Mark before. Luke makes the connection of the

[1] Klostermann, *Das Markusevangelium* (1936), p. 131.

tribulation with the siege of Jerusalem explicit, xxi. 20–3, and gets over the difficulty that the Parousia did not follow by introducing a period called 'the times of the Gentiles' between the fall of Jerusalem and the return of Christ (24). It is not clear that Matthew has successfully evaded the difficulty; if, as seems probable, the Temple was already in ruins when he wrote, he may have intended some other undefined sanctuary by the words 'standing in *a* holy place' (Greek and R.V. m.). Streeter has suggested that if we follow the Sinaitic Syriac reading of Matthew xxiv. 15, omitting 'standing in the holy place', the connection of the passage with the temple is broken.[1] It seems therefore that while to Luke part of the prophecy has already been fulfilled and part awaits fulfilment, to Matthew the whole still lies in the future.

Several reasons have led scholars to follow the suggestion that Mark incorporated an early Christian apocalypse which contained much beside genuine utterances of Jesus (a theory which Colani put forward in 1864 in his *Jésus Christ et les croyances messianiques de son temps*).

(*a*) Many expressions arouse suspicion, as they are not found elsewhere in the teaching of Jesus and seem alien to His message. Such phrases as 'the abomination of desolation', 'for the elects' sake He shortened the days', 'the sun shall be darkened', 'stars shall be falling from heaven' are unusual upon the lips of Jesus and unlike His customary language.

(*b*) This is the only connected discourse of any length in Mark. 'In Mark it stands apart from even the parabolic collection in iv as the only long speech put into the mouth of Jesus' (Moffatt).

(*c*) The words, 'Let him that *readeth* understand' (14), are very strange if the original was actually spoken as Jesus sat on the Mount of Olives. They cannot refer to

[1] *Four Gospels*, p. 519.

the Book of Daniel, as that is not mentioned; it is Matthew who adds the reference to Daniel in his version. The words seem to betray the secret that part of this chapter was originally a document, not a speech.[1]

Attempts have been made to distinguish the foreign material from genuine words of Jesus. Most agree that some passages, such as 9-13, are reminiscent of His words elsewhere. But it is precisely the other parts about the Parousia and the end of the world which arouse most suspicion. Many attempts to identify the alien matter have been made and though they differ in detail all include 24-7.

As noticed above many who believe most emphatically that Jesus prophesied His return in glory are convinced that we have in this chapter much which did not come from His lips. Schweitzer, for instance, who makes the Parousia central in the teaching and thought of Jesus, nevertheless accepts the theory of the Little Apocalypse. (C. H. Turner, in his commentary on Mark, strangely writes, 'the Eschatological School of Albert Schweitzer and his followers lays primary stress on this chapter as containing the quintessence of the message of Jesus'. Schweitzer, however, has made it quite plain that, far from laying stress on the chapter, he accepts the theory we are discussing, which indeed is essential to his own interpretation.)

Dr. Moffatt, in his *Introduction to the Literature of the New Testament*, gives an imposing list of scholars who have given their adherence to the theory, and concerning it he writes: 'It is now a *sententia recepta* of synoptic criticism.'[2]

A fuller treatment of the Little Apocalypse must be reserved for Part Three, where it will take its place in a discussion of the teaching of the early Church. At the

[1] '*Donc ce discours n'a pas été prononcé primitivement, mais écrit*' (Colani).
[2] 3rd ed., p. 209.

moment our only concern is to point out that this chapter, especially the central section, and its parallels in Matthew and Luke cannot be used with confidence if we are making a serious inquiry into Jesus' teaching on the subject of His return.

CHAPTER 9

PROPHECIES OF JERUSALEM'S FALL

REFERENCE has already been made to the words of Jesus concerning the Temple when the disciples had drawn attention to its architectural splendours (Mark xiii. 1–2). A similar saying was brought up at the trial, false witnesses alleging that they had heard Him say, 'I will destroy this temple that is made with hands, and in three days I will build another made without hands' (Mark xiv. 58). Though their testimony is described as false, it is clear that Jesus had made some utterance of this kind which they maliciously construed as a threat that He would destroy it. During the Crucifixion the mockery included the words: 'Ha! Thou that destroyest the temple, and buildest it in three days' (Mark xv. 29). A pronouncement of the same sort seems to lie behind the accusation brought against Stephen: 'We have heard him say that this Jesus of Nazareth shall destroy this place, and shall change the customs which Moses delivered unto us' (Acts vi. 14). The evidence suggests that Jesus not only foretold the passing away of the Temple religion, but that He also foresaw towards the end of His ministry that its material fabric would be destroyed together with the city.

All the leading parties in the nation had rejected His mission for very varied reasons; in the north and the south the people did not repent; and Jesus saw that the same false desires and values which caused them to ignore His appeal would finally bring about their own undoing. To mention but one aspect of a complex situation: subsequent events showed that their preference for Barabbas the revolutionary was in line with the very factors which

F

later initiated the fatal conflict with Rome. It may be
that the injunction, 'Agree with thine adversary quickly,
etc.' (Matthew v. 25–6: Luke xii. 58–9) had the political
situation in mind. In any case, the warnings of Luke
xiii. 1–5 suggest a national peril: 'Except ye repent, ye
shall all in like manner perish.'[1]

Then we have the apostrophe to the city beginning, 'O
Jerusalem, Jerusalem' (Matthew xxiii. 37 *f*.: Luke xiii.
34 *f*.) and the words to the women as Jesus journeyed to
Calvary:

Daughters of Jerusalem, weep not for Me, but weep for
yourselves, and for your children. For behold, the days are
coming in which they shall say, Blessed are the barren and
the wombs that never bare and the breasts that never gave
suck. Then shall they begin to say to the mountains, Fall on
us; and to the hills, Cover us' (Luke xxiii. 28–30).

The Parable of the Vineyard too (Mark xii. 1 *ff*.)
implies that through Israel's failure to respond to His call,
the hour of great opportunity had been missed and henceforth the purpose of God must find a new organ, the
vineyard would be given to others; or as Matthew's
addition phrases it, bringing out what is already implicit
in the parable, 'The kingdom of God shall be taken away
from you, and shall be given to a nation bringing forth
the fruits thereof' (xxi. 43).

As O.T. prophets had foreseen from time to time the
fate of surrounding nations, so to Jesus fell the more
sorrowful task of announcing the doom of His own nation.
It was not some magical power of soothsaying, but rather
a matter of insight and the grasp of moral and spiritual
principles. If a man is rushing towards the edge of a cliff,
there is no magic in foreseeing the result before it happens.
Nor was it, of course, a prophecy that God would arrange
some punitive intervention; but Jesus saw that the attitude

[1] cf. C. J. Cadoux, *The Historic Mission of Jesus.*

and condition of the nation could have only one issue; the same forces which had led them to reject Him were leading them to sure destruction, and it was to Him a matter of deep sorrow. In contrast with Nahum with his whoop of triumph over the doom of Assyria, and with Jonah whose delight at the prospect of Nineveh's overthrow is scarcely veiled, Jeremiah had with an aching heart seen the people follow a path which could only lead to disaster (cf. Jeremiah ix. 1). In the same spirit, Jesus found this the bitterest part of His task. He was overwhelmed with grief as He thought of the city's future; 'and when He drew nigh, He saw the city and wept over it, saying, If thou hadst known in this day, even thou, the things which belong unto peace! . . .' (Luke xix. 41–4).

The agony of Gethsemane is not to be explained as the shrinking of a sensitive nature from pain. Surely the bitter cup was the fact that He who had come to save and to bless, to fulfil the long hopes of the nation, to lead it to its true destiny, now seemed to be involving it in its worst sin. Though His sacrifice was regarded as a necessary part of His task, the part that Israel was playing in the event aroused a terrible conflict in His soul.

It is in the light of the foregoing that we must examine the passage recorded in Luke xvii. 22–37. (There are parallels to a good deal of it in Matthew xxiv mingled with the Little Apocalypse.) This is sometimes thought to be an apocalypse referring to the Parousia, but let us look at it more closely. 'In that day' (we read in verse 31), 'he which shall be on the housetop, and his goods in the house, let him not go down to take them away: and let him that is in the field likewise not return back.' Now, this is clearly inappropriate to the sudden arrival of the last judgement; no one would think then of going into his house to collect his belongings or to wrap up provisions for a journey. The language suggests some one running away from a sudden danger, and it is a matter of urgency.

Again, the words 'Remember Lot's wife' (32) do not
suit the day of judgement or the end of the world. It was
Lot's wife who looked back during the flight from Sodom,
a doomed city. If the end of the world suddenly arrived,
of what use would it be to remember Lot's wife? The
passage speaks of escape, of fleeing from impending ruin,
running away from a definite area, a danger zone, and
it deals with the same theme as the passages mentioned
above which treat of the fall of Jerusalem. It is a warning
to the disciples to flee for their lives when the time should
come, not to wait in the city, but to leave without delay.
In fact, the matter was so urgent that if a man were having
a siesta on the flat roof of his house, he must run down the
outside steps and not even wait to enter his house to get
his belongings together, but run like the wind. If a man
should be working in the field, he must not return to the
house, but go straight off for his life.

Jesus illustrates this by referring to two Old Testament
stories—the Flood and the destruction of Sodom. In both
these stories there was a great disaster which came suddenly upon a careless generation, a disaster from which
some were saved to make a new beginning. In the days
of Noah they ate, they drank, they married, they were
given in marriage, until the day that Noah entered into
the ark, and the flood came and destroyed them all
(26-7). So it was in the days of Lot; men were eating,
drinking, marrying, building, planting, and sudden
destruction came upon them (28-9). And now, says
Jesus, this kind of thing is to happen again. But this time
the doom will fall upon the holy city itself; again there is
to be a time of careless living followed by sudden calamity,
and those who heed the warning will escape; for the rest
there can be no deliverance; and thus 'the one shall be
taken and the other shall be left'. [On the other hand,
the last words (34-5) may possibly refer to havoc caused
among the population by the invasion.] And 'where the

body is there will the vultures[1] gather' (37)—there is perhaps a reminiscence here of Jeremiah vii, the chapter from which Jesus took the words 'den of robbers' in Mark xi. 17; it speaks of national apostasy and the approaching desolation of the Temple; cf. Jeremiah vii. 4, 10–11, 12–15, and 33: 'the carcases of this people shall be meat for the fowls of the heaven.'

It is true that Luke (probably following Q) interprets the passage as a reference to the Second Advent, but, as we have seen, this does not agree with the main drift of the context, and it tends to reduce to mystery a passage which is otherwise fairly consistent and intelligible. Since '*that day*' (31) looks back to the 'day' mentioned in 24 and 30, and since the events associated with 'that day' in 31 *ff.* can only refer to the fall of the city, it is likely that an expression similar to 'in that day' was used by Jesus throughout and was altered in the earlier cases to the forms found in Luke and Matthew.

If we place these three events together, (*a*) the Flood, (*b*) the destruction of Sodom, and (*c*) the doom which is to come upon Jerusalem, we find in each case 'days' followed by a 'day'. The 'days of Noah' (26), the time when men lived heedlessly, were followed by 'the day' when the flood came. The 'days of Lot' (28) worked to a climax in 'the day' when destruction came upon Sodom. Similarly there will be 'the days of the Son of man' (26) corresponding to the days of Noah and reaching their climax in a 'day' (30 and 31).

What Jesus originally called this day is difficult to decide and we cannot even be sure about the expression which stood in Q. Corresponding passages in Matthew xxiv have: 'so shall be the coming [Greek, *parousia*] of the Son of man'; but we have already seen that the word *parousia* only occurs in this chapter in the whole of the Gospels. We know by comparing Matthew xxiv. 3 with

[1] This Greek word is used of the griffon vulture in Micah i. 16, LXX.

Mark xiii. 4 that the word has been added by the Evangelist there, and it is almost certain that in all the four cases where the word occurs in Matthew xxiv it is due to the Evangelist (verses 3, 27, 37, 39). It is common in the Epistles and this suggests that Matthew has imported an expression from the vocabulary of the early Church.[1] The Lucan equivalents in xvii. 24 and 30 are also dubious, as both are unique in the Gospels:

24: 'so shall the Son of man be in his day.' BD, etc., omit 'in his day'. Other authorities have: 'so shall be the coming [*parousia*] of the Son of man', evidently a gloss from Matthew, and others: 'so shall be the day of the Son of man'.

30: 'after the same manner shall it be in the day that the Son of man is revealed'. ἀποκαλύπτεται is only found here in the Gospels in an advent sense and rather reflects the ἀποκάλυψις which is used of the coming of Christ several times in the Epistles.

31 has 'in that day', which may have been Jesus' original expression in all three places.

This is more likely than the suggestion of a 'day of the Son of man' corresponding to the O.T. 'day of the Lord'. (If the disputed words 'in his day' are included in 24, then the one word common to the three expressions is the word 'day'.)

The day is not a literal one, since it is also a night (verse 34). But the historical development it represents will come with alarming suddenness upon the unsuspecting, as in the case of the two Old Testament stories. This

---

[1] Harnack (*Sayings of Jesus*, p. 107) thinks that *parousia* stood in the passage of Q behind Matthew xxiv. 27=Luke xvii. 24. 'St. Luke', he writes, 'has avoided the word, which belonged to the sphere of Jewish Messianic dogma and was an unsuitable term for that Second Coming in which Christians believed.' But this cannot be correct, for there is not the slightest evidence that the word had ever been associated with the Messiah. As Lagrange says in a note on this word: '*on ne saurait prouver que cette expression ait jamais été employée du Messie juif*' (*S. Matthieu*, p. 459, cf. also civ).

is brought out by the comparison to lightning (24). As it now stands, the verse refers to the Parousia, but if the argument of this chapter is valid, it originally referred to the swiftness with which the event foretold would arrive. Several similes of this kind are to be found in the Bible: the snare—travail suddenly coming upon a woman with child—a thief in the night; and none of them is to be taken literally. They are different ways of making one point, that the day of crisis comes without warning, it is sudden and unexpected. The simile of the lightning is another way of saying the same thing; it too gives no warning of its coming. This fits the rest of the passage admirably. The men of Noah's generation were eating and drinking in careless ease, and sudden judgement came upon them as swiftly as lightning; and so with the men of Sodom. So shall it be in 'the days of the Son of man', men will be living in careless disregard of the great issues of the Kingdom of God until at length there will come a day of judgement. No one would dream of finding a meaning in the dishonest intention of the thief, in his jemmy or his criminal greed, or of dwelling upon the material with which the snare is made. The transit of the lightning from one part under heaven to another part under heaven is just as irrelevant. The significance is in the one point they all have in common, a sudden crisis breaking into careless ease.

Verse 22 cannot be interpreted with certainty and is difficult on any view; 25 and 33 are also missing from the parallels to the whole context which are found in Matthew xxiv, and may be out of place. But the broad meaning of the passage up to 30 is that a period of time will reach its climax in a great crisis. Then from 31 the crisis is taken up in more detail and the disciples are bidden to make good their escape.

It is significant that in each case attention is drawn to *the survivors*. The time of crisis is described, not as the day when the flood came, but 'the day that Noah entered into the ark', not the day when it rained fire from heaven, but 'the day that Lot went out from Sodom'. Had it been the purpose of Jesus merely to illustrate sudden judgement, there would have been no need to mention Lot at all. But there is a note of hope as well as doom.

As hinted earlier this may be the meaning of the cryptic words, 'one shall be taken and one left'. Lot and Noah respectively were living side by side with their contemporaries. They were all linked together in their daily lives, and yet there was a secret division between them which the day of crisis made open and clear. The flood took away the careless generation, and, as the O.T. puts it, 'Noah alone was *left* and those who were with him'. This perhaps is the key to 34–5; men and women will be living a common life, two men sleeping on the same bed, two women grinding together, and though their outward circumstances are so similar there is a vital spiritual distinction between them which the crisis will bring to light; and once again some will be taken and some left.

Jesus is concerned that His followers shall not be overwhelmed in the city's fate. That the warning was known and heeded is suggested by the tradition that at the time of the siege of Jerusalem the Christians escaped to Pella.

CHAPTER 10

THE PARABLES

A NUMBER of references to the Parousia occur in association with parables and these call for special notice. It is usually in the interpretations that these references are found and this in itself is significant. Reference has already been made in connection with Matthew (in Chapter 7) to the allegorical treatment of the parables in Matthew xiii, and what was said there has wider applications. Our Lord's parables were spoken in order to stimulate thought, to encourage men to do their own thinking. Many of them were obscure and cryptic, providing, as it were, a shell which kept the truth from the careless and preserved it for the earnest. It does not seem to have been our Lord's habit to give an interpretation of His parables; it was precisely the hearer's personal discovery of the meaning which brought the truth home to him.

In such brief sayings as, 'Which of you that is a father. . . . If ye then being evil . . . how much more shall your heavenly Father, etc.' (Luke xi. 11–13), it is true that Jesus made the interpretation plain. But in parables of the story type He usually left the hearers to find the message for themselves. However, some of the longer parables as we now have them in the Gospels have interpretations attached, and many authorities maintain that these do not go back to the teaching of Jesus. The early Church was not satisfied to leave the parables to convey their own message; it added interpretations of its own and these were not always what the Master intended, but were rather in keeping with the circumstances and needs of the Church. Sayings therefore at the end of parables pointing the moral must be looked at with great care. This does not apply to the apocalyptic interpretations alone; it is widely held, for instance, that the allegorical explanation of the Parable of the Sower does not go back to Jesus' own words.[1]

In some cases we have two versions of the same parable in different Gospels and it is instructive to compare them; e.g. it is likely that the Great Supper of Luke xiv. 16–24 goes back to the same original as Matthew xxii. 1 *ff*. We notice that in the latter 6–7 are peculiar to Matthew and evidently refer to the destruction of Jerusalem in A.D. 70. The addition has been inserted rather clumsily, since after the involved military operations of verse 7 the meal is still apparently on the tables! 'He sent his armies, and destroyed those murderers, and burned their city. Then saith he to his servants, The wedding is ready, etc.' This instance confirms the point that later additions were made.

We must therefore be on the look-out for any additions made to the parables of Jesus, either in the substance of the story itself or in the appended explanations. It is exactly at these points, where there is reason to suspect the influence of the Evangelist, that several references to the Second Advent occur.

In Luke xviii. 1–8 we have the story of the Unjust Judge. The narrative itself ends at 5, and it is possible that the original words of Jesus end with 6: 'And the Lord said, Hear what the unrighteous judge saith.' It would be in keeping with Jesus' usual practice to leave His hearers to find the message for themselves. If this is so, then we must ascribe 7–8 to early Christian interpretation. We have already seen that the language of 7–8 is very reminiscent of Ecclesiasticus, a work which was known to Luke. Moreover, the subject of the parable is persistence in prayer, not vengeance; as in the case of

[1] e.g. cf. Klostermann on Mark iv. 13–20.

the Friend at Midnight, the nature of the request is not a material point. It would seem therefore that 7-8, in its faulty interpretation, introduced the subject of divine retribution, and this in turn occasioned a reference to the coming of the Son of man, when in the view of the early Church the retribution would take place. The words, 'shall he find faith on the earth', may be a hint of the 'apostasy'; if so, this would be another indication that the words were not spoken by Jesus.

Even some who accept 7-8*a* as genuine words of Jesus are doubtful concerning 8*b* ('Howbeit when the Son of man cometh, shall he find faith [or, the faith, R.V. m.] on the earth?'). J. M. Creed, in his commentary on Luke, writes: 'The interpretation of the parable is complete with 8*a*. 8*b* appears to be an independent reflection which has been added later. . . . The saying, perhaps, echoes the anxiety of a Church leader distressed at the inroads of strange teachings' (pp. 222 and 224).[1]

Let us now turn to Luke xix. 11-27, the Parable of the Pounds. In spite of important differences, it is likely that this is an alternative version of the parable found in Matthew xxv. 14-30, the Talents. There are significant additions in Luke. We are told in the introduction that the parable was spoken 'because he was nigh to Jerusalem and they supposed that the kingdom of God was immediately to appear'. The nobleman is then described

[1] C. J. Cadoux writes concerning 6-8*a*: 'It is doubtful whether this addition to the Parable actually comes from the lips of Jesus' (*Historic Mission of Jesus*, p. 325); 8*b* he describes as dubious (292-3). T. W. Manson, who accepts 8*b* as a genuine saying of Jesus, suggests two alternatives in his *Teaching of Jesus*, p. 223 *f*. 1. The words refer to the Parousia. 2. They refer to the situation at the time when Jesus spoke. 'The sense will then be: this parable shows what ought to be the attitude of men, but when a man (*sc.* Jesus) comes in search of this faith does he find it?' He compares Luke vii. 9, 'I have not found such faith, no, not in Israel.' He inclines, though with great hesitation, to the second interpretation; cf. the later *Mission and Message of Jesus*, where he writes: 'I still think the second line of explanation the better' (p. 600).

as going into a far country as in the Matthean version, but
14 is peculiar to Luke: 'But his citizens hated him, and
sent an ambassage after him, saying, We will not that this
man reign over us' (xix. 14). Again, at the close of the
parable, 27 has no parallel in Matthew: 'Howbeit these
mine enemies, which would not that I should reign over
them, bring hither, and slay them before me.' Here
again we can trace an alien intrusion into the parable,
depicting Christ's destruction of the wicked at His return.
The extra matter is allegorical and introduces Advent
details where they did not stand in the original parable
of Jesus.

It may be said that even if we remove these verses
peculiar to Luke, the parable still speaks of the return of
Christ. It is not now a question of the Evangelist's
addition to a parable; the return of Christ is involved in
the substance of the original story. The master who goes
away, leaving his servants in charge, and later returns and
takes a reckoning with them, can only stand (so it is
maintained) for Christ's departure from the earth, His
absence for an indefinite period and His final return. But
was this necessarily the meaning of Jesus? Would not the
conception of the lord and the servants suggest to His
hearers God and the people of Israel? Jesus thought of
His own mission as a divine visitation, and if we apply the
parable to the actual situation at the time when He spoke
the reference would be to the state of Judaism when He
came, not to the recompense of the Christians at some
future coming. This gives an excellent sense. The man
who stored his pound in a napkin, or buried his talent,
would refer to the strict Jew who jealously guarded the
treasure of his faith instead of putting it into circulation.
Later the Church, losing sight of the original application
of the parable, would naturally refer it to their own
situation, and the lord and the servants would now
become Christ and His people.

The Form Critics have insisted that the pericopes of which the Gospels are made up must be examined in the light of the needs of the early Church and the situation of the time. As this principle suggests, it was inevitable that words of Jesus spoken in the context of *His* situation would be quoted in reference to *theirs*, and at times would be coloured by this new application.

Similarly, the Parable of the Ten Virgins probably referred to the situation in Israel when Jesus came (Matthew xxv. 1–13). We think of other sayings in which He complained of unreadiness and the failure of the people to recognize the crisis of their history. One is tempted to quote some words of Tagore, the Indian poet, in reference to a time of crisis and opportunity in the life of India.[1] 'At the moment when Europe came to our door the whole of Asia was asleep; the darkness of night had fallen over her life. Her lights were dim . . . the East was not ready to receive the West in all her majesty of soul.' Tagore was probably not thinking of the parable of the Virgins, but the imagery is strikingly similar— 'came . . . asleep . . . darkness . . . her lights were dim . . . not ready'.

The parable of Jesus referred to a similar time of crisis and opportunity in Israel's life, a day of divine visitation for which the majority were not ready. This would bring the parable into line with that of the Marriage Feast or the Great Supper; it is clear in these cases that the reference is not to some future consummation but to the attitude of the Jewish leaders who treated lightly the great invitation. Luke xii. 35–6 and xiii. 25–7 appear to be doublets of the beginning and end of the parable of the Virgins and may be included here. Whether Matthew or Luke comes nearer to the original it is difficult to say. Some suggest that Matthew composed the parable out of the passages which we have in Luke. On the other hand, it is more likely that

[1] Quoted in C. F. Andrews, *India and Britain*, pp. 36–7.

the original parable of Jesus was broken or parts of it quoted separately.

The judgement scene of Matthew xxv. 31–46 is not strictly a parable, but an apocalypse, and will be considered later.[1]

Some have suggested that in such passages as we are considering Jesus was referring merely to life's responsibility, but this is not adequate. The historical event of His mission was conceived as a divine visitation—see Luke xix. 42–4; 'If thou hadst known . . . because thou knewest not the time of thy visitation.' (For the usage, cf. Luke vii. 16 and i. 68.) We may compare the parable of the Vineyard where Jesus' description of the man who went into another country refers to God. The time of this divine 'departure' as it were lay, of course, in the past; the language is not intended to be pressed literally, but indicates that there are times when man appears to be left in independence. There are other times when the call and presence of God are especially urgent and vivid, and Jesus evidently held that His own ministry was such a time. He complained that while men could read the indications of the weather in the sky, they could not 'discern this time'—they were not watching, they were not ready for God's hour. Looked at in this light, the parables fit admirably into the picture. It is a mistake, therefore, to regard them as Advent teaching.

There are other brief parables of crisis, as they have

---

[1] C. H. Dodd, in his *Parables of the Kingdom*, has endeavoured to show how practically all the parables had their original setting in the life of Jesus. I am particularly indebted in this chapter to his discussion of the eschatological parables (pp. 146–74 in the 1938 ed.). He concludes this section with the words: 'They were intended to enforce His appeal to men to recognize that the Kingdom of God was present in all its momentous consequences, and that by their conduct in the presence of this tremendous crisis they would judge themselves as faithful or unfaithful, wise or foolish. When the crisis had passed, they were adapted by the Church to enforce its appeal to men to prepare for the second and final world-crisis which it believed to be approaching.'

been called, to which the same may apply. There is the
Householder and the Thief (Matthew xxiv. 43–4; Luke
xii. 39–40). In its present form the parable contains an
explicit allusion to the Parousia: 'in an hour that ye think
not the Son of man cometh.' The passage is probably
from Q and consists of two verses, the former giving the
parable or simile, the latter the application. Here again
it is likely that the original pronouncement had a different
crisis in mind from the one indicated, the application to
the Parousia being added later. Harnack, in his *Sayings
of Jesus* (pp. 31, 34), suggests that the latter verse in Luke,
i.e. xii. 40, is perhaps an interpolation from Matthew.
'If so,' he says, 'we cannot be sure that it stood in Q.' It
is true that in some MSS. this verse is missing from Luke;
but most important authorities include it. Quite apart
from this textual point, the passage is probably another
instance of the tendency noticed earlier to add applications.

Another parable of this category is that of the Servants
awaiting their Master, Mark xiii. 33–7. Luke xii. 41–6 =
Matthew xxiv. 45–51 (Q) may be a doublet of this, and
it is possible that Luke xii. 37–8, which is peculiar to Luke,
is a third version of the same original. What was said
above of the Parable of the Talents may apply here too.
But even if we take this view only in reference to *some* of
the parables of crisis, it does not necessarily follow by any
means that the others refer to the Second Advent. The
duty of watchfulness, wherein so many had disastrously
failed, was urged by Jesus upon His disciples apart from
any reference to the end of the world. 'Watch and pray'
was His word in the Garden of Gethsemane, but such an
injunction can scarcely be called Advent teaching.

The situation which obtained in Jesus' ministry included, not only the nation and its unreadiness, but also
His own disciples and their need of alertness in view of
the testing-time which was coming to them, in the events of

the approaching Passion, and beyond that in the terrible happenings which He foresaw for the nation. It is possible therefore that one or two of the shorter parables inculcating watchfulness did refer originally to the disciples. Further, Jesus also taught that death sometimes came unexpectedly, as in the case of the Rich Fool, Luke xii. 16–21. Thus the idea of being prepared was not bound up with the Parousia hope and is adequately explained apart from it.

CHAPTER II

FURTHER PASSAGES

So far we have discussed passages of the Gospels which for various reasons cannot be appealed to with any confidence as giving us references to the Parousia in the words of Jesus. It has been maintained that in His reply to Caiaphas He was not speaking of a Second Advent and that other sayings originally had other topics in mind; evidence has been given that some of the Parousia sayings are due to the Evangelists. The factors pointed out must be taken into account by everyone who wishes to find the actual teaching of Jesus, and some of them are among the commonplaces of New Testament study.

We now turn to the Gospels again to find a surer foundation on which to base the belief that Jesus taught the essentials of the Parousia doctrine.

1. *Mark xiii. 32* is often quoted in this connection:

But of that day or that hour knoweth no one, not even the angels in heaven, neither the Son, but the Father.

Mark xiii is the chapter containing the Little Apocalypse and where exactly its influence ends is uncertain, possibly at 30 or 31; but 32 is almost certainly a genuine saying of Jesus. Some critics have objected that He would not have referred to Himself absolutely as 'the Son'; but surely no Christian would have invented a saying ascribing ignorance to Christ.

It is not at all obvious why the saying should be referred to the Parousia. It makes no mention of a glorious descent from heaven, or of a return of Christ. It is a detached verse which without its original context is cryptic. In its present position in the chapter it no doubt suggests to the reader the time indicated in verses 26–7 when the Son of man shall come with great power and send forth His angels to gather His elect from the four winds. But as we have seen earlier, this passage, 26–7, is part of the Little Apocalypse. The view that 32 must refer to the glorious return of Christ is perhaps a legacy of the days before the theory of the Little Apocalypse was advanced, when the discourse in which the words now find their setting was regarded as a genuine unity.

In itself the phrase 'that day or that hour' tells us nothing; it could have many different meanings. The words are apparently a reply to a question and we have no means of finding what the question was. 'That day' is used of the fall of Jerusalem in Luke xvii. 31: In that day, he which shall be on the housetop, and his goods in the house, etc. The words of Mark xiii. 32 may have been an answer to a question about the end of the world or the last day.

2. *Matthew xxiii. 37–9:* O Jerusalem, Jerusalem, which killeth the prophets, and stoneth them that are sent unto her! how often would I have gathered thy children together, even as a hen gathereth her chickens under her wings, and ye would not! Behold, your house is left unto you (desolate). For I say unto you, Ye shall not see me henceforth, till ye shall say, Blessed is he that cometh in the name of the Lord.

The closing sentence is a quotation from Psalm cxviii and originally meant, Blessed is he that cometh to the feast, or to the temple, in the name of the Lord. Pilgrims to Jerusalem were welcomed with these words, and they were, of course, used on the occasion of the Triumphal Entry.

Various interpretations have been suggested, and among them is the view that they refer to the Second Advent: Jesus will be absent from Jerusalem until the Jews welcome Him on His glorious return.

It should be observed that in Matthew xxiii the words of verses 37–9 (=Luke xiii. 34–5) form a continuation of a section (34–6) which is found separately in Luke (xi.49–51) 'Therefore, behold, I send unto you prophets', etc., or as Luke has it: 'Therefore also said the wisdom of God, I will send unto them prophets,' etc.

The two passages have clear affinities and it is very probable that they were together in Q, that Matthew has preserved the sequence and that the separation into two parts is due to Luke.

Luke's phrase, 'Therefore also said the wisdom of God', is remarkable. Matthew has omitted it; it probably stood in Q, as it is easier to understand its omission than its intrusion. Some have thought that the passage is a quotation from a lost apocryphal writing entitled, 'The Wisdom of God'. It is more likely, however, that Jesus, like the Old Testament prophets, is here speaking in God's name and that the clause means, 'God, in His wisdom, said.' It is true that Jesus usually spoke in his own name: 'Verily, I say unto you', but this appears to be an exception. C. H. Dodd, in an essay on 'Jesus as Teacher and Prophet',[1] after referring to the O.T. formula, 'Thus spoke Jahweh', continues: 'He [Jesus] does not, however, appear to have made common use of any such formula, though we probably have one example in Luke xi. 49, "The Wisdom of God said . . .". Such a periphrasis for the divine Name is in the manner of the period, for the Talmud has similar expressions: "The Righteousness of God saith . . .", "the Holy Spirit saith." '

On this view, it is God who says, 'I send unto you prophets and wise men and scribes', or, as Luke has it, 'prophets and apostles'; cf. Mark xii. 2–5. If the two sayings which in Luke are separate were together in Q, as Matthew xxiii suggests, it is probable that Jesus spoke them as one connected whole in God's name, announcing in O.T. style the divine departure from Jerusalem (cf. Jeremiah xii. 7, 'I have forsaken mine house', and

[1] Contributed to *Mysterium Christi* (ed. Bell and Deissmann).

Ezekiel's description of God leaving the Temple and city, x, xxxix. 23). The meaning on this view is that God is speaking through Jesus and reviewing the long history of Israel—'How often would I have gathered thee as a hen gathereth her brood under her wing'—the words are very appropriate if God is regarded as the speaker (cf. Isaiah xxxi. 5; Psalm xci. 4, etc.). The long story of Israel has now reached its climax and once more the city and the Temple are to be bereft of the divine presence—'Your house is left unto you.'

This interpretation makes good sense except in relation to the closing verse (Matthew xxiii. 39), where God can hardly be regarded as the speaker—unless the meaning is that the divine absence will continue until the nation as a whole emulates the ovation accorded to Jesus by the Galilean crowds as they entered the city, i.e. until they recognize Jesus and cease to reject Him. This somewhat resembles Plummer's view that the words refer to 'the conversion of the Jews throughout all time. . . . Converted Israel will thus welcome the spiritual presence of the Messiah.'[1]

It seems more likely that verse 39 should be detached from the earlier verses. The words, 'Behold, your house is left unto you (desolate)', make an impressive close to the passage regarded as a declaration in the name of God. It may well be that 39 was a saying of Jesus in His own name spoken on a different occasion, and joined by the compiler of Q to the other passage. It will be noticed that 39 does not flow straight on, but begins with the words, 'For I say unto you'. In that case the words of this verse may have been spoken at the close of an earlier Jerusalem ministry as an intimation that He would not return until the Feast of Passover, when the traditional and familiar words of greeting would be heard.

There are several reasons which tend to confirm the

[1] *I.C.C.*, Luke, p. 353.

suggestion that 39 should be separated in this way. (*a*) It is, of course, a common feature of the Gospels that sayings spoken on different occasions became linked together through some real or imagined affinity (e.g. Mark ix. 49–50; Luke xvi. 9–13). In addition to (*b*) the rather loose connection and (*c*) the fact that the speaker in 39 is Jesus in His own person, while in the earlier portion the words are best regarded as spoken in the name of God, (*d*) there are similar words in 2 Esdras i (one of the Christian chapters of that book), and the part which coincides with the Gospels ends with 'Your house is desolate' and has nothing resembling 39:

'Thus saith the Lord Almighty . . . I gathered you together, as a hen gathereth her chickens under her wings: but now, what shall I do unto you? . . . I sent unto you my servants the prophets, whom ye have taken and slain, and torn their bodies in pieces, whose blood I will require of your hands, saith the Lord. Thus saith the Lord Almighty, Your house is desolate, I will cast you out as the wind doth stubble' (2 Esdras i. 28–33).

We do not know the exact source of this quotation, but it is noteworthy that the speaker is here said to be the Lord Almighty.

(*e*) Harnack, who thought that the whole passage (Matthew xxiii. 34 *ff.*) was a quotation from an apocryphal Jewish writing where it was spoken by the Wisdom of God, regarded verse 38 as the limit of the quotation. He maintained that the passage 34–8 stood in Q as a quotation used by Jesus, 'to which 39 was appended as a real utterance of our Lord Himself'. This, he suggests, caused uncertainty about the limits of the quotation and Matthew accordingly did not treat the passage as a quotation at all, while Luke has torn it asunder (*Sayings of Jesus*, pp. 168–70). While we have not accepted the view of a lost apocryphal writing, the point at the moment is that Harnack's treatment of the passage recognizes 39 as separate in nature from the rest.

(*f*) C. F. Burney has shown that verses 37–8 fall readily into the Kina rhythm, familiar in Hebrew lamentations; verse 39, however, does not respond to this rhythmical arrangement (*The Poetry of Our Lord*, p. 146). One notes the impressive close made by the two final stresses of 38 in Burney's translation:

> 'Behóld there remáineth to ýou
> your hóuse a desolátion.'

In Q there were probably no indications of the time of speaking. Matthew places the whole passage in the closing episode at Jerusalem shortly before the Crucifixion.[1] Luke, however, includes both sections of his version much earlier (xi. 49 *ff.*, xiii. 34 *f.*) and it may be that he understood the latter saying as a reference to Jesus' next visit to Jerusalem at the Passover. It has often been interpreted in this fashion,[2] but the main difficulty has been that the saying as a whole is far too solemn to bear this meaning; but if, as suggested above, we regard the closing words ('Ye shall not see me,' etc.) as spoken on a different

[1] It is perhaps worth mentioning that in the 'Dialogue of Athanasius and Zacchaeus' (which contains some valuable and early elements—see F. C. Conybeare's edition, *Anecdota Oxoniensia*, Classical Series, viii) it is said that at His trial Jesus only said, 'Behold, your house is left desolate'.

[2] e.g. Otto, *in Kingdom of God*, writes, p. 172: 'According to Goguel's recent investigations, . . . Jesus went up to Jerusalem for the Feast of Tabernacles. After working there for a rather long time, he went away. On departing, he referred to his return for the Passover festival, and lamented the unresponsiveness of the people of Jerusalem. He closed with the words (verse 39): "Ye shall not see Me henceforth, till ye shall say, Blessed is He that cometh in the name of the Lord." Granted that even Matthew plainly interpreted this salutation eschatologically, as a greeting to the Son of man appearing in glory, yet the latter is nowhere saluted with such an exclamation. It is rather the typical salutation given to pilgrims coming to the Passover festival. Jesus says that He will leave Jerusalem on account of its hard-heartedness, and only the Passover feast will bring him back. Here again Matthew has charged with mystery a simple saying original to Jesus.'

occasion from the preceding words the obstacle is removed. We may conclude therefore that Jesus was simply referring in the course of one visit to Jerusalem to His absence until the Feast of Passover.[1]

3. *Matthew x. 23*: But when they persecute you in this city, flee into the next; for verily I say unto you, Ye shall not have gone through the cities of Israel, till the Son of man be come.

These famous words form a part of the precarious foundation for Schweitzer's imposing superstructure. He insists that all the words attributed to Jesus in this chapter were spoken by Him on sending out the twelve disciples, ignoring Synoptic criticism on the matter. 'This discourse is historical as a whole and down to the smallest detail' (*Quest of the Historical Jesus*, p. 361). He ridicules the idea of regarding the great Matthean discourses as composite structures.

Synoptic study, however, which has been carried to a greater pitch of certainty since 1906, when Schweitzer wrote his great work, has shown that most of Matthew's 'discourses' are composite, and we can usually trace which source he is following. Matthew x has elements which come from Mark and other elements from Q; still other parts are peculiar to Matthew. Probably nothing beyond verse 14 was spoken by Jesus on this occasion. It is inconceivable that after telling the disciples not to go outside Jewish territory (5–6) Jesus should on the same occasion say that they would be brought 'before governors and kings . . . for a testimony to them and to the Gentiles' (18).[2]

The question remains whether Jesus at any period uttered the words of Matthew x. 23*b* and what meaning

[1] Thus while Matthew xxiii. 37 may have no bearing on the Johannine question of the Jerusalem ministry, verse 39 has.

[2] cf. Streeter, *Four Gospels*: 'Schweitzer's whole argument depends on the assumption that Matthew x is word for word an exact report of what was said at the time. The demonstration . . . that Matthew x. 5–23 is a late conflation of at least two sources, Mark and Q, would alone be a sufficient refutation of his argument' (p. 255).

is to be attached to them. Schweitzer, of course, holds that Jesus expected His Parousia to take place before the disciples returned from their mission; He did not at that period envisage His death—He was, rather, to be caught up to heaven and then to come again in glory almost immediately! (p. 363).

This verse, unlike those which precede it and those which follow, has no parallel in the other Gospels. It reminds one of conditions in the early Church when persecution arose: before the harassed Christians have exhausted the places of refuge which Palestine holds, the end will have come.[1]

T. W. Manson, in his *Teaching of Jesus*, p. 221, points out that x. 23a 'presupposes circumstances of which there is no trace in the other accounts of the charge; and it may quite well represent the ideas of the early Church rather than the words of Jesus himself'. He goes on to say that the second half of the verse is 'just as much open to suspicion as the first', and concludes (as many other scholars have concluded) that 'the evidence of Matthew x. 23 is therefore to be regarded with grave suspicion; and we cannot build anything on it with confidence'.[2]

4. The remaining passage which speaks of a return of Christ is also from *Matthew—xxv. 31*:

When the Son of man shall come in His glory, and all the angels with Him, then shall He sit on the throne of His glory.

It has previously been noted that the last clause of this sentence is very similar to one found in the Similitudes of

[1] It has been suggested that the words express the hope of the Christians who fled to Pella at the time of the siege, that Christ would come before they were driven out of Palestine.

[2] cf. C. J. Cadoux, *Historic Mission of Jesus*. Matthew x. 23b 'was almost certainly framed under the stress of the controversy between Paul and the Jerusalem Church' (p. 303, footnote; see also 95 and 292–3). Since Cadoux and Manson believe that Jesus expected His Parousia and the Last Judgement to take place during the lifetime of that generation, their views of this and similar passages have additional weight.

Enoch. It occurs in only one other place in the New Testament, in Matthew xix. 28. In the Lucan parallel to Matthew xix. 28 the words do not occur (xxii. 28–30), and in view of Matthean usage it is likely that both in xix. 28 and xxv. 31 they are due to the Evangelist and have been taken from Enoch. This throws suspicion on the remainder of the verse, and it is generally held that the whole passage, 31–46, owes a good deal to the Evangelist.

The following comment is typical: Dr. Cadoux in the *Historic Mission of Jesus*, after speaking of Matthean alterations and additions of an apocalyptic nature continues:

'All this added to our hesitation in accepting Matthew xxv. 31–46 . . . as a close report of what he had explicitly said.'[1]

We shall return to the whole passage under the subject of Judgement in a later chapter.

There are no other passages in the Synoptic Gospels which either speak, or appear to speak, directly of Christ's Parousia beyond those considered in the foregoing pages; and it is a striking fact that when we set aside the passages mentioned in Chapters 6–10, such as the Little Apocalypse, the obvious Matthean additions, etc., the residue is very small indeed. Of the four sayings discussed in this chapter, two in all probability do not refer to the Parousia at all, and even the staunchest believers that it was a genuine part of Jesus' teaching have the gravest doubts concerning the other two.

But so far we have confined ourselves fairly narrowly to the one point of Christ's Parousia, His visible manifestation and return in glory. Account must also be taken of His teaching concerning the Kingdom of God, the Messiah, and the Judgement. It has been contended that He conceived of all these in an apocalyptic fashion and that they imply the Parousia. To this wider subject we now turn.

[1] cf. T. W. Manson, *Teaching of Jesus*, p. 37.

CHAPTER 12

THE KINGDOM OF GOD

For the interpretation of the phrase 'the Kingdom of God', which is very rare in the apocalyptic writings, we must go rather to the Old Testament and to rabbinic sources. It had three main senses:

1. God is now and always King; behind all things stands His sovereignty; cf. Psalm cxlv. 13:

> Thy Kingdom is an everlasting Kingdom,
> And Thy dominion endureth throughout all generations.

The Lord reigneth (Psalms xciii, xcvii, xcix).

2. The sovereignty of God is, however, only partially recognized at present. Israel is peculiarly His people and among them the Kingdom resides and finds expression. Elsewhere evil rules and the kingship of God is openly violated. Connected with the thought of the Kingdom as a covenant relationship is the rabbinic phrase, 'taking upon oneself the yoke of the Kingdom'.

3. The time will come, however, when all men will have to recognize the kingship of God. An effective struggle against evil will be joined and supreme blessing will come upon the whole world. At present God's sovereignty is veiled, but there will come a time when He will interpose, when the New Age foretold by the prophets will dawn. This sense is intimated in such places as Daniel ii. 44: 'in the days of those kings shall the God of heaven set up a kingdom, which shall never be destroyed.'

We may call these respectively the eternal sovereignty, the covenant relationship, and the divine intervention. They may be gathered up in a single definition by the sentence: The eternal sovereignty of God (1), now acknowledged in Israel (2), will one day embrace the whole world through the conquest of evil (3).

To the Jews the Kingdom in the third sense indicated above corresponded with the Messianic Age, and in this Israel was to have a dominant place. In Daniel ii and vii the four empires of worldly might are followed by a fifth; in vii this fifth empire, the Kingdom of God, is mediated through a community, 'the saints of the Most High', and to the writer this meant the faithful Jews. In the days of Jesus, 'looking for the Kingdom of God' was a synonym for 'looking for the consolation of Israel' or 'looking for the redemption of Jerusalem' (Luke xxiii. 51, ii. 25, 38).

While 'divine intervention' is not a happy phrase, and may suggest bizarre associations, it rests ultimately upon the conviction that God cannot be impassive in the face of a desperate human situation, that He is the living God and will 'devise means' by which His true purpose for mankind will be fulfilled, and that His will in the world cannot finally be thwarted.

In the teaching of Jesus, the Kingdom of God does not usually imply the eternal sovereignty in the first of the three senses outlined, but there are several sayings which make contact with the second. In such passages as Mark xii. 34 the sense of personal obedience and relationship is implied: 'Thou art not far from the kingdom of God.'

But there are other passages which go much farther than this. When Jesus said, 'If I by the finger of God cast out demons, then is the Kingdom of God come upon you' (Luke xi. 20), He was not referring to men taking upon themselves the yoke of obedience to God's will; His words speak of a dramatic arrival. They declare that the conquest of evil powers has begun and the divine intervention has taken place. We are clearly in the context of the third meaning.

Jesus said on another occasion that what men had been awaiting for centuries had now arrived:

Blessed are the eyes which see the things that ye see: For I say unto you, that many prophets and kings desired to see the things which ye see, and saw them not; and to hear the things which ye hear, and heard them not (Luke x. 23-4; cf. Matthew xiii. 16-17).

This gives the key to such sayings as Matthew xii. 6, 'something greater than the temple is here', . . . 'something greater than Jonah . . . than Solomon' (41-2). This 'something' (neuter in each case) is the Kingdom.

It is obvious that Jesus re-interpreted the conception of the coming of the Kingdom of God. If the Kingdom was already present, Jesus' view of it must have been radically different from the popular one. For one thing, Jesus referred to it in language which had no nationalistic colour. But more important still, while His compatriots were mainly concerned with deliverance from the Gentile yoke and from political oppression, Jesus found the signs of the Kingdom's presence in the conquest of evil in men's lives, and in the powers made manifest in His own ministry of healing and saving and preaching to the poor.

Another important modification which Jesus introduced was that the Kingdom did not in His view come as a complete whole, destroying the forces of evil and creating a miraculous new order. It was a kind of wedge driven into the actual world. In the mission of Jesus the Kingdom came germinally. The Kingdom, He said, is like a Seed; and in the parable of the Mustard Seed He illustrated its small beginnings and its vast ultimate results. The same thought was brought out in the parable of the Leaven. Again, the Seed growing Secretly (Mark iv. 26-9) illustrates the idea of growth and development; the seed had been sown and the results were as sure and dependable, and as silent in their advance, as the forces of Nature. Stages of development are indicated: the blade, the ear, the full corn in the ear. There is something inevitable about it all; men may sleep and rise night and day, but the ground brings forth of itself. Here we have the sublime faith of Jesus, that however small and unpretentious the beginnings were, a great tree would inevitably grow, the harvest would surely come.

This interpretation of Jesus was highly original. It is true that there was great variety, as we saw earlier, in the conceptions of the New Age and its coming; and that some looked for a kingdom on the present earth, others (perhaps under Zoroastrian influence) looked for a new creation, while the Book of Jubilees, according to Charles, held that the Messianic kingdom 'was to be brought about gradually by the progressive spiritual development of man and a corresponding transformation of nature'.[1] Jeremiah in his prophecy of the new age emphasized the spiritual factors of the New Covenant rather than sudden cataclysms in nature, but the prevailing view at the time of Jesus was undoubtedly that the Kingdom would arrive through certain miraculous and coercive events. Men were expecting the sudden destruction of evil and the forcible establishment of righteousness by the sheer power of God operating through a military success or in some other way. Jesus, however, taught that the Kingdom had come germinally; a new divine element had been introduced into the world, and like Mark Antony in the play, He could stand by and say, 'Now let it work'.[2] Evil was not to be overthrown by sudden divine fiat; this was surely the original meaning of the Wheat and the Tares—for the present both good and evil would remain side by side in the world.[3]

Thus the Kingdom is present and future. In the mission

---

[1] *Apocrypha and Pseudepigrapha*, II. 9. The references, i. 29 and xxiii. 30, hardly bear the weight of this exegesis.

[2] *Julius Caesar*, Act III, Scene ii.

[3] Lagrange on Matthew xii. 28 ('If I by the Spirit of God,' etc.): '*Ce texte, clair par lui-même, jette une vive lumière sur le mode d'avènement du règne de Dieu. Ce n'est pas quelque chose de foudroyant, amenant un changement total, mais une pénétration des influences surnaturelles dans le monde actuel.*'

of Jesus it has arrived; supreme blessing is available for men as a present possession; what prophets and kings had longed for is now here; the struggle with evil has begun, and Satan has fallen from heaven. But as yet the Kingdom is like seed and leaven, and stages of development will follow. The Kingdom will only come completely when the will of God is 'done in earth as it is done in heaven', and it is for this consummation that we are bidden to pray in the Lord's Prayer.

But even this is not the full story. There are a few sayings which speak of the Kingdom's future in a way which is not explained by reference to the harvest of an already planted seed. Such a saying is Mark ix. 1: There be some here of them that stand by, which shall in no wise taste of death, till they see the Kingdom of God come with power.

Now, there are indications that Jesus saw that His death on the Cross would have far-reaching results, and it will be helpful in this connection to consider the striking words of Luke xii. 49–50:

> I came to cast fire upon the earth;
> And how I wish that it were already kindled![1]
> But I have a baptism to be baptized with;
> And how am I straitened till it be accomplished!

At first sight 'fire' (49) and 'division' (51) seem to go together—the passage continues: Think ye that I am come to give peace . . . nay; but rather division. His coming produced disturbance and strife; not that He aimed at this, but it was the inevitable result of His ministry. Closer examination, however, shows that this interpretation cannot be sustained and that the sayings were placed together because, as in so many cases, the compilers thought that they referred to the same subjects. The co-ordination of 'fire' and 'division' is artificial and

[1] cf. *Grammar of N.T. Greek*, II. 472 (J. H. Moulton and W. F. Howard).

literary, for (a) the fire is not yet kindled while the division has already begun; and the words suggest that the fire cannot be kindled until the baptism had taken place; (b) He earnestly desires the kindling of the fire; Jesus surely did not desire strife and discord.

Fire can stand for other things than war and judgement. The word of God is fire in Jeremiah xxiii. 29; cf. xx. 9; Psalm xxxix. 3. The pillar of fire was a symbol of the divine presence. In Song of Songs viii. 6–7 the burning jealousy of love is described as a very flame of the Lord which many waters cannot quench nor the floods drown. It may be that Charles Wesley was not very wide of the mark when he wrote, 'O Thou that camest from above, The pure celestial fire to impart'. Jesus repudiated the fire of judgement in Luke ix. 54–6; but this fire is something which He intensely desires to be kindled. He came for this very purpose, but He must die to achieve it. If one may say so, He is the new Prometheus—and He must pay the same price.

The word συνέχομαι is also worthy of attention. It may mean: 'I am hampered, straitened, until my baptism of blood has taken place.' The word is sometimes said to imply anguish, suffering, affliction, but in these cases the cause of the trouble is usually indicated (συνεχόμενοι πυρετοῖς). The root meaning of the word is 'held, confined'. Obviously a man is in anguish if he is held by a fever; but the anguish is brought by the fever. A man can be held or constrained by the love of Christ (2 Corinthians v. 14). In Philippians i. 23, the only other place in the N.T. where the word is used without a dative to explain it, it does not mean, 'I am afflicted from two sides', but 'I am hemmed in from two sides'. Thus, before the Crucifixion, Jesus felt hemmed in, confined, straitened. . . . Liddell and Scott include among the meanings 'check', 'hinder'. Further, if we have to choose between (a) I have anguish in my spirit until it is all over, and (*b*) My work is handicapped and cabined until I have given my life, the second is the one which suits the context (49–50). He is concerned with the fulfilment of His mission.

But apart altogether from the meaning of 50*b*, the remainder of the saying (49–50*a*) implies that the real aim of Jesus' mission could not be fulfilled without the Cross. 'How I wish . . . but I have a baptism.' Thus, the Kingdom could not come with power until He had been crucified.[1] See also Luke xiii. 32, 'and the third day I am perfected'.

It is in the light of this that we may interpret Mark ix. 1. The words 'some of them that stand by' imply that others would taste of death, and this suggests at first sight the lapse of a good number of years. But the meaning may be that not all would escape death before the Kingdom's coming with power—for Jesus Himself would not, and it is probable that He believed at that time that some of His disciples would die with Him; cf. His words to John and James: 'with the baptism that I am baptized withal shall ye be baptized' (Mark x. 39). But when the time came, He alone went to the Cross and 'tasted death for every man'. A few weeks later the Kingdom of God came with power, and the conflagration began.[2]

The saying of Jesus at the Last Supper should

[1] cf. E. F. Scott, *Kingdom and Messiah*, p. 229, a valuable passage ending with the words: 'Jesus here implies that He is subject as yet to conditions that imprison and fetter Him. He cannot move at freedom till He has undergone His baptism; and He looks forward to it with passionate eagerness as to the great event which will mark the beginning of His true activity.'

[2] cf. (Bishop) C. Gore: 'Thus if Jesus, standing among His disciples, speaks of some among them who, before they die, shall have "seen the Kingdom" or "seen it come with power", and if, standing before Caiaphas, He declares that "henceforth" or "from this moment" they shall see realized Daniel's vision of the Son of man in divine power, His words are satisfied by the events which followed His death and gave the Church that sense of glory and power reflected from Christ, which was the secret of its surprising success, and which inspired in its adversaries a kind of terror' (*Jesus of Nazareth*, 1929, Home University Library, p. 119).

be considered here; there are different versions of it:

Mark xiv. 25: Verily I say unto you, I will no more drink of the fruit of the vine, until that day when I drink it new in the Kingdom of God.

Luke xxii. 18: For I say unto you, I will not drink from henceforth of the fruit of the vine, until the Kingdom of God shall come.

We cannot be sure whether Luke is here following the special Passion source which he used, or varying Mark's words, and there is therefore uncertainty about the original saying. There is no doubt that Jesus is drawing attention to the fact that this is His last earthly meal. But He is confident that it is not the end, and in the remainder of the saying He may be speaking (*a*) of the heavenly bliss which awaited Him after His death, (*b*) or the thought may be of some future re-union with His disciples;[1] this is evidently how Matthew understood the words in Mark, since he adds 'with you' (Matthew xxvi. 29), (*c*) or the words may be another indication that Jesus expected some great development to result from His death.[2]

The close connection of the Kingdom and the Cross is observed by those who hold that the Kingdom was future and catastrophic. Thus Schweitzer holds that when the disciples returned from their mission and the Parousia had

---

[1] The spirited words of P. Dearmer may be quoted: Mark xiv. 25: 'But this surely means no more than (*a*) "We are drinking now for the last time together", and (*b*) "But we shall drink a wine of another kind together in a better world than this". It does really seem that the discovery of so many Hebrew apocalyptic books has upset the judgement of some theologians. There is nothing here about an apocalyptic eruption or any second coming. A man of the present day, steeped in evolutionary science, might say it if he believed in immortality and a future life. Surely we shall never arrive at the truth while we are so unimaginative in our interpretation of One who, because His mind was of the highest type, was a poet as well as a teacher' (*Legend of Hell*, p. 217).

[2] cf. V. Taylor, *Jesus and His Sacrifice*, pp. 141–2.

H

not taken place in fulfilment of Jesus' guarantee (Matthew x. 23), He had to re-think the subject. According, it is said, to the fixed eschatological programme by which Jesus' thoughts were ruled, tribulation was to precede the coming of the Kingdom. Jesus finally came to the conclusion that He must bear the suffering of this pre-ordained tribulation Himself; when He had done so there would be nothing further to prevent the coming of the Kingdom. He therefore went up to Jerusalem in order to bring about His own death for this purpose. On the Cross He realized that He had been following a fantasy, His whole world crashed in ruins around Him, and He died with a cry of heartbroken despair (*Quest of the Historical Jesus*, p. 284, and chapter xix). Why Jesus should have become disillusioned in this way is not explained by this remarkable interpretation.

It is true that Jesus believed that by His death certain developments would be set in operation and that shortly afterwards some great event would take place—nor was He deceived; great results did follow. But what kind of events did Jesus expect? Did the coming of the Kingdom with power mean (*a*) the end of the world, sudden catastrophe, judgement, and new creation, or (*b*) the outburst of spiritual power which brought the Christian movement into existence and began a new era in human history, so that the early Church felt that it was already living in a new world? The advantage of the second view is that this is what actually happened. It is very strange to maintain that Jesus expected something entirely different, and that the emergence of the Christian Church was an undesigned accident, the chance precipitate of an experiment that went wrong!

We may summarize by saying that Jesus re-interpreted the Kingdom, and announced its presence. Yet although it was already in the midst of men it was present only in its initial stages. Through the death of Jesus it would come in victorious strength. The planted seed must be watered by the bloody sweat of His Passion.

Additional Note

Some have explained the statements about a present Kingdom as the *proleptic* activity of a Kingdom that was strictly future and catastrophic. The following may be taken as representative of this viewpoint. 'He thought of the Kingdom as future, but yet as so near at hand that its power could be felt already. The influences sent forth from it were beginning to act on the present; it was possible for men to discern those influences and allow them to operate in their lives. This in our judgement is the true significance of those sayings of Jesus in which a present realization of the Kingdom appears to be contemplated' (E. F. Scott).[1] But such an interpretation does not appear to do justice to statements like Luke xi. 20, x. 23-4—such sayings imply the arrival and presence of a sphere of blessing and power not available before. Scott says, 'The consummation which kings and prophets hoped for is on the verge of its fulfilment'; the new age is 'all but come'. Jesus' words hardly leave room for 'all but'. The strong man is already bound, and Satan has fallen; something greater than the temple is *here*. According to the thought of Jesus, evil spirits were being cast out because the 'strong man' had previously been bound. He was not on the verge of being bound for his goods were already being spoiled.

Otto should be included with those who hold the 'proleptic' view. He deals at some length with the Kingdom as a present reality, the Kingdom exercising its power. He maintains that in Mark ix. 1 'the particular addition "with power" distinguishes and presupposes an earlier existence and presence of the Kingdom which is not yet the same as the latter, and is not yet in existence "with

[1] *Kingdom and Messiah*, pp. 111-12.

power", but which is, nevertheless, already in existence and at hand'. At times we seem in these pages to be in the realm of 'realized eschatology', but he makes it quite plain that in his view of Jesus' teaching, the real inception of the Kingdom is future and catastrophic. It is, however, so near that we may speak of it as already 'breaking in'. '*The Kingdom of God was for Christ always the future Kingdom of the new age and was conceived on strict eschatological terms. It was to follow on the Messianic woes and the divine judgement.*' But already its powers had penetrated into the world. In Otto we have a rather exceptional form of the proleptic view.

It is strange that such cataclysmic events as the Parousia, Resurrection, Last Judgement, and the setting up of the Kingdom by irresistible divine power, should have manifested themselves by anticipation in One who did not strive nor cry, who did not break the bruised reed or quench the smoking flax—strange that a drama of violence should begin with a prologue of tenderness and love!

There is a sense in which, as we have seen, the ministry and death of Jesus were acts of inauguration and initiation, but they prepared the way for something of the same character, for a fuller manifestation of the same forces and the same aims. The powers that worked in Jesus were, as it were, released and extended in the later developments which His sacrifice occasioned.

CHAPTER 13

THE MESSIAHSHIP OF JESUS

IT has been maintained by some scholars that Jesus never claimed to be the Messiah or thought of Himself as such. It was the Church, it is alleged, which gave Him this designation and the references to His Messiahship in the Gospels are to be explained as alien views ascribed to Him by the Evangelists. It seems, however, quite groundless to treat the Gospels with the scepticism which this entails, and the way in which Messiahship is re-interpreted and gradually disclosed bears the stamp of truth upon it. In the Fourth Gospel there is no secrecy about the Messiahship of Jesus; all is openly announced and acknowledged from the start. But the gradual unfolding recorded in the Synoptics is more likely to correspond with the facts.

That Jesus thought of Himself in Messianic terms is suggested by the following:

1. The words at the Baptism imply that the Messianic consciousness came to Jesus on that occasion (Mark i. 11).

2. The Temptation is best explained as Jesus working out the methods and meaning of His Messiahship (Matthew iv).

3. The reply to John the Baptist is virtually a Messianic claim (Matthew xi. 2–6).

4. On the occasion of Peter's confession at Caesarea Philippi, Jesus qualified but did not deny His Messiahship (Mark viii. 27 ff.).

5. The Triumphal Entry cannot be divorced from the passage in Zechariah ix, and here we have an indirect claim to Messiahship (Mark xi. 1 ff.).

6. The words of Jesus to the High Priest give us the only explicit claim on record. To the question, 'Art thou

the Christ, the Son of the Blessed?', Jesus replied 'I am' (Mark xiv. 61–2).

It may be pointed out that 1 and 2 are concerned with the consciousness of Jesus; 3 and 4 with His disciples and John; with 5 and 6 the circle is widened still farther and the claim becomes open and explicit.

The accounts of 1 and 2 can only have come from Jesus Himself; we may well believe that He expressed to His disciples, in a way they could grasp, something that happened within His own mind. The account of the Temptation in particular is too profound to be merely a legendary creation.

It must also be insisted that whatever we think of the Form Critics' claim to have shattered the framework of the Gospel narrative, the sequence of these events is not vitally affected. It is not true that Form Criticism has destroyed every trace of development. Even if we concede that the arrangement of the pericopes is often artificial and that itineraries may be geographically uncertain, Form Criticism has no exclusive right to pronounce upon historicity; and if these things happened, they happened in this order—they arrange themselves in a sequence which (apart from the relative order of 3 and 4) can scarcely be varied.

The evidence shows that while Jesus looked upon Himself as Messiah, He was reluctant to make the claim openly; He sternly charged them to tell no man that He was the Christ. One reason for this is obvious. The word had dangerous associations, and if He had openly given Himself forth as Messiah, political upheaval and misunderstanding would have followed. Practically all the instances cited above show that Jesus re-minted the conception. The insistence at Caesarea Philippi that the Son of man must suffer is in harmony with what we find elsewhere. The position may be summarized by saying that (*a*) Jesus thought of Himself as Messiah, (*b*) He re-interpreted the conception, (c) He was hesitant in employing the word openly lest it should suggest the popular connotation and not His.

But let us look more closely at these incidents. We cannot treat them exhaustively, as our main concern in these pages is with the Parousia; but if we can discover how Jesus conceived His Messiahship it will throw further light on this related subject.

1. In Mark's account of the Baptism, it is Jesus Himself who sees the heavens rent asunder and the Spirit as a dove. The words too are addressed to Him: 'Thou art my beloved Son, in thee I am well pleased.' It is likely that these features represent something which passed in the mind of Jesus and that the account came from Him.

The words from heaven are remarkable in that they combine two O.T. passages: Psalm ii. 7 and Isaiah xlii. 1. Psalm ii speaks of a king reigning in power; it was usually regarded as Messianic, and it gives the Messiah the title Son of God and describes him as receiving the nations for his inheritance and the uttermost parts of the earth for his possession. But it goes on: 'Thou shalt break them with a rod of iron; and thou shalt dash them in pieces like a potter's vessel.'

Isaiah xlii. 1 *ff.* speaks of the Servant of God, the chosen. He too is connected with the nations and establishes judgement in the earth, but his ministry is quiet and tender; he is so gentle that he does not break the bruised reed.

The combination of these two passages is a stroke of genius. They correct and supplement each other. One speaks of sovereignty, the other of service. Together they imply that the Messiah is to achieve his goal by the methods of the Servant of God.[1] Instead of a rod of iron,

---

[1] The above suggestion is found to be substantially the same as that expounded in an essay on the Baptism of Jesus contributed by D. Plooij to *Amicitiae Corolla*, the Rendel Harris *Festgabe*.

there is the tenderness which does not even break the bruised reed or quench the smoking flax.

We may be sure that during the hidden years at Nazareth Jesus had been studying the Scriptures. There is something very original and fresh about His use of them. One of the most striking things is that He did not give great prominence to the Law as most Jews did. Jesus evidently studied the Prophets and Writings with great thoroughness, and it appears that He had formed His own interpretation of the Messianic prophecies. It may be that long before the Baptism He had made this striking conjunction of the Messiah and the Servant of God; and that at His Baptism the consciousness fully dawned on Him that He Himself was to fulfil the office.

2. The Temptation follows the Baptism. If Jesus is the Messiah, He must get alone to work out His plans and His course of action. Here again the story must have come from Jesus Himself. It is an inner struggle described in pictorial form. 'Here is the record of long days of sifting thought, and patient disentangling of confused issues, of resolute discrimination between the best and the good which is the enemy of the best.'[1] Many had thought of the Messianic age in terms of material advantages, in terms of world-domination, in terms of sheer miracle and supernatural display, and even in the O.T. these three elements are present among others of a nobler type. Jesus rejected all three. The recurring words, 'If thou art the Son of God', show that the Messiahship was the theme of the temptations; and they take up the words by the Jordan, 'Thou art my beloved Son'.[2]

It may appear strange to say that parts of the O.T.

---

[1] Dr. W. R. Maltby, *Significance of Jesus*, pp. 23–4.

[2] Cadoux (p. 103) suggests that the Temptation was the occasion when the 'strong man' was bound (Luke xi. 21–2). One may add that behind this pictorial language lies the spiritual law that the measure of a man's victory over sin in his personal experience is the measure of his ability to deliver others. Those who first bind the strong man can spoil his goods.

were a source of temptation to Jesus, that the great variety of Messianic prophecies had to be discriminated and assessed. But we may notice that in the temptation story itself the devil is represented as quoting Scripture.

The incident throws a flood of light on the way Jesus conceived His Messiahship.

3. The reply to the Baptist too is most instructive. John had foretold a cataclysmic destruction of evil and had spoken of one who would have an axe and a winnowing-fan. 'The chaff he will burn up with unquenchable fire.' This was in line with one type of O.T. Messiah who was to smite the earth and slay the wicked (Isaiah xi. 4). Little wonder that John found difficulty in recognizing in Jesus the one who should come. Jesus was spending His time in healing the sick, reclaiming the wanderers and bringing good news to the poor.

It has been asked: Did John's question arise from dawning faith, or from doubt clouding a former faith? The latter seems to be the case. Jesus' reply concluded with the words 'Blessed is he, whosoever shall find none occasion of stumbling in Me'; and this implies that Jesus was a stumbling-block and a disappointment to John. In a sense there was here a foreshadowing of the 'scandal' of the Cross.

We cannot discover when John first realized that Jesus was the Messiah; but there is evidence that John and Jesus were associated at one time, and it is possible that He had been John's disciple. Thus, while the Master did not openly speak of Himself as Messiah, John was nevertheless in a position to know who He was on account of this special relationship. With the populace it was different; Jesus' message to them concerned the Kingdom; He upbraided the cities because they did not recognize the signs of the Kingdom's presence, not because they did not recognize Him (Matthew xi. 20-4).

This incident too throws light on the way He conceived

His Messiahship. John was impatient at the lack of catastrophic intervention, and, like many good souls to-day, wished evil to be forcibly uprooted from the earth; but Jesus followed the quiet path of service and love. His method and programme did not consist in force and domination, but in joyous and redemptive ministry.

4. The Confession of Peter at Caesarea Philippi is in line with the foregoing. When Peter said, 'Thou art the Christ', Jesus 'charged them that they should tell no man of Him. And He began to teach them that the Son of man must suffer many things.' In other words, (*a*) He did not repudiate the title, (*b*) but enjoined strict silence upon the subject, and (*c*) gave an entirely new conception of Messiahship by combining it with suffering. Nothing had previously been written concerning a suffering Messiah— it seemed to be a contradiction in terms. 'And Peter took Him, and began to rebuke Him.' (The 'scandal' of the Cross now emerges quite plainly: cf. 1 Corinthians i. 23). Jesus then rebuked Peter, 'Get thee behind me, Satan'; the same temptation which arose in the wilderness comes again and is repelled with the same words.

We notice in this incident the title 'Son of man', probably Jesus' first use of the term. It is unnecessary to repeat here what was said in Part One concerning Jesus' use of this term. The conclusion reached there is in complete harmony with the findings of the present chapter. Evidence was given to show that Jesus took the designation from Daniel vii, but it is vital to notice that in this first mention of the title it is coupled with suffering. There is nothing in Daniel about this. Once again we are confronted with the fact that Jesus had His own interpretation of Messiahship.

The statement, 'the Son of man must suffer', is probably an allusion to O.T. prophecy (cf. Mark ix. 12, 'how is it written of the Son of man that He should suffer many things and be set at nought'; xiv. 21, 'for the Son of man goeth, even as it is written of Him'). The view which has commended itself to many is that Jesus has combined the Son of man with the Suffering Servant of Isaiah liii. As Dr. V. Taylor writes: 'This identification of the Son of man with the Suffering Servant is so firmly established in the mind of Jesus that He can say of the former what in the O.T. is said only of the latter.'[1] It was suggested earlier that Jesus combined in His thought the Messiah and the Servant of God (Psalm ii and Isaiah xlii); if that is true, then we have now a similar instance of the same procedure. In Daniel vii. 13–14 the Son of man is given world-sovereignty; yet this lofty claim is linked by our Lord with the man of sorrows of Isaiah liii. Thus the passage which claims the greatest glory is linked with the one which describes the greatest humiliation. In Philippians ii. 5–11 Paul is virtually repeating the teaching of Jesus, the lowliest humiliation and the highest glory are joined together; the One who took the form of a servant becomes Lord of all. As the words at the Baptism had combined sovereignty with service, so now sovereignty is combined with sacrifice.

The thought is further illustrated in Mark x. 35–45, the request of John and James. Jesus does not deny His kingship, but it is contrasted with the kingdoms of the world. Instead of thrones, He offers a cup and a baptism. Potentates may desire to dominate, but His kingdom is different; He came to serve and to give His life a ransom for many. His supreme service for mankind is His sacrifice, and His death is of a piece with His life. The principles of service enunciated in 43–5 reach their climax in sacrifice, just as the Servant Songs of Isaiah reach their climax in liii.

In the early days of His ministry it appears that Jesus did not speak of His death. That event was occasioned by historical circumstances; we are not to think of Him

[1] *Jesus and His Sacrifice*, p. 256.

slavishly following some hard-and-fast prophetic chart. If we were writing a life of Christ much more would have to be said of this. His first call was to the nation, and when rejection came and death was threatened He found in Isaiah liii the pledge that death itself could startle many nations and could be a gateway into a more glorious ministry.

5. Jesus' choice of an ass on the occasion of His entry into Jerusalem is again significant. It is difficult to avoid the impression that Zechariah ix was in His mind, with its message of a king who was 'meek and lowly'. On entering the city, His first action was to visit the Temple and to 'look round about upon all things' (Mark xi. 11); the next day He made His protest against the neglect of its purpose of providing 'a house of prayer *for all the nations*' (17). He is reminding the nation again of its true vocation, religious leadership.

It is sometimes wrongly said that Jesus had to choose between two conceptions of the Messiah, the warrior son of David and the apocalyptic Son of man. The choice was rather between two conceptions of national destiny developed in the Old Testament—one which thought of the nation as destined to material greatness and political supremacy, another which thought of the nation as 'the sacred school of the knowledge of God and of the spiritual life for all mankind'. These involved different conceptions of the Messiah, but the Messianic figure corresponding to the second had not been developed in the O.T. Jesus accordingly created it Himself, not out of nothing, but by skilfully combining strands of O.T. teaching into a new synthesis. A Messiah who was also prophet had scarcely been thought of before; by His emphasis upon the Servant conceptions Jesus included the prophetic task as an essential part of the Messianic vocation.

6. The reply to Caiaphas has been dealt with earlier, with similar results.

In the light of all this, it is surely foolish to say that the Messianic thought of Jesus was entirely eschatological, that He was Messiah simply in the sense that He believed He was destined to come again upon the clouds in the near future. When we consider the facts set forth in the foregoing, the whole argument that Jesus' thought and ministry were entirely controlled by the Parousia—hope simply falls to pieces.

It may be asked: If Messiahship was open to misunderstanding and the disclosure would have run the risk of political upheaval, and if Jesus re-interpreted it in such a radical manner, why did He employ the conception at all? The answer is that though He transformed it, it was hardly possible for Him to ignore it altogether. Had He not accepted the designation, had He left it unabsorbed, the disciples would have still looked forward for the coming of the promised one and the inevitable question would have arisen again and again, 'Art thou he that should come or look we for another?' Their attitude to the Scriptures, and His own, did not permit them to abandon the conception altogether. There are signs, as we have seen, that He was somewhat dissatisfied and embarrassed by the title. He appeared to avoid the word 'Messiah', and His use of the rare phrase 'Son of man' allowed Him to pour into it His own meaning.

It was a sound instinct which led the Jews to look for some outstanding person as the fulfilment of their hopes. Many other nations have had similar Messianic hopes, longings not only for a divine order, but also for a captain of salvation. Jesus was conscious of His uniqueness, and His task as He conceived it could best be explained by the employment of these categories.[1] If Jesus was, and is, what the Christian Church believes Him to be, then it is not strange that He Himself was conscious of that unique

[1] 'He was conscious of speaking the last and final word; He felt that what He did was final and that no one would come after Him' (Bousset, *Jesus*).

relation with God which His words imply, and it was not lack of humility, but recognition of the truth which led Him to admit that in His ministry God's final struggle against evil had been joined.

But this is very different from maintaining that Jesus slavishly modelled His life upon a pre-ordained programme or followed the fixed Messianic scheme of which some speak. The prophecies concerning the Messiah were so varied and inconsistent that it would have been impossible for Jesus to have attempted to follow them all. Further, in Christ we find far more than the prophets ever dreamed of; He fulfilled and transcended their loftiest conceptions.

So far, indeed, is the Christ of the Gospels from being the studied and self-conscious realization of the Messianic hope of the past, that it was not till the Christ had lived on earth that the true inwardness and meaning of those ancient ideals became manifest, and found at once their interpretation and fulfilment in the various natural expressions of the unique personality of the Son of Man (R. H. Charles).[1]

[1] *Between the Old and New Testaments*, p. 96.

CHAPTER 14

JUDGEMENT

In Matthew the Parousia is linked with the Judgement, and we must therefore make some reference to this subject as it appears in the teaching of Jesus. Some authorities have held that He never spoke of Himself as Judge, and it is noteworthy that references to this effect are confined (among the Synoptic Gospels) to Matthew.

Luke xiii. 25–8 speaks rather of a shut door than a judgement scene. Dr. C. H. Dodd contends that the source of this passage is the same as that of Matthew xxv. 10–12, 'but whereas in Matthew we have the natural conclusion of a quite realistic story, in Luke the only remnant of parable is in the word "householder".'. The final stage he finds in Matthew vii. 22–3 where the 'bridegroom' of Matthew xxv and the 'householder' of Luke xiii has become unequivocally the Lord Jesus speaking in His own person, and the scene is laid on the day of judgement.[1]

The fact of man's accountability to God's judgement is undoubtedly present in Jesus' teaching, but for the most part the statements are general and lack pictorial details. This is the case with the Marcan saying, 'these shall receive greater condemnation', κρίμα (xii. 40), and the Q saying, 'Judge not, that ye be not judged' (Matthew vii. 1; Luke vi. 37). In these and in similar references nothing is said of Jesus as judge, or of a day of judgement, near or remote—a Great Assize at the end of the world.

In Matthew, however, specific details of this kind are given. Matthew xvi. 27b speaks of Christ as judge: 'then

[1] *Parables of the Kingdom*, p. 173–4.

shall he render unto every man according to his deeds', but comparison with the corresponding passage of Mark shows that Matthew is responsible for the addition of these words, which apparently come from the O.T. (Psalm lxii. 12).

It is more than doubtful whether Jesus ever spoke of 'the day of judgement', an expression which is found only in Matthew as is 'judgement of Gehenna'. The word κρισις, which does not occur in Mark is used much more frequently in Matthew than in Luke.

Luke has references to 'the judgement' in x. 14, xi. 31, 32. These are all sayings in which Jesus contrasts His contemporaries unfavourably with certain people of the past. The expression 'rise up in the judgement' must not be pressed to mean that at a great assize a group of people who once lived at Nineveh will rise to their feet and condemn another group consisting of Jesus' contemporaries; Wellhausen and others have pointed out that the Aramaic behind ἀναστήσονται (ἐγερθήσονται) ἐν τῇ κρίσει would mean simply 'will accuse, will condemn'. The reference is not to a future judgement day at all; the meaning is: Contrasted with them this generation stands condemned because it has sinned against greater light. We may compare Matthew xii. 27=Luke xi. 19: 'And if I by Beelzebub cast out devils, by whom do your sons cast them out? therefore shall they be your judges', i.e. their action shows you to be in the wrong.[1]

In Luke x. 12–15 (=Matthew xi. 20–4) the meaning clearly is that a worse fate awaits Chorazin and Capernaum than befell Sodom. To press the words literally and to say that 'the land of Sodom' will be punished again on judgement day is surely mistaken. The judgement of Sodom lay in the past; let Capernaum be warned, let its inhabitants repent lest in view of their fuller

[1] ἔσονται represents an Aramaic imperfect, not a definite future (McNeile).

advantages they have a worse fate. Jesus had a message for communities as well as individuals. He believed in a judgement of God which runs through history. His language to the northern cities is reminiscent of Isaiah xiv. 13–15, the oracle on Babylon. The implication is that as Babylon had perished and descended to the realm of the dead, so would the cities which rejected the Kingdom of God.

As a matter of fact, Capernaum has so perished. Jesus saw that survival is dependent on moral and spiritual qualities. Communities which violate divine laws cannot endure. The thought is not of some future day of judgement at the end of time, but it is rather a philosophy of history. This is confirmed by the statement that if Sodom had repented, as it would have done had it witnessed the mighty works of Jesus' ministry, '*it would have remained until this day*' (Matthew xi. 23). Dr. Cadoux connects these pronouncements against the northern cities with the advance of Roman armies marching south towards Jerusalem.[1] Jesus foresaw the breach between the Jews and the Empire; it was involved in their rejection of His ethical teaching. Capernaum and the rest lay on the path of the Roman armies.

We come now to the great judgement scene of Matthew xxv. 31–46, of which some mention was made in an earlier chapter.

(1) Many authorities believe that Matthew is responsible for the framework, but it seems clear that some genuine words of Jesus lie behind this passage. The sentence, 'Inasmuch as ye did it to one of the least of these, my brethren, ye did it unto me', surely goes back to the Master Himself. But other features arouse misgivings. Some phrases belong to stock apocalyptic imagery of the kind in which Matthew delighted. The word ἀφορίζω (32) is found also in xiii. 49 in Matthew's

[1] *Historic Mission of Jesus*, p. 268.

I

midrash on the Dragnet: 'so shall it be in the end of the world; the angels shall come forth, and sever the wicked from among the righteous.' The word occurs nowhere else in the Gospels in this eschatological sense. (Luke vi. 22 is the only other occurrence in the Gospels: 'when men separate you from their company'.)

T. W. Manson points out that Matthew's special source has a particular interest in separating men into two classes and that its material is reminiscent of John the Baptist. 'The parables of the Wheat and Tares, of the Dragnet, of the Sheep and Goats . . . are all of them just variations, more or less elaborate, on the theme of John the Baptist—wheat and chaff' (*Teaching of Jesus*, pp. 34–8). C. J. Cadoux's opinion on Matthew xxv. 31–46 has been quoted earlier in Chapter 11.

We may take the passage as a Matthean construction; the main picture is just an expansion of such teaching as is found in xiii. 40–3, Matthew's explanation of the Tares parable. But it has at its heart genuine words of Jesus similar to the sayings found elsewhere: 'He that receiveth you receiveth Me . . . whosoever shall give to drink unto one of these little ones a cup of cold water only, he shall in no wise lose his reward' (Matthew x. 40–2). Matthew or his source had developed this thought, placing it within an apocalyptic framework (probably under the influence of Enoch lxii) and working it out in the light of his preference for two ways, two classes, two destinies.

(2) Another treatment of the passage has been suggested, in the light of its opening reference to 'all nations'. It is urged that literal nations are envisaged, not individual Gentiles. This would be completely in keeping with the usage of the O.T. prophets; the only judgement of which they speak is that of nations. Sometimes, like Amos, they dealt with specific peoples one by one; and sometimes they spoke of nations in general. It would have been natural for Jesus, after dealing on several

occasions with the fate which awaited Israel, to turn to
Gentile nations and in doing so to draw upon the imagery
of the Valley of Jehoshaphat, where God was to plead
with all nations and vindicate His own people (Joel iii. 2
and 12). But in Jesus' version what is the standard and
the test by which the nations are judged, and who are
the people to be vindicated? The test is the nations'
treatment of the poor and the unprivileged; He identifies
Himself with the prisoner, the naked, the sick, the stranger
—these are His brethren; and by their treatment of His
brethren the nations are judged.

cf. Psalm ix. 17–18:

> The wicked shall return to Sheol,
> Even all the nations that forget God.
> For the needy shall not always be forgotten,
> Nor the expectation of the poor perish for ever.

and Psalm lxxvi. 9:

> When God arose to judgement,
> To save all the meek of the earth.

On this view the passage may be taken as pictorial
representation of a judgement which runs through history.
Reference has been made earlier to this thought in the
teaching of Jesus. The passage would thus give a magni-
ficent philosophy of history with very practical bearings
upon national policy. The survival of a nation depends
upon compassion and goodness, upon its treatment of the
unprivileged, for God is the friend of the poor and needy;
cf. Homeric morality, in which Nemesis is aroused by
any wrong or treachery toward the helpless, the stranger,
the suppliant, and the aged.[1] This is why Nineveh and
Babylon perished; behind the glittering façade of their
splendour there was cruelty and oppression, and so they

[1] Gilbert Murray, *Encyclopaedia Britannica* (14th ed.), xi. 698.

have passed to the realm of the dead, to the rubbish tip of Gehenna.

It must be admitted that this is a most attractive interpretation of the pericope; and while parts of the passage in its present condition read rather awkwardly for the national application, it is possible that the words of Jesus which lie behind it had the nations in view.

But whether we adopt this interpretation or the one suggested earlier, the fact remains that the evidence of this passage is not strong enough to warrant us in revising our conclusion that Jesus did not regard Himself as judge of all humanity quick and dead in a great assize at the end of time.

There are also positive statements inconsistent with the view that Jesus looked for such an assize.

1. In the discussion with the Sadducees, Jesus refers to 'the God of Abraham, and the God of Isaac, and the God of Jacob' (Mark xii. 26), and adds, 'He is not the God of the dead, but of the living', for as Luke's account adds as a legitimate inference, 'all live unto Him'. This implies that men go to whatever fate awaits them immediately after death, and are not kept waiting until sentence has been passed at the great judgement.

The questioners used the phrase 'in the resurrection', but the reply of Jesus speaks of the present (not future) state of the patriarchs and implies that they already live the risen life. As Otto writes: 'They had received deliverance from the condition of death, and they were with God. But they never rose from their graves. They had arisen—if the word arisen is at all appropriate—from Sheol, but not from the grave. The story of the beggar Lazarus corresponds exactly' (p. 239). Otto maintains that in the mind of Jesus the conception of resurrection simply combined with that of a life with God generally, a life renewed from death. The vivification of the body, he says, had no special emphasis—indeed, was not really and necessarily included in the conception.

The incident is also important as showing that Jesus did not share the materialistic views set forth in some of the apocalypses (Mark xii. 25).

2. In the Parable of Dives and Lazarus (Luke xvi. 19 *ff.*), the two principal characters go respectively to torment and to Abraham's bosom immediately after death. It would be wrong to insist that Jesus accepted all the details of the popular story which probably lie behind this parable; but it is legitimate to point out that here again there is no room for a judgement day.

The view that Jesus expected a speedy arrival of a great judgement at which all the race would be judged by Himself does not survive close study of our original documents. That Jesus believed in human responsibility and men's accountability to God is indisputable. He taught that this life was closely linked to the next, that men's actions and character would be reflected in their future destiny. The question we have been discussing is whether Jesus clothed these thoughts in a certain way.

It is true that Jesus divided men, but this division belonged to the present and was brought about by the challenge of His mission. Men had to take sides, they were either for Him or against Him, and in a sense this was a judgement, for the true character of a man was revealed by his response to the call. John the Baptist had foretold a day of wrath and the separation of wheat and chaff; the coming One would have a fan in His hand and would thoroughly cleanse His threshing-floor. This prophecy received an unexpected fulfilment; there was no forcible separation of good and bad, but nevertheless in the ministry of Jesus there was a sifting of human souls. By their reaction to His message men fell into two camps, and they thus judged themselves. Some gathered with Him, others scattered. We can see the sifting process in action in such passages as Mark x. 22; Luke ix. 57–62; cf. Luke xii. 51–3: 'There shall be from henceforth five in one house divided, three against two, and two against three; they shall be divided. . . .' Men revealed their true characters, they judged themselves (as they do to-day), by the different attitudes which they assumed towards Him.

CHAPTER 15

JESUS AND THE FUTURE

It is taken as axiomatic by many scholars that Jesus expected a speedy end of the world.[1] His announcements concerning the Kingdom of God are, it is said, a proof of this. But it has been pointed out earlier that while Jesus expected some great development to result from His death He spoke of the Kingdom as already present during His ministry, transmuting its meaning in terms of a present salvation. 'Transmuted eschatology' was expounded by Von Dobschütz in his *Eschatology of the Gospels* (1910), and he stressed the point that Jesus fulfilled in His ministry and work what was expected for the Messianic time: 'What was spoken of in Jewish eschatology as to come in the last days is taken here as already at hand in the lifetime of Jesus; it is transmuted at the same time in the other sense that what was expected as an external change is taken inwardly.'[2]

But apart from the fact that Jesus spoke of the Kingdom of God as already initiated, His whole attitude and the spirit of His teaching is inconsistent with the view that He expected a world catastrophe to arrive at any moment.

---

[1] '*Es ist unbestreitbar, dass Jesus sich das Kommen des Gottesreichs zugleich als eine nahe kosmische Katastrophe vorgestellt hat*' (Bultmann).

[2] The point was, of course, not new; e.g. Colani in 1864 emphasized the fact that the Kingdom had already come in the ministry of Jesus and underlined Matthew xii. 28, ἔφθασεν ἐφ' ὑμᾶς, xi. 4–6, Luke xvii. 20–1, and similar sayings (*Jésus Christ et les croyances messianiques de son temps*, p. 95). Hoskyns and Davey, in their stirring *Riddle of the New Testament* (1931), showed that underlying Mark's Gospel was the thought that the Messianic prophecies of Isaiah xxxv, etc., were now fulfilled, and thus the whole ministry of Jesus is the advent of precisely those things which were sighed for in the Messianic hope. C. H. Dodd prefers the term 'realized eschatology'.

Where in His teaching is this universal cataclysm described?

We know for a certainty that Jesus studied the processes of Nature, but we do not know that He ever saw the pseudepigraphs extant in His day. The references to Nature are abundant; they are fresh, original, and belong to the most characteristic part of His teaching. He was impressed by its mystery and beneficence, its quietness and dependability, the steady and sure growth revealed in its processes. Even the grace of God is symbolized by the impartiality of the sunshine and the rain. The bearing of Jesus is not that of a distraught, wild-eyed apocalyptist shrieking out the vain message that millions now living will never die; it is rather that of the patient farmer who has perfect confidence that the harvest is sure, that one stage of development will inevitably follow another, that small and unpretentious beginnings will have great results. One finds nothing to veto but much to confirm the belief that Jesus looked down the vista of the future knowing that the triumph of His cause was sure.

The parables show how deeply Jesus loved the actual world. The everyday life of ordinary people was to Him a matter of absorbing interest. One who knows Nature and life as intimately as Jesus did does not take kindly to the view that God is about to destroy the present universe by some sudden cataclysm. On the contrary, there is much in Jesus' teaching to support the view that to Him human history had a long period before it. Jesus spoke of a New Covenant rather than a new universe. The Old Covenant had lasted for 1,500 years. Now, He says in effect, a new dispensation has begun.

There are many incidental factors in the Gospels, too, which confirm the view that Jesus did not expect the end of the world to supervene almost immediately. In the story of the anointing at Bethany, for instance, the well-known words occur, 'The poor ye have always with you, and whensoever ye will ye can do them good; but Me ye have not always' (Mark xiv. 7). These words alone, whose genuineness is surely beyond question, show that Jesus did not expect the end of the world in the near future. Opportunities for ministry to the poor would continue after His removal. Again, in the same story, 'Wheresoever the gospel shall be preached throughout the whole world, that also which this woman hath done shall be spoken of for a memorial of her' (9). Many critics have thrown doubt upon these words, but His readiness to defend the maligned woman is thoroughly in keeping with the character of Jesus, and the idea of making her action a part of the imperishable Gospel seems too beautiful to be the invention of the early Church—especially as no name is given. But in any case verse 7 quoted above remains.[1]

But apart from such incidental touches which are so revealing, let us look more closely at three considerations which show that Jesus did not believe the end was at hand and would follow shortly after His Crucifixion: His ethical teaching, His references to the New Israel, and to the Gentiles.

A. *Ethical Teaching*

The ethical teaching of Jesus, which figures so prominently in His recorded words, would be inexplicable on the view that He expected a catastrophic divine intervention to take place shortly; cf. Matthew v: 'It was said to them of old time . . . but I say unto you.' Why should Jesus take the trouble and risk of revising a legal code, which had existed for centuries, if He expected the end of the world in a short time? The Sermon on the Mount cannot

[1] W. R. Maltby in his book, *Jesus and His Cross*, shows in Chapter 3 that in the later stages of the ministry one can trace a widening of the horizon; Jesus is 'concerned with a far wider audience than His own contemporaries'.

represent the ethics of the new creation for persecution is spoken of.

Schweitzer, of course, held that eschatology was the main obsession of Jesus and that this was the secret of His ethical greatness. The apocalyptic hope enabled Him to take a detached view of human life and lifted Him above the fashion of the times into the eternities:

That which is eternal in the words of Jesus is due to the very fact that they are based on an eschatological world-view, and contain the expression of a mind for which the contemporary world with its historical and social circumstances no longer had any existence. They are appropriate, therefore, to any world, for in every world they raise the man who dares to meet their challenge, and does not turn and twist them into meaninglessness, above his world and his time, making him inwardly free, so that he is fitted to be, in his own world and in his time, a simple channel of the power of Jesus.[1]

The relevance of Jesus' words to every age is not in dispute, but the alleged eschatological basis. The ethical teaching of Jesus sprang from His vision of the Father, not from apocalypticism. Men were called to model their lives upon the divine character. They must love their enemies because God does so; He sends His rain upon the just and the unjust. 'Ye therefore shall be perfect, as your heavenly Father is perfect' (Matthew v. 48). By likeness to God men establish their divine sonship. 'Love your enemies and do them good . . . and ye shall be sons of the Most High; for he is kind towards the unthankful and evil. Be ye merciful, even as your Father is merciful' (Luke vi. 35–6). This conception of imitating the divine goes back to the O.T.; e.g. Leviticus xix. 2: 'Ye shall be holy; for I the Lord your God am holy.' The supreme commands, said Jesus, were to love God, and one's neighbour. How does this lofty teaching spring from apocalyptic?

[1] *Quest of the Historical Jesus*, p. 400.

It is true that in some parts of the N.T. the influence of apocalyptic upon ethics can be traced. One example is Paul's teaching on marriage in 1 Corinthians vii, where the eschatology has had a warping and lamentable effect. Again, the fervid apocalyptic hopes of the Thessalonians did not sharpen their moral perception, but led them to neglect their work and to offend against the community to which they belonged. But the ethic of Jesus was a corollary of His revelation of the divine character. Incidentally, this shows how futile it is to separate the ethic of Jesus from His teaching about God.

B. *The New Israel*

The Church spoke of itself as the new Israel, e.g. Galatians vi. 16, and it seems certain that this thought goes back to Jesus Himself. The sorrow of the Master over the refusal of His countrymen to respond to His call, their blindness to the presence of the Kingdom of God, have already been mentioned. The parable of the Vineyard gives a pictorial representation of their failure, and it ends with the words, 'What therefore will the lord of the vineyard do? he will come and destroy the husbandmen, and will give the vineyard unto others' (Mark xii. 9). The purpose of God must find a new organ. The pains which Jesus took with the Twelve are explained by the fact that He regarded them as the nucleus of the new community. Such sayings as Mark x. 43–4 refer to the disciples as a distinct society: 'But it is not so among you; but whosoever would become great among you, shall be your servant, etc.'[1]

In the same way, the destruction of the Temple is coupled with the building of a new one 'without hands'. As we saw earlier, the accusation at the trial of Jesus evidently rested upon some genuine words of His whose

[1] Dr. R. Newton Flew, in *Jesus and His Church*, demonstrates by a five-fold argument that Jesus 'had in view a community of a new kind' (pp. 48 *ff.*).

original form is not certain, though there is little doubt of their meaning; cf. Mark xiv. 58; John ii. 19, etc. It is unlikely that Jesus had in mind the prophecy that the Messiah would build a temple (Zechariah vi. 12–13). We have rather another form of the idea that the reverse side of the rejection of Israel is the creation of a new Israel. Otto's comment is interesting (p. 62):

> The saying anticipates a time in which there will arise from the work of Christ a temple not made with hands, i.e. a service of God in opposition to that with which Israel was acquainted, and which the law had sanctified—one is almost compelled to say a new religion instead of the old. This opposition is not that between God's kingdom and the present mundane period, and the saying does not speak of the inbreaking of the eschatological order. Rather, the latter conception now recedes, and the reference is to something in the mundane period itself, opposed to, dissolving, and surpassing what has gone before—and it is indeed a something which will have a future, a stability, and duration, as against what had been wiped away, and was of a provisional and transitory character.

In writing this, which is the correct meaning of the words, Otto appears to be abandoning his main contention. But this is not so, for he goes on:

> Thus we encounter a peculiar double-sidedness, which must appear paradoxical. On the one hand the liveliest feeling of the immediate inbreaking of the supramundane future; on the other hand a message which is completely undisturbed by the former fact in its relation to time, the world, and life, which reckons on duration, on continuance in time and in temporal and world affairs, and is related thereto. This it is which we call the irrationality of the genuine and typically eschatological attitude.

Otto thus maintains that at one and the same time Jesus held two inconsistent ideas: (1) that the end of the world was imminent, and (2) that from His work a new community of God and a new religion would arise on earth! It is significant that we have advanced beyond 'consistent eschatology'. We can no longer regard apocalyptic as the key to every problem in the life and teaching of Jesus, and indeed it can only be retained by sacrificing His consistency.

Related to the new Israel and the new temple are the new covenant and the new law (Matthew v. 21, 27, etc.) and the saying, 'The law and the prophets were until John: from that time the gospel of the Kingdom of God is preached' (Luke xvi. 16). Again, there is the new wine and the old wineskins, the new patch and the old garment (Mark ii. 21-2).

The logion of Luke xii. 32 is also relevant in this connection: 'Fear not, little flock; it is your Father's good pleasure to give you the Kingdom.' The words seem to be an echo of Daniel vii. 27: 'the kingdom shall be given to the people of the saints of the Most High'. In both passages we have 'the kingdom' without any epithet; in both, the kingdom is 'given'; and in both mention is made of the people to whom the kingdom is given—the writer of Daniel obviously meant the Jewish nation, but Jesus identifies the recipients of the kingdom with His own disciples, the 'little flock'.

The same thought gives the key to the difficult saying which we have in different versions in *Matthew xix. 28* and *Luke xxii. 28-30*:

Matthew: Verily I say unto you, that ye which have followed Me, in the regeneration when the Son of man shall sit on the throne of His glory, ye also shall sit upon twelve thrones, judging the twelve tribes of Israel.

Luke: But ye are they which have continued with Me in my temptations; and I appoint unto you a kingdom, even as My Father appointed unto Me, that ye may eat and drink at My table in My kingdom; and ye shall sit on thrones judging the twelve tribes of Israel.

Luke probably gives the more reliable version of this saying, which can hardly be from Q, Matthew and Luke rather taking it from their special sources. Suspicion attaches to Matthew's word, παλινγενεσια,[1] and also, as noted before, to the words 'when the Son of man shall sit on the throne of His glory'. Again, Luke's setting is more likely to be the true one, as Matthew has intruded it into the story of the Rich Ruler.

Luke xxii. 24–30 forms a coherent unity and it was probably a continuous sequence in Luke's special source.[2] If we therefore consider it as a whole the meaning will emerge more clearly. The disciples are contending as to who is the greatest (24) and Jesus gives them a contrast between the overbearing conduct of earthly kings (25) and the principle of service which must characterize *their* community (26),[3] a spirit which they have seen in Him (27). Yet He is a king, and as they have shared His trials (28) so they will now share in His kingship (29–30).

God had appointed to Him a kingdom, or rather kingly authority (29b);[4] He had the right to sit at the table and yet lived as a servant:

For whether is greater, he that sitteth at meat, or he that serveth? is not he that sitteth at meat? but I am in the midst of you as he that serveth (27).

The words sum up the whole ministry of Jesus and do not, of course, refer to a literal feast. They have seen the kind of royalty for which He stands—the royalty which He now assigns to them—so different from that of pagan

[1] Dalman, *Words of Jesus*: 'It must be attributed to the Evangelist himself'; 'distinctly Greek, and cannot be literally translated either into Hebrew or Aramaic' (p. 177).

[2] cf. V. Taylor, *First Draft of St. Luke's Gospel*, 34.

[3] J. M. Creed on verse 26: 'Readers of the Gospel would naturally think of the Apostles as future rulers of the Church.'

[4] Βασιλεια is anarthrous and means 'kingly authority' rather than the Kingdom of God.

rulers. Theirs is to be of the same kind: he that is chief let him become as he that doth serve. It is true that they are to be leaders in the New Israel, but their leadership is to be modelled on the example of Christ, not that of secular rulers.

The passage thus makes a logical unity and is bound together by the idea of the disciples and their 'greatness'— a theme which occurs in the first verse (24) and the last (30) and indeed in every verse except 28. Verse 30 is also linked to the earlier part by the imagery of a table and a feast. As the passage began with kings, so it returns at the end to the imagery of thrones. From beginning to end, the question of leadership and greatness is in view.

We have not yet finished with the words '*the twelve tribes of Israel*', and if Luke is right in connecting them with the Last Supper, further light is thrown on their meaning.

Luke xxii. 24–7 is similar to Mark x. 42 *ff.*, but this is not fatal to the view that the words of the former were spoken at the Last Supper. (*a*) As several authorities hold, Mark may have joined together two units which were originally separate; x. 35–40 and 41–5 both deal with the same theme. (*b*) There are important differences between the two passages in Luke and Mark, and it may be that Jesus dealt with the same subject in a rather similar way on two occasions; the contention about precedence apparently came up again and again, and it would not be surprising that Jesus should give roughly the same reply on more than one occasion.

Further, the imagery of reclining at a meal (Luke xxii. 27 and 30) would have been appropriate at the Last Supper.

If then Luke is correct in his placing of 24–30, Jesus had previously spoken of a New Covenant in His blood (20). It is true that there is doubt on the grounds of MS. variation about 19*b*–20 and this passage may have been interpolated into Luke's account; but for our present purpose this point is immaterial. Our concern is with what actually happened in the Upper Room, and we know from other sources that Jesus spoke of covenant blood (Mark xiv. 24); and our oldest account of the Last Supper (1 Corinthians xi) contains the words now found in Luke: 'This cup is the New Covenant in My blood.'

These words look back to two passages of the O.T. which were presumably in the mind of Jesus, Jeremiah xxxi and Exodus xxiv. *Jeremiah xxxi* had spoken of a New Covenant, a new divine-human relationship, superseding the old one of external laws and sanctions. This New Covenant was to be with 'the house of Israel'. The disciples of Jesus were both the 'remnant' of the old Israel and the nucleus of the new.

Exodus xxiv; cf. verse 8: 'Behold the blood of the Covenant.' This chapter describes how the first Covenant was established and the nation constituted.

In primitive times when two men made an alliance or friendship they sometimes sealed their union by cutting themselves and allowing their blood to mingle—a piece of symbolism as rational as the ring at a wedding given as a token of the 'Covenant now made betwixt me and thee'. In the incident recorded in Exodus xxiv, Israel and God are symbolically joined together in an analogous way and the equivalent of the blood ceremony is the sprinkling of animal blood partly on the altar (representing God) and partly on the people.[1] Thus the Covenant is ratified.

And so when Jesus in the gathering shadows speaks of the New Covenant, He says in effect, 'This Covenant too is to be sealed with blood—My own'. It will not be aimlessly poured out, His death is to bear His meaning and not that of His enemies—it will not be merely a martyrdom and a crime. He knew that it was not the

---

[1] According to T. H. Robinson, the slaying of the victims here 'is not strictly a "sacrifice", because the offering is not made to any one' (*Moffatt Commentary on Matthew*, p. 216).

end for Himself, but the point in view here is that it was
not the end of 'the people of God'. The Cross marked an
end and a beginning—the end of the Old Covenant with
its external laws, but also the founding of the New Israel
and the beginning of a new era in the story of God and
man. Since the Last Supper is indissolubly linked to the
Cross and took place in its shadow, the Supper itself, with
its 'cup of the New Covenant in My blood' and its
symbolism of a common meal, marks the constituting of
the Christian Church.[1] The phrase 'making history' has
perhaps become cheapened by common use; but when
Jesus went through the events of the Last Supper and the
Crucifixion He was consciously making history. The
world Church of to-day, which traces its origin from the
Upper Room at Jerusalem, is the direct result of His
action.

As the Old Covenant was made with 'the twelve tribes
of Israel' (Exodus xxiv. 4) and was sealed with blood, so
the New Covenant envisages the twelve tribes of a New
Israel and its validity is assured by One who paid the
uttermost sacrifice and had no limit to the lengths He was
prepared to go in His task of bringing men to God.

It is noteworthy that the phrase '*the twelve tribes of
Israel*' occurs in the chapter to which the words of Jesus
take us back. 'Moses . . . builded an altar under the
mount, and twelve pillars[2] according to the twelve tribes
of Israel' (Exodus xxiv. 4). The phrase is found nowhere
else in the O.T., except Genesis xlix. 28, and the reference
cannot have been to that passage. This is a striking confirmation of the view taken above that in Luke xxii. 30
Jesus was speaking of the New Israel.

The defection of Judas is not a fatal objection to Luke's
placing of the logion. 'Twelve tribes of Israel' is symbolic

---

[1] '*Das Abendmahl ist der Akt der Gründung seiner ἐκκλησια, seiner "Gemeinde"
als solcher, gewesen*' (Kattenbusch).
[2] It is only a coincidence that in Galatians ii. 9 the Apostles are 'pillars'.

language for the new community as a whole, and in
Luke's version there are not twelve thrones. The usage
may be illustrated by reference to James i. 1, where the
greeting to the Church universal is expressed in the words
'to the twelve tribes which are of the Dispersion'.

C. *The Gentiles*

There are many indications that the ultimate purpose of
Jesus embraced the Gentiles. It is true that He regarded
His own mission as one to Israel, and during His ministry
He concentrated upon His own countrymen. But again
and again His thoughts went out to the Gentile world
from which men would one day come from the East and
West and sit down in the Kingdom of God. He spoke
with approval of the Queen of Sheba and the men of
Nineveh, and according to Luke made pointed references
to the widow of Zarephath and Naaman the Syrian. He
had special words of kindness for Samaritans and for the
Roman Centurion. When cleansing the Temple, Jesus
referred to its original purpose as a house of prayer 'for
all the nations'. This suggests that though His immediate
task had the nation in view, it was that the nation itself
might fulfil its divine mission of bringing blessing to all
the families of the earth.[1] Again, the Messianic passages
of the O.T. which are suggested by different stages in the
life of Jesus have a super-national reference (Psalms ii, cx;
Daniel vii; Zechariah ix). We must consider also such
expressions as 'the light of the *world*', and 'the salt of the
earth'. This question has an important bearing on Jesus'
thoughts concerning the future.

We are nevertheless told by many scholars that Jesus
could not have contemplated the mission to the Gentiles
which His followers later carried out, because in the early
Church there was a dispute on this matter. Such sayings
as Mark xiv. 9 ('wheresoever the gospel shall be preached

[1] cf. R. N. Flew, *Jesus and His Church*, p. 85.

throughout the whole world') are swept aside, and it is argued that if such words existed the later controversies would have been impossible. The real answer to this is that the controversy was about the terms on which Gentiles should be admitted to the Church. But before we come to this point it is perhaps worth noting that when the missionary movement began in this country 150 years ago, many Christian people opposed the historic work of William Carey. The Rev. Sydney Smith, in the *Edinburgh Review*, 1808–9, spoke of 'routing out a nest of consecrated cobblers'; and while making the formal concession that it was 'the general duty of Christian people to disseminate their religion among the Pagan nations who are subjected to their empire', he nevertheless wrote: 'We see not the slightest prospect of success; we see much danger in making the attempt; and we doubt if the conversion of the Hindoos would ever be more than nominal.' In one article he developed at length four reasons 'for giving up the task of conversion'. It would be precarious to conclude from this that Sydney Smith's Bible lacked the missionary commands of the N.T.! If such an attitude was possible in the nineteenth century, it was surely possible in the first.

Would not words of Jesus have been quoted, it is urged, if they had been known? As hinted above, such questions miss the point. The dispute in the early Church was about the terms on which Gentiles were to be admitted to the Church. The Judaistic party did not wish to stop the missionary work of the Church. Judaism had for centuries welcomed Gentiles into the fold; indeed, some of the Pharisees compassed sea and land to make one proselyte, and we cannot imagine that the Church was narrower than the Synagogue. The point at issue was this: on what terms were Gentiles to be admitted as Christians? must they become full Jews and obey the Mosaic law, or not? There was genuine ground for dispute here, and the debate of Acts xv, the hesitation of Peter in x–xi, and his vacillation in Galatians ii, do not prove that Jesus had not envisaged the Gentile mission. They do suggest that He had not left clear guidance on the details of procedure. The First Gospel and Paul's letters illustrate the two sides of the dispute; both agree that Gentiles must be evangelized (cf. Matthew xxviii. 16–20), but while Paul maintains that the law of Moses has been abrogated, the First Gospel insists that no jot of it must be disregarded.

Words of Jesus no doubt could have been and were adduced on both sides of this dispute. He appeared indirectly to abrogate the dietary rules of Leviticus by His pronouncement that a man is not defiled by what goes into his mouth, but by what comes out. 'This He said, making all meats clean' (Mark vii. 19). But He had given no explicit instructions concerning circumcision and many other questions which were bound to be provoked by work among the Gentiles.

We cannot, of course, rest anything upon Mark xvi. 15 or Matthew xxviii. 19–20, and probably the same must be said of Acts i. 8; but there is much to support the view that the purposes of Jesus went far beyond national barriers and were indeed world-wide. The Servant passages which apparently meant so much to Him constantly reach out to other nations; e.g. Isaiah xlix. 6:

It is too light a thing that thou shouldest be my servant to raise up the tribes of Jacob, and to restore the preserved of Israel: I will also give thee for a light to the Gentiles, that thou mayest be my salvation unto the end of the earth.

It follows from all this that if the ultimate aims of Jesus in His ministry and His death reached out to the Gentiles it is difficult to maintain that He expected a speedy end of the world.

All the evidence brought forward in this chapter,

concerning the ethical teaching of Jesus, the Church and the Gentiles, encourages the view that He looked forward to a long period in which the Kingdom of God would spread through the world until at last the old prophecies would come to pass and the knowledge of the Lord would cover the earth. Thus the seed would become a great tree; the leaven would permeate the whole; the meek would inherit the earth and the will of God would be done in earth as in heaven.

The question arises, What then did Jesus teach about the end of the world? If human history was not about to draw to a close with His dramatic descent in glory, what did He actually teach about the ultimate end? Apart from the fact that we have little evidence on the matter, it may be asked in reply, Why do we assume that He must have made some pronouncement on the subject? Are there no marks of reticence in His teaching? Jesus did not set out to construct a complete system of dogmatic theology. There were many subjects on which He was silent. He gave no chart of the future; and though He foresaw the fall of Jerusalem and the triumph of the Gospel, He may well have regarded other questions as matters which the Father had set within His own authority.

Looking back over the four preceding chapters, we may say that a consideration of the wider teaching of Jesus does not remove but strengthens the doubt aroused by the discussion in Chapters 6–11.

It may be added that if the two main sources for the study of the Gospels, Mark and Q, be examined, the following facts emerge:

In Mark there is only one verse outside the Little Apocalypse which indubitably teaches the Parousia— viii. 38; it is the doublet of a saying which in its Q form does not mention the Parousia (cf. Chapter 7).

In Q, as reconstructed by Harnack, there are fifty-nine sections; the Parousia is absent from fifty-six of them.

The remaining three are passages, such as Matthew xxiii. 37–9, which probably referred to other matters when originally uttered.

Nor must we forget the demonstration of Part One that the Messiah's Parousia was not a current Jewish doctrine. This makes it imperative to find very strong evidence to convince us that Jesus originated it.

One ground of hesitation, however, still remains: How can we account for the belief of the early Church in an imminent and glorious coming of Christ to judge the world except on the assumption that He taught it Himself? We turn therefore in Part Three to an examination of the teaching of the early Church.

The Parousia in the Early Church

CHAPTER 16

THE PRIMITIVE CHURCH

St. Paul's letters to the Thessalonians were written about the middle of the first century, and they show that at that time the Christian Church held very definite beliefs concerning the Second Coming of Christ which they considered to be very near. Full and detailed descriptions of the great event are given, and it appears to be one of the main preoccupations. It is, however, very important to notice that this state of affairs is twenty years after the Resurrection of Christ and much can happen in a period of that length, especially in a new movement. What warrant is there for maintaining that these views were held in the earliest days of the Church? It is precisely in the eschatology of these Epistles that we find strange material which does not seem to be a natural development of the teaching of Jesus, e.g. the Man of Sin who was to be destroyed at the Parousia.

It is widely taken for granted that the early Church from the very start believed that the Parousia was imminent. But the evidence for this 'axiom' is difficult to find. The early speeches of the Acts of the Apostles do not substantiate this view. Much has been written concerning the reliability of these chapters as correct records of the speeches of Peter, and while it can hardly be maintained that we have no traces of later beliefs, all would agree that Luke has been extraordinarily successful in giving just the kind of teaching that was likely at that time. While we are not warranted in pressing every phrase and sentence as though we were dealing with shorthand reports, we are justified in appealing to the general trend and atmosphere of the speeches. The main emphasis is on the Resurrection; Jesus is exalted at the right hand of God and the Apostles are witnesses of His living power; the gift of the Spirit and the forgiveness of sins are freely offered in His name. The Christology and the words concerning the Cross are still at a fitting stage of primitive fluidity. These speeches of Peter in ii–v are practically devoid of the idea of the Second Coming; the exception is iii. 19–22 where it is not included among the facts about Jesus, but is an expansion of the offer and the promise; the Advent is apparently contingent on the Jews' repentance. The passage as a whole is suggestive of delay—'whom the heavens must receive until the times of restoration', etc. The only other mention of the return of Christ in these early chapters is i. 11, where two angels are said to state on the occasion of the Ascension that this same Jesus 'shall so come in like manner as ye beheld him going into heaven'. The historicity of this is, of course, more than questionable.

If we try to reconstruct the contents of the original message of the primitive Church, the Kerygma, we find first a statement of fact, then an offer. The first part declares that the promises of God have been fulfilled in the death, Resurrection and Exaltation of Christ, the Apostles being witnesses of the Resurrection; the second offers to those who repent forgiveness and the gift of the Spirit. Thus in Acts ii we have first of all the O.T. reference which is said to be fulfilled (14–21), the life, death, Resurrection and Exaltation of Jesus (22–36), the call and the promise (38–40). The central section which is most important of all is concerned with what has happened in the immediate past; no mention is made of the Parousia, for the climax is reached in the exaltation of Christ. Similarly, repentance and pardon immediately follow the Exaltation in v. 30–2, which may be taken as a concise summary of the Apostolic preaching:

The God of our Fathers [the O.T. allusion is implicit here] raised up Jesus, whom ye slew, hanging Him on a tree. Him did God exalt with His right hand to be a Prince and a Saviour, for to give repentance to Israel, and remission of sins. And we are witnesses of these things; and so is the Holy Spirit, whom God hath given to them that obey Him.

cf. Paul's sermon at Antioch in xiii, where the message of the death and Resurrection of Jesus is immediately followed by the offer of forgiveness: 'But he whom God raised up saw no corruption. Be it known unto you therefore, brethren, that through this man is proclaimed unto you remission of sins. . . .' (37–8).

The quotation from Joel in Acts ii. 16–21 is sometimes put forward as a proof that the Second Advent was expected immediately. Concerning this quotation in Peter's speech the following points may be noticed:

1. The Parousia of Christ is nowhere mentioned.

2. The quotation is given to show that the promises of God are now fulfilled; and the point of this passage is the reference to the outpouring of the Holy Spirit. Joel's prophecy, it is claimed, is fulfilled in the events of Pentecost. 'This is that' (16). The Day of the Lord (20) is not the main point of the quotation which is given primarily because of its reference to the Spirit and to prophecy; it is extended beyond these limits, not with the idea of giving a 'representation of great spiritual changes under physical imagery',[1] but rather in order to include the final words: 'And it shall be, that whosoever shall call on the name of the Lord shall be saved' (21, cf. Romans x. 13).

[1] The phrase comes from Westcott on Hebrews xii. 27.

3. The O.T. quotations are the least reliable parts of the Acts, as Rendel Harris has shown in his second book on the 'Testimonies'. Many of the O.T. passages quoted are found in Testimony books which have come down to us, and though some may have been taken from Acts, Harris thinks that others were in the collection of Testimonies first and that Luke took them from this source. It is doubtful if at such an early stage Peter would have quoted Psalm lxix. 26 and cix. 8 as applying to Judas (Acts i. 20). Again, a testimony from Amos is placed upon the lips of James in xv, but the point of the quotation only occurs in the LXX, which he surely did not use on this occasion; the Hebrew has *Edom* not *'adam*. This quotation is apparently due to the writer, and the same may apply to other O.T. references in his pages.

An attempt may be made to reconstruct the Kerygma from the speeches in Acts by placing five of them side by side—those recorded in ii, iii, v, x, and xiii—and tracing the recurring themes. According to Luke's presentation, the speeches in x and xiii are subsequent to Paul's conversion and therefore considerably later than the others, several years having elapsed since Pentecost; but the general framework is the same in all five cases. There are differences of detail, e.g. the gift of the Spirit is not mentioned in iii or xiii, while the work of John the Baptist is introduced in the later speeches of x and xiii. But if we trace the features which occur in all five we find the following:

1. Fulfilment of the O.T. promises:
   ii. 16–21, 25–8, 34–5, iii. 18, 22–5, v. 30, x. 43, xiii. 17–23, 27, 29, 32–5.
2. The death of Jesus:
   ii. 23, iii. 14–5, v. 30, x. 39, xiii. 27–9.
3. The Resurrection of Jesus:
   ii. 24, 31–2, iii. 15, v. 30–1, x. 40, xiii. 30, 34–7.

4. The offer of forgiveness:
   ii. 38, iii. 19, v. 31, x. 43, xiii. 38–9.
5. The Apostles as witnesses:[1]
   ii. 32, iii. 15, v. 32, x. 41, xiii. 31.

Here we have the irreducible minimum, the essential skeleton, of the Christian Kerygma. The result is confirmed by the fact that the same five factors, and no others, are found in 1 Corinthians xv. 3 *ff*.:

For I delivered unto you first of all that which also I received, how that Christ died [cf. 2, above] for our sins [4], according to the scriptures [1], and that he was buried; and that he hath been raised on the third day [3] according to the scriptures [1 again]; and that he appeared to Cephas, then to the twelve, etc. [5].

Other witnesses of the Resurrection follow; cf. the word 'witnesses' in verse 15; cf. also Luke xxiv. 44–9.

The Parousia clearly did not form a part of the original Gospel; this was concerned with events which had already happened and of which the Apostles were witnesses.

One would certainly not gather from these speeches as a whole that the members of the primitive community lived from the very first in momentary expectation of the end of the world, as they are often represented. The promise of the Spirit is 'to you and to your children and to all that are afar off, even as many as the Lord our God

---

[1] Repentance is mentioned three times (ii. 38, iii. 19, v. 31) and the exaltation of Jesus three times (ii. 33, iii. 13, v. 31). It is noteworthy that the witness of the Apostles occurs in all five speeches, and the word 'witnesses' is found throughout. The essential qualification of an Apostle was that he was a witness of the Resurrection (i. 22). The personal testimony of an eye-witness cannot be transferred or delegated. The only way he can perpetuate his witness after his death is by leaving a written record—hence the New Testament, which is essentially the apostolic witness. The books of the N.T. were not selected because they were profound or inspired, but because they were apostolic or were believed to be. This explains why the N.T. comes from a single brief period, while the O.T. is the product of a thousand years.

shall call unto him' (ii. 39). Even if, as seems likely, the reference in the words 'all that are afar off' is to proselytes, the passage implies that a process of future evangelism is contemplated. Again, in these chapters we have the message of Stephen who was charged with speaking words against the Temple and the Law, and with affirming that Jesus of Nazareth would 'change the customs which Moses delivered unto us' (vi. 13–14).

Those who maintain that Jesus must have foretold His imminent return, because we cannot otherwise account for the unanimity with which the early Church believed in it, fail to see that there is no good evidence that this belief was held immediately after the Resurrection. We find it twenty years later in the Thessalonian correspondence, and a great deal can happen in twenty years. Dr. G. G. Coulton has shown that twenty years after the death of St. Francis far-reaching changes had taken place in the tenets of the Franciscan order. He uses this illustration to show that we must not be surprised at great doctrinal developments in a similar period following the death of Jesus.

The evidence considered in this and the earlier chapters suggests that the doctrine of the Parousia emerged during this period. How the doctrine was formed and developed is the question to which we must now turn. St. Paul was not responsible for it, and in his earliest letters he was apparently following an eschatology derived from common Christian teaching. Some conception of the last things would be an early need of the young community, and we may assume that the first few years after Pentecost would see the gradual formation of a primitive theology.

CHAPTER 17

THE INFLUENCE OF THE OLD TESTAMENT

It is evident that the early Christians studied the Old Testament intensively and made great use of it in the construction of their theology. It has been powerfully argued by Rendel Harris that the first Christian book ever produced was a collection of O.T. proof-texts, the original Testimony Book.[1] Whether we accept this or not, all will agree that it was to the O.T. that the early Christians turned for the interpretation of the great events which figured in their message. By showing that the life and death of Jesus and the developments which followed were all foretold, they were able to prove that all was part of the divine plan. When opponents alleged that the sufferings of Christ disproved His claims, the Christians showed that those sufferings were clearly foretold in the Law and the Prophets. Further, the new movement of the Church preserved the valuable factor of continuity with the past by demonstrating that their bold innovations were really the fulfilment of ancient prophecies, and that Christians were heirs of the promises made to the fathers.

As far as the events of the life of Christ were concerned, there was here the control of a genuine historical tradition; but it was different in the case of doctrines and interpretations not bound by restraints of this kind. Even in the case of the life of Christ there are minor touches in

[1] J. Rendel Harris, *Testimonies I and II*; cf. F. C. Burkitt: 'To collect and apply the Oracles of the Old Testament in the light of the New Dispensation was the first literary task of the Christian Church' (*Gospel History and its Transmission*, p. 127). C. H. Dodd: 'The study of testimony books has led to the conclusion that the application of prophecy was probably the earliest form of Christian theological thought' (*History and the Gospel*, p. 60).

all the Gospels which appear to be due to the desire to bring the events into closer agreement with O.T. prophecy. For example, Matthew in his account of the Triumphal Entry has provided both an ass and a colt because of Zechariah ix. 9, not appreciating Hebrew parallelism; similarly the gall of xxvii. 34 (absent from the Marcan source) is apparently derived from Psalm lxix. 21. The underlying argument evidently was that these things were foretold of the Messiah: Jesus was the Messiah: and therefore these things happened to Jesus. This form of reasoning is still in existence in certain circles. A devotional book published in 1939 refers to an O.T. 'prophecy of Christ' and adds the comment: 'The Gospels do not tell us this. Even the beloved disciple, John, may not have known of it. But there it is, plainly stated. We find prophecies that fill out the records of the Evangelists.' Some scholars have suggested that the influence of the O.T. upon the Gospel narrative extends farther than mere matters of detail, and that the whole story of the Virgin Birth, and even the connection of Jesus with Bethlehem, have no more basis than O.T. prophecy, the narratives being imaginative constructions.

In those parts of Christian teaching, however, where there was no historical control, e.g. in eschatology, there would be much more freedom in developing Christian doctrine in the light of the O.T., which was regarded, of course, by the early Church as the authoritative word of God. There are some Christian doctrines which have no warrant in the teaching of Jesus. They are not necessarily untrue on that account; but the Church had to say something about matters on which they could not find clear guidance in any remembered words of the Master, and it was to be expected that the O.T. should be used in filling up these gaps. Even in modern manuals of theology proof-texts from the O.T. are supplied in cases where no saying of Jesus can be adduced.

One of the most striking features in the Christian use of the O.T. and the most important for our present purpose, is that not only Messianic proof-texts, but also passages originally written about God were applied to Jesus. To the Church, Jesus was Lord as well as Christ. During His lifetime He was apparently addressed as 'Lord' in the sense of 'Rabbi', but afterwards the word had a far richer content. The dying Stephen prayed, saying, 'Lord Jesus, receive my spirit' (Acts vii. 59), and Christians were known as those who called upon His name. That this usage was not confined to the Hellenists is shown by 1 Corinthians xvi. 22, where the Aramaic expression for 'Lord' is found. The Hellenists who called Jesus '*Kyrios*' (Lord) found the same word used of God in the LXX and thus had little difficulty in applying to Jesus passages originally written of God. But this practice, as the passages themselves show, did not depend upon terms and titles. What lay behind this striking procedure is not our immediate concern, though it is of great importance in connection with the Person of Christ. Our sole point at the moment is to draw attention to the undoubted fact that words originally written about the God of Israel were applied to Jesus. It was not Paul alone who followed this practice, which is found in all the main writings of the N.T.:

Paul:
Two examples may be given

Joel ii. 32: And it shall come to pass that whosoever shall call on the name of the Lord shall be delivered.

Romans x. 13: For, whosoever shall call upon the name of the Lord shall be saved.

Isaiah xlv. 32: Unto me every knee shall bow, every tongue shall swear.

Philippians ii. 10: That in the name of Jesus every knee should bow . . . and every tongue should confess that Jesus Christ is Lord.

Peter:

Isaiah viii. 13: The Lord of hosts, him shall ye sanctify; let him be your fear.

1 Peter iii. 14–15: Fear not their fear . . . but sanctify in your hearts Christ as Lord.

Isaiah viii. 14: And he (the Lord of hosts) shall be for a stone of stumbling and for a rock of offence.

1 Peter ii. 8: A stone of stumbling and a rock of offence.

Hebrews:

Psalm cii. 25–27:
Of old hast thou laid the foundation of the earth,
And the heavens are the work of thy hands, etc.
But thou art the same,
And thy years shall have no end.

Hebrews i. 10–12 quotes the passage in full as 'of the Son'.

John:

Isaiah vi. 1 *ff*.: I saw the Lord high and lifted up, etc.

John xii. 40–41 quotes Isaiah vi. 10 and adds: 'These things said Isaiah because he saw His glory; and he spake of Him.'

Revelation:

Isaiah xliv. 8: I am the first and I am the last.

Revelation i. 17: I am the first and the last.

Jeremiah xvii. 10: I the Lord search the heart, I try the reins even to give every man according to his ways.

Revelation ii. 23: . . . all the churches shall know that I am he which searcheth the reins and the hearts: and I will give unto each one of you according to your works.

Synoptics:

Isaiah xl. 3: The voice of one that crieth, Prepare ye in the wilderness the way of the Lord.

Used of John the Baptist preparing the way for Jesus in Mark i. 3; Matthew iii. 3; Luke iii. 4-6.

These are a few examples of this type of quotation or allusion. But one highly significant class has been reserved for special consideration in the chapters which follow.

CHAPTER 18

THE COMING OF THE LORD

Many passages of the O.T., especially those connected with the Day of the Lord, declare that at some future time Jahveh will descend in glory from heaven to destroy His enemies or to judge the world; this Advent is in some cases preceded by tribulation and followed by the Lord's reign.

These passages draw their imagery as a rule from the manifestation at Sinai, which may be described as the original Theophany:

The Lord will come down in the sight of all the people upon mount Sinai (Exodus xix. 11). . . . And it came to pass on the third day, when it was morning, that there were thunders and lightnings, and a thick cloud upon the mount, and the voice of a trumpet exceeding loud; and all the people that were in the camp trembled. And Moses brought forth the people out of the camp to meet God; and they stood at the nether part of the mount. And mount Sinai was altogether on smoke, because the Lord descended upon it in fire: and the smoke thereof ascended as the smoke of a furnace, and the whole mount quaked greatly. And when the voice of the trumpet waxed louder and louder, Moses spake, and God answered him by a voice. And the Lord came down upon mount Sinai, to the top of the mount (16–20).

This incident, whose historical origin may have been a thunderstorm,[1] is referred to again and again in the O.T., e.g. Deuteronomy xxxiii. 2; Judges v. 4–5; and it is amplified in the great theophanic poem in Habakkuk iii. Its imagery is borrowed in describing a great personal deliverance in Psalm xviii. 7–15 and a national deliverance in Psalm xcvii. 3–6.

[1] cf. Driver, Exodus, *Cambridge Bible*, pp. 176–7.

But our main concern is with the great coming of the Lord which, in the prophetic view, still lay in the future. The following passages may be quoted. In some of these the imagery of Exodus xix is again laid under tribute, and it was evidently felt that as God had descended in glory at the beginning of Israel's story, so He would come again in glory at the great crisis of the future.

The significance of such passages for our present purpose is that nearly all of them are applied to Christ either in the N.T. or in other early Christian writings, and that their influence can be clearly traced in the earliest epistles.

1. Isaiah ii describes a day of the Lord when men will hide 'from before the terror of the Lord, and from the glory of his majesty' (10) when he ariseth to shake mightily the earth (19 and 21).

2. Isaiah xl. 3:

Prepare the way of the Lord.

5 and the glory of the Lord shall be revealed.

10 Behold, the Lord God will come as a mighty one, and his arm shall rule for him.

3. Isaiah xlii. 13:

> The Lord shall go forth as a mighty man;
> He shall stir up jealousy like a man of war;
> He shall cry, yea, he shall shout aloud;
> He shall do mightily against his enemies.

4. Isaiah lxiii. 1–6: Jahveh comes from Edom with garments sprinkled with blood, having trodden down the peoples in anger. 'Glorious in his apparel, marching in the greatness of his strength' (1). 'The year of my redeemed is come' (4).

5. Isaiah lxvi. 15–18:

For behold, the Lord will come with fire, and his chariots shall be like the whirlwind; to render his anger with fury, and his rebuke with flames of fire.

6. Zechariah xiv, when the nations gather to attack Jerusalem:

Then shall the Lord go forth, and fight against those nations . . . and his feet shall stand in that day upon the mount of Olives (3–4).

And the Lord my God shall come, and all the holy ones with thee (5).

7. Psalm l. 3–6:

Our God shall come, and shall not keep silence:
A fire shall devour before him,
And it shall be very tempestuous round about him.
He shall call to the heavens above,
And to the earth, that he may judge his people:
Gather my saints together unto me;
Those that have made a covenant with me by sacrifice.
And the heavens shall declare his righteousness;
For God is judge himself.

8. Psalm lxviii. 1–8 gives another theophanic description with reminiscences of Sinai:

Let God arise, let his enemies be scattered . . .
As wax melteth before the fire,
So let the wicked perish at the presence of God.

9. Psalm lxxxii. 8:

Arise, O God, judge the earth;
For thou shalt inherit all the nations.

10. Psalm xcvi:

He shall judge the peoples with equity (10). . . . for he cometh;
For he cometh to judge the earth;
He shall judge the world with righteousness,
And the peoples with his truth (13).

All the above are connected with Christ's coming either in the N.T. or in other Christian writings, especially those which contain testimony material drawn from earlier sources. The use made of Isaiah xl. in the Gospels suggests that the coming of the Lord spoken of here was fulfilled in the First Advent of Christ. The others are connected with the Second Advent.[1]

The following 'Day of the Lord' passages which speak of the divine Advent are also of importance. They have all influenced the N.T. Advent teaching, as will be shown in detail later:

Isaiah xiii-xiv is a typical description of a day of the Lord, with heavenly portents, the coming of the Lord, destruction of his enemies, deliverance and prosperity for Israel:

They come from a far country, from the uttermost part of heaven, even the Lord, and the weapons of his indignation to destroy the whole land (xiii. 5).

Isaiah xxvi-xxvii is more important. It is part of the apocalypse, xxiv-xxvii, and includes the resurrection of the dead (xxvi. 19) as well as the divine Advent, the gathering of dispersed Israel, and the reign of peace.

For, behold, the Lord cometh forth out of his place to punish the inhabitants of the earth for their iniquity (xxvi. 21).

Isaiah xxxiv-xxxv: The day of the Lord's vengeance is followed by the age of prosperity and peace for the redeemed.

Behold, your God will come with vengeance, with the recompence of God; he will come and save you (xxxv. 4).

The two chapters were probably written by the same author and form a unity; but the Christians usually connected xxxv with the first coming of Christ; cf. Justin, *First Apology*, xlviii; Tertullian, *Against Marcion*, iv. 10,

[1] cf. the references at end of chapter.

and *Answer to Jews*, ix; Irenaeus, *Against Heresies*, IV. xxxiii. 11; etc.

The following passages on the divine Advent are also of interest. Most of these, too, are applied to Christ by Christian writers, but they are not of great importance for the N.T.; Isaiah xxxi. 4 ('So shall the Lord of hosts come down to fight upon mount Zion'), lix. 16–20, lxii. 11; Micah i. 3 ('For, behold, the Lord cometh forth out of his place, and will come down'); Zechariah ii. 10; Malachi iii-iv.

References for the first ten quotations:

1. 2 Thessalonians i. 9; Tert., *Adv. Marc.*, iv. 30; Iren., IV. xxxiii. 13.

2. Luke iii. 4–6; John i. 23, etc.; Justin, *Dial. Tryph.*, 1.

3. Cyprian, *Testimonies*, ii, 28; *Advantage of Patience*, xxii-xxiii.

4. Revelation xix. 11–16; Tert., *Adv. Marc.*, iv. 40.

5. 2 Thessalonians i. 8; Cypr., *Patience*, xxii; *Pseudo-Clement*, xvii.

6. 1 Thessalonians iii. 13; Did., xvi. 7.

7. Cypr., *Test.*, ii, 28, *Patience*, xxii; Iren., V. xviii. 3, III. vi. 1.

8. Cypr., *Test.*, ii. 28.

9. Cypr., *Test.*, ii. 28; Justin, *Dial. Tryph.*, cxxiv.

10. Justin, *Dial. Tryph.*, lxxiii., etc.

CHAPTER 19

THE PAROUSIA IN 1 AND 2 THESSALONIANS

Iᴛ is possible that 2 Thessalonians is slightly earlier than
1 Thessalonians, and a number of authorities have
advocated this order.[1] 2 Thessalonians may thus be the
earliest of all Christian writings to come down to us in its
original form, and, though the point is immaterial for our
present purpose, we will consider them in this order.

The influence of the O.T. on the Epistle is clear,
especially in passages dealing with the Second Advent.
The first of these is i. 7–8: 'at the revelation of the Lord
Jesus from heaven with the angels of his power in flaming
fire, rendering vengeance to them that know not God.'
The conception is derived from the theophanic passage
Isaiah lxvi. 15: 'For behold the Lord will come with fire
. . . to render his anger with fury, and his rebuke with
flames of fire.' Paul used the LXX and this shows closer
agreement: ἀποδοῦναι ἐν θυμῷ ἐκδίκησιν αὐτοῦ. . . .
ἐν φλογὶ πυρός.

Paul: ἐν πυρὶ φλογός, διδόντος ἐκδίκησιν . . . .

The Apostle goes on to speak in the next verse of
'eternal destruction from the face of the Lord and from
the glory of his might when he shall come', etc. (9).
These words come from the description of the Day of the
Lord in Isaiah ii, where it is said that God will arise to
shake mightily the earth and men will hide 'from before
the terror of the Lord, and from the glory of his majesty'
(10). Again there is closer agreement with the LXX:

Isaiah: ἀπὸ προσώπου τοῦ φόβου Κυρίου καὶ ἀπὸ τῆς
δόξης τῆς ἰσχύος αὐτοῦ ὅταν ἀναστῇ θραῦσαι τὴν γῆν.

---

[1] J. Weiss points out that the letters of Paul have been arranged in the
N.T. roughly according to size; Romans comes first because it is longest,
and 1 Thessalonians precedes 2 Thessalonians for the same reason.

2 Thessalonians: ἀπὸ προσώπου τοῦ Κυρίου καὶ ἀπὸ τῆς δόξης τῆς ἰσχύος αὐτοῦ ὅταν ἔλθῃ . . . This is not a mere reminiscence; a dozen consecutive words of Paul are taken bodily from the LXX. The words were originally written of Jahveh, but they are here applied to Jesus. The next verse in 2 Thessalonians has the words, 'in that day', ἐν τῇ ἡμέρᾳ ἐκείνῃ, a phrase found in the next verse of the corresponding passage in Isaiah ii.

Isaiah lxvi, the chapter quoted above, may also be the source of 2 Thessalonians i. 12, 'that the name of our Lord Jesus may be glorified in you', ὅπως ἐνδοξασθῇ τὸ ὄνομα τοῦ Κυρίου Ἰησοῦ ἐν ὑμῖν.

cf. Isaiah lxvi. 5: ἵνα τὸ ὄνομα Κυρίου δοξασθῇ.

Similarly the words 'when he comes to be glorified in his saints and to be marvelled at' (i. 10) may be compared with the theophanic passages Isaiah xxiv. 23 and Psalm lxviii. 35.

The source of this doctrine is not the teaching of Jesus. We cannot conceive Him talking of Himself as coming with flaming fire rendering vengeance upon them that know not God. Nor is the conception due to Paul; there is nothing distinctively Pauline about it as there is in the case of Justification by Faith, 'in Christ', and the 'fruit of the Spirit'. This Parousia teaching was evidently part of the Christian tradition at that time and the language betrays its origin in the O.T.

In 1 Thessalonians the Lord, it is said, will descend from heaven and He will come with all His saints. This again is familiar theophanic language. Nowhere in the whole range of O.T. prophecy, pre-Christian apocalyptic, and Gospel teaching, is the word 'descend' used of the Messiah. But it is often used of God, particularly in reference to the coming Day of the Lord. For example, Micah i. 3 reads: 'For, behold the Lord cometh forth out of his place, and will come down'; the LXX has Κύριος

ἐκπορεύεται ἐκ τοῦ τόπου αὐτοῦ καὶ καταβήσεται. In
1 Thessalonians iv. 16 the words are: 'The Lord . . . will
descend from heaven', ὁ Κύριος...καταβήσεται
ἀπ' οὐρανοῦ; cf. LXX of Exodus xix. 20, xxxiv. 5;
Numbers xi. 25; Isaiah xxxi. 4.

Paul's phrase, 'with all his saints', μετὰ πάντων τῶν
ἁγίων αὐτοῦ (1 Thessalonians iii. 13), is again from the
same source, i.e. O.T. theophanies. 'The Lord my God
shall come, and all the saints with him' (Zechariah xiv. 5,
ἥξει Κύριος . . . καὶ πάντες οἱ ἅγιοι μετ' 'αὐτοῦ).

Zechariah xiv. 5 is quoted literally in Didache xvi, and
applied to the Second Advent. The idea of holy ones
accompanying Jahveh in his theophanic descent is
familiar in the O.T. (e.g. Deuteronomy xxxiii. 2).

The shout, too, the trumpet, the gathering of the elect,
figure in several O.T. theophanies. In Exodus xix. we
have (1) the divine descent, (2) in fire, (3) the voice, (4)
the trumpet. This is a theophany in the past, but it may
be noticed that all these features are present in 1 and 2
Thessalonians, for the same factors reappeared in the
prophets' descriptions of the future theophany.[1]

Isaiah xxvi-xxvii is another passage whose influence
can be traced in the N.T. and the Fathers. It is another
description of the Day of the Lord and it speaks of:

---

[1] It would be interesting to speculate on the possibility that the process
by which the Theophany became a Christophany was facilitated by the
Aramaic paraphrases of the O.T., which would be familiar to the Jewish-
Christians through their use in the synagogues, and in which statements
concerning God's movements and appearances were softened down, by
such expressions as 'The Shekinah of God appeared', etc. (If James'
Epistle is a sample of Judaistic Christianity, it is interesting to note that in
ii. 2 Jesus is called the Glory, and the translation has been suggested: 'the
faith of our Lord Jesus the Shekinah' (Mayor; see *H.D.B.*, iv. 489).)

But this is speculation, and we must base our case upon the evidence of
the N.T. As noted earlier the application to Jesus of passages about God
did not rest upon the word *Kyrios*; it sprang from something deeper than
terms and names. And while on some subjects it is possible to distinguish
between the beliefs of the Aramaic-speaking wing and the Hellenists, there
is no indication or likelihood that on these matters they were divided.

1. The Lord's Coming (xxvi. 21: 'The Lord cometh forth out of his place').

2. Judgement (xxvi. 21: 'to punish the inhabitants of the earth').

3. The Resurrection (xxvi. 19: 'Thy dead shall live; my dead bodies shall arise'). LXX: ἀναστήσονται οἱ νεκροί.

4. The Trumpet (xxvii. 13).

5. The Gathering of the Elect (xxvii. 12).

All these appear in the Thessalonian correspondence in connection with the Second Advent of Jesus:

1. The Lord's Coming (1 Thessalonians iv; 2 Thessalonians i, etc.).

2. Judgement (2 Thessalonians i. 9, ii. 8).

3. The Resurrection (1 Thessalonians iv. 16: οἱ νεκροί ἀναστήσονται).

4. The Trumpet (1 Thessalonians iv. 16).

5. The Gathering of the Elect (1 Thessalonians iv. 17).

We may notice that in Isaiah xiii-xiv, another Day of the Lord's passage whose influence can be seen again and again in the N.T. and the Fathers, we have the 'day of the Lord', xiii. 6 (ἡμέρα Κυρίου, anarthrous), followed by 'pangs shall seize them . . . as a woman in travail', verse 8. Similarly, in 1 Thessalonians v the 'day of the Lord' of verse 2 (ἡμέρα Κυρίου) is likened to travail coming upon a woman with child, verse 3.

It will be remembered that in Part One we failed to find in the Similitudes of Enoch any mention of the shout, trumpet, fire, angelic escort—features prominent in the N.T. We now find these very phrases in abundance, in the Theophanies of the O.T. We also noticed that in Enoch the Messiah was never separated from God as He is in the N.T.; the reason is now obvious.

While the eschatologies of Enoch and the N.T. both derive from O.T. theophanies, they represent independent lines of development. They are different branches of the same tree. The Old Testament said: 'The Lord will come.' The Enoch literature underlined this, and embellished the picture of coming judgement, the Dream Visions (lxxxiii-xc) adding that God would be assisted in the judgement by Michael, and the Similitudes (xxxvii-lxxi) that He would be assisted in the judgement by the Messiah. The New Testament repeated the O.T. message, 'The Lord will come', but interpreted it as 'the Lord Jesus'. In Enoch the Messiah comes with the Lord; in the N.T. the Messiah and the Lord are the same person. The N.T. view could not have grown out of Enoch (whatever the date we prefer for the Similitudes); it grew directly out of the O.T. and the language shows the contact was immediate, Jesus being identified with the Lord. Jesus comes not because He is Christ, but because He is Lord.

To find the true origin of the Parousia teaching of 1 and 2 Thessalonians we are not to go to the teaching of Jesus and then to Enoch and then to Persian eschatology. Rather, as the language suggests, we are to go straight from these passages of 1 and 2 Thessalonians, as representing early Church teaching, to the O.T. The connecting link was the conviction that Jesus was Lord.

We have not yet accounted for the belief that the Advent was near; nor have we examined the remarkable passage about the Man of Sin. But before we turn to these questions it will be as well to adduce further evidence for the main point we have already reached.

CHAPTER 20

FURTHER EVIDENCE

THE strong Old Testament element in 1 and 2 Thessalonians may be related to the Testimony collection mentioned earlier. H. A. A. Kennedy, in *St. Paul's Conceptions of the Last Things*, refers to Weizsäcker's hypothesis that Paul 'arranged a kind of system of doctrine in the form of proofs from Scripture for use in giving instruction' and to Bornemann's suggestion that 2 Thessalonians i. 7b–10a is a portion of an early Christian psalm based on O.T. passages (pp. 48 ff.). That there was a collection of proof-texts in the earliest days of the Church is almost certain. But Paul was not the compiler; it was pre-Pauline. Much that used to be called Pauline is now known to be simply primitive Christianity; and the O.T. passages which lie behind 1 and 2 Thessalonians were probably taken by the Apostle from an early collection of Testimonies.

The testimony collection of course passed through many stages, and various editions were made from time to time. Some passages were dropped and many others were added, but when the same proof-texts from the O.T. are found associated together for centuries in writers who are not dependent one upon the other, the conclusion is warranted that they are drawn from the Testimony book. Rendel Harris, in his two books on the subject, has given numerous illustrations of this and has also given reasons for the view that the Testimony book was produced before any of the N.T. writings and that its influence can be traced throughout the N.T. The suggestion that the Testimonies were the famous Logia drawn up by Matthew is possibly true but it is not a really vital point.

The question now arises: Is there any evidence that the usage we have traced in 1 and 2 Thessalonians was a feature of the Testimony collection? If so, it will strengthen the suggestion that Paul was drawing upon such a source. If we examine the Testimony material which has survived in various forms, we find that the evidence is abundant. Cyprian's *Testimonies against the Jews*, for instance (especially Parts 1 and 2), presents a collection of O.T. material the core of which both in arrangement and substance goes back to the earliest times. (For example, the Stone testimonies, ii. 16; cf. 1 Peter ii and Romans ix). If we turn to the section dealing with the Second Advent, ii. 28, 'That Jesus Christ shall come as a Judge', we find five O.T. proof-texts: Malachi iv. 1; Psalm l. 1–6; Isaiah xlii. 13–14; Psalm lxviii. 1–7; Psalm lxxxii. 8—every one of them exactly the kind of passage with which we are concerned.

In his tract, *On the Advantage of Patience*, Cyprian refers in chapter xxii to the following passages in connection with the coming of divine vengeance: Malachi iv. 1; Psalm l. 3–6; Isaiah lxvi. 15–16; Isaiah xlii. 13–14, an almost identical list, suggesting that he is selecting from a recognized collection. He goes on, xxiii: 'But who is this that says that he has held his peace before' (as in Isaiah xlii just quoted) 'and will not hold his peace for ever? Surely it is He who was led as a sheep to the slaughter', etc. We note (1) the recurrence of the same sequence of Testimonies and (2) the definite equating of 'the Lord' in these passages with Jesus. The presence of Isaiah lxvi. 15–16 which we found in 2 Thessalonians is interesting.

Justin Martyr's writings are saturated with Testimonies, many of which go back to early days. It is remarkable that his first *Apology for Christianity*, written in the middle of the second century, is based upon the O.T., not the New. In the *Dialogue with Trypho* we see again O.T. passages about God applied to Jesus; e.g. lxxiii: 'For he comes to judge the earth. He shall judge the world with righteousness and the people with his truth' (Psalm xcvi).

In his treatment of the point that in the O.T. more than one divine Lord is indicated, he shows that many passages which appear to speak of God should be understood of the Logos, though he is here speaking of past theophanies (cf. cxxvii). This treatment of past divine appearances perhaps has a bearing upon the idea that future manifestations are to be taken in the same way. Thus a difficulty would be removed; the O.T. prophecies of God's descent are hard sayings to those who believe that He is omnipresent and spiritual, and that no one hath seen God at any time. Modern readers of the Bible would be inclined to regard these predictions as unworthy survivals of a more primitive conception of God; but the early Church held that all that was written must be fulfilled and it was not surprising that these prophecies of the divine coming should be applied to Christ, the Lord of the Church's worship.[1] Since the Advent was for purposes of judgement, it came about that this function was ascribed to Jesus too.

Testimony material can be traced in Christian writers through the centuries, and it frequently gives further instances of the same kind. Blocks of old Testimonies turn up in all kinds of places; some are found, for instance, in a late Treatise on the Triune Nature of God (translated from the Arabic in *Studia Sinaitica*, VII). One block (at f. 108*b*) consists of the following passages which are applied to Christ: Isaiah lxiv. 1 ('Lord, bend the heavens and come down to us'); Psalm lxxx. 1; Isaiah lxiii. 9; Psalm cvii. 20; Habakkuk ii. 3; Psalm cxviii. 26–7;

---

[1] Some of these, but not all, were intended by the original writers to be taken figuratively. This is probably the case with the anthropomorphic language of Psalm xviii. See Kirkpatrick's note on verse 8 (*Cambridge Bible*, Psalms, p. 90). This note is quoted with approval by the Chief Rabbi, Dr. J. H. Hertz, in his edition of the *Pentateuch and Haftorahs* (1938), p. 905.

Psalm l. 3. In this case all are rather surprisingly referred to the First Advent of Christ.[1]

In trying to discriminate between Testimonies which a writer has added himself, and those which belonged to the main testimony tradition handed down from earlier times, special attention must be given to those which persist through the centuries. And among these, outstanding importance attaches to cases where the same testimonies are found linked together in writers who are not dependent one upon the other.

Now, if we look again at the two groups of testimonies quoted above from Cyprian, we find some passages among them which are linked together in other writers. Cyprian's references are repeated for convenience: *Malachi iv. 1* (twice); *Psalm l* (twice, 1–6 and 3–6); *Isaiah lxvi.* 15–16; Isaiah xlii. 13–14 (twice); Psalm lxviii. 1–7; Psalm lxxxii. 8.

Nearly two centuries later, Augustine, in his *City of God*, dealing in Bk. xx. 21–30 with the subject of Judgement, dwells upon the following O.T. passages: Isaiah xxvi. 19; *Isaiah lxvi.* 12–16, 18, 22–4; Daniel vii. 15–28; Psalm cii. 26–7; *Psalm l.* 3–5; *Malachi iii–iv.* (His concern to show that, though these passages were written of God, they should be understood as referring to Christ is noteworthy.)

Pseudo-Clement (second century) refers to *Malachi iv. 1* in xvi and to *Isaiah lxvi*, 18 and 24 in xvii ('I come to gather together all the nations', etc.).

All the writers are obviously independent of one another

---

[1] The practice of applying theophanic passages to Christ persisted through the centuries and up to modern times. Even in Charles Wesley's Advent hymn, 'Lo, He comes with clouds descending', there are the words, 'Jah, Jehovah, Everlasting God, come down'. Similarly the first line of the famous Latin hymn on Christ's coming to judge the world, '*Dies irae, dies illa*', is the Vulgate of Zephaniah i. 15—a Day of the Lord context. Thus, in spite of its Christian dress, the doctrine of the Parousia never succeeds completely in concealing all the traces of its origin.

in regard to their quotations, and the striking coincidences in their selection cannot be accidental. It is significant that *Isaiah lxvi*, which occurs three times in the above groups, lies behind 2 Thessalonians i. 8, as we saw in the last chapter. It may also be the case that *Psalm l. 3 ff.* was in Paul's mind when he wrote 2 Thessalonians ii. 1: 'the coming of our Lord Jesus Christ and our gathering together unto him'. In Psalm l the divine coming in 3–4 is followed by 5: 'Gather my saints together unto me.'

But whatever view we take of the Testimony book—whether Paul is drawing upon it or not—the main argument is unaffected. That O.T. passages concerning God were applied to Jesus, and that among them were descriptions of the Lord coming for judgement, is beyond dispute, and this is sufficient for the present purpose. Here we have an adequate source for the doctrine that the Lord Jesus would descend in glory from heaven with His angels and would judge the world, a doctrine for which we could find no solid foundation in His own teaching.

In a sense, the doctrine of the Parousia was not new; all the essential details are found in the O.T. description of the coming theophany. Broadly speaking, the Christians took over the O.T. doctrine of the Advent of the Lord, making the single adjustment that the Lord was the Lord Jesus.

The terms used in the N.T. provide additional confirmation. Consider the word *Parousia*:

1. In normal speech this Greek word means simply 'arrival' or 'presence', and it bears this sense in the few places where it is found in the LXX, e.g. 2 Maccabees xv. 21; Judith x. 18.

2. But it acquired in pagan circles a technical sense in addition to the normal usage, and came to mean a divine manifestation: a theophany or else a divine act of healing. (See Dibelius' excursus on the word in his commentary on

1 and 2 Thessalonians,[1] p. 13 in the 1925 edition, and the quotation from Diodorus Siculus on p. 31). We cannot be sure whether the Jews had ever used the word in connection with a divine manifestation prior to Christian times. In the Greek version of the Testaments of the XII Patriarchs the words occur, ἕως παρουσίας τοῦ θεοῦ τῆς δικαιοσύνης (Testament of Judah xxii. 3), but we do not know when this Greek version was made. Late in the first century, Josephus used the word several times of a divine manifestation and it is interesting to note that he employed it in his account of the Theophany at Sinai.[2]

3. Another technical meaning of the word applied it to the visit of a king or ruler. This was possibly connected with meaning 2, as divine language was often used of kings in pagan circles.

In the N.T. this word, which had been used of divine manifestation, has become a technical term to describe the return of Jesus. It is also used a few times in the normal sense of arrival or presence, as of the coming of Titus (2 Corinthians vii. 6) and the coming of Antichrist (2 Thessalonians ii. 9). But when it is applied to the glorious coming of Christ with the holy angels, it is obviously being used in the theophanic sense. In this technical sense it is found in 1 and 2 Thessalonians, 1 Corinthians xv. 23, James, 1 John, Matthew, and 2 Peter (of the Transfiguration, i. 16, as well as of the future advent, iii. 4). The word had never been associated with the Messiah by the Jews; it was a theophanic word,

---

[1] Lietzmann's *Handbuch*, 11.

[2] *Antiquities*, III. v. 2: 'But on the third day, before the sun arose, a cloud settled down over the whole camp of the Hebrews, who had seen not the like before, enveloping the spot whereon they had pitched their tents; and, while all the rest of heaven remained serene, blustering winds, bringing tempestuous rain, came sweeping down, lightning terrified the beholders, and thunderbolts hurled from aloft signified the *advent* of God propitious to the desires of Moses' (H. St. J. Thackeray's translation, Loeb Library). καὶ κέραυνοι κατενεχθέντες ἐδήλουν τὴν π α ρ ο υ σ ι α ν τοῦ θεοῦ . . . .

M

and thus conclusions reached along other lines are confirmed by philology.

Since some of the O.T. prophecies of the divine advent were held to be fulfilled in the first coming of Jesus, it is not surprising that this came to be known as a Parousia too; cf. Justin, *1 Apol.*, xlviii: 'There are these words, At His coming [*parousia*] the lame shall leap as an hart, etc.' (Isaiah xxxv. 4,6). Thus in some writers we find mention of the 'first' Parousia and the 'second'.

Epiphany (Greek, *epiphaneia*) is another theophanic word used in the N.T. of Christ's coming: 2 Thessalonians ii. 8 and the Pastorals (cf. 2 Maccabees xii. 22, xv. 27).

1 Peter prefers the word *Revelation* (Greek, *apokalypsis*), which is used three times of the Second Advent, as also in 1 Corinthians i. 7 and 2 Thessalonians i. 7. 'The revelation of His glory' (1 Peter iv. 13) is reminiscent of Isaiah xl. 5, where similar words are used of God: 'the glory of the Lord shall be revealed.' (It is interesting to note that Delitzsch, in his commentary on this passage of Isaiah, refers to 1 Peter: 'When the way is made ready for Jehovah the Coming One, the glory of the God of salvation will be revealed; His *parousia* is ἀποκάλυψις τῆς δόξης αὐτοῦ, 1 Peter iv. 13.')

Not many books of the N.T. are as rich in advent teaching as 1 and 2 Thessalonians, but the Apocalypse has an even stronger eschatological element, and it is not surprising that we find similar evidence there. The description of the Parousia in Revelation xix draws upon several O.T. passages, and the influence of Isaiah lxiii can be clearly traced:

> Who is this that cometh from Edom,
> With dyed garments from Bozrah?
> This that is glorious in his apparel,
> Marching in the greatness of his strength?
> I that speak in righteousness, mighty to save.

> Wherefore art thou red in thine apparel,
> And thy garments like him that treadeth in the winefat?
> . . . their lifeblood is sprinkled upon my garments,
> And I have stained all my raiment (lxiii. 1–3).

In Revelation xix Christ comes from the opened heavens to fight against the gathered armies of the kings of the earth;

Verse 13: And he is arrayed in a garment sprinkled with blood, etc.

Verse 15: And he treadeth the winepress of the fierceness of the wrath of Almighty God.

The theophany of Isaiah lxiii is combined with Messianic passages from Psalm ii and Isaiah xi (cf. Revelation xix. 15).

The description of the Day of the Lord in 2 Peter iii shows the influence of Isaiah xxxiv. 4 (which we shall meet again when we examine the Little Apocalypse) and of Isaiah lxv. 17, lxvi. 22 (new heavens and a new earth).

As time went on, even passages from pseudepigraphs descriptive of God's coming for judgement were applied to Christ. In Jude, for instance, there is a quotation from the Book of Enoch, chapter i. There is no mention of the Messiah in the first thirty-six chapters of Enoch, and this passage describes in familiar O.T. imagery the coming of God:

> Behold the Lord came with ten thousand of His holy ones, to execute judgement upon all, and to convict all the ungodly of all their works of ungodliness which they have ungodly wrought, and of all the hard things which ungodly sinners have spoken against Him.

It is almost certain that 'Jude' understands these words (originally written concerning the coming of God to judge the world) as a reference to the Parousia of Jesus; cf. verse 21. If so, this is a very clear instance of the usage we have found to be so important.

CHAPTER 21

THE MAN OF SIN

THE Thessalonian correspondence shows that in constructing their doctrine of the last things, the early Christians employed not only the prophecies of the Day of the Lord, but also the Jewish legend of an evil being who should appear in the last days. The idea that the Advent was near is associated with this and with the mystery of iniquity which was already at work (2 Thessalonians ii. 7).

This teaching was based upon various O.T. passages, especially the later chapters of Daniel. The references in Daniel originally applied to Antiochus Epiphanes, but since his demise was not immediately followed by the resurrection and the age of gold, it was held that the prophecies still awaited fulfilment. Apocalyptic, of course, arose in part through the non-fulfilment of prophecy; thus Jeremiah's prediction concerning a period of seventy years received a new interpretation in Daniel, becoming seventy weeks of years; and when Daniel's prophecy was not fulfilled this in its turn was re-interpreted and projected into the future. Accordingly, the Jews still looked for a Man of Sin who should concentrate in himself the powers of evil and whose appearance would be a sign of the last time.

Bousset, in his *Antichrist Legend*, has shown that the Christian Fathers have a vast amount of material on this subject, much of which is quite unexplained by the N.T. It is clear that they derived it from the Jewish form of the legend, and this can be traced in such writings as Psalms of Solomon, Assumption of Moses, Testaments of the XII Patriarchs, etc. It was natural that this doctrine should pass over into Christian theology even though it had no warrant in the teaching of Jesus. The Christians added characteristic modifications to the original version.

Daniel's prophecy had foretold an apostasy (xi. 30, 32), an impious king who would 'magnify himself above every god' (xi. 36-7, etc.), and the profaning of the sanctuary (xi. 31), the events reaching their climax in the destruction of the evil king and the deliverance of the people of God (xi. 45, xii. 1 *ff.*). All these features reappear in 2 Thessalonians ii. The language shows traces of this passage of Daniel[1] and others, such as Ezekiel xxviii. 2 and Isaiah xiv. 13-14. (Isaiah xiv particularly was much used by the Fathers in reference to Antichrist, and it probably passed early into the tradition.)

It is probable that the old myth of a primeval struggle between God and the dragon of the deep provided the background of the Antichrist legend (on the principle that the end of the world will resemble the beginning, *Endzeit=Urzeit*), but the influence of the later chapters of Daniel led to the view that the great adversary in the final struggle would be a man, and a man after the stamp of Antiochus. It was not difficult to find others who in later times showed similar tendencies, and the Psalms of Solomon show that Pompey was regarded in the light of this tradition. Earnest men have always recognized the signs of the great apostasy in their contemporaries, and in that period particularly every generation threw up some monster of iniquity who suggested that at last the Man of Sin had taken shape.

According to Paul, the mystery of wickedness (i.e. the spirit of Antichrist) was already at work when he wrote 2 Thessalonians, and this was a sign that the personal incarnation of evil could not be far distant. The attempt of the Emperor Caligula to set up his image in the Temple at Jerusalem in A.D. 40 would account for this conviction. Caligula's desire to be worshipped as a god provoked

---

[1] Daniel xi. 36: μεγαλυνθησεται επι παντα θεον. 2 Thessalonians ii. 4: ὑπεραιρομενος ἐπι πάντα λεγομενον θεον.

tremendous disturbance in the minds of the Jews. The language of Josephus concerning the incident is interesting in comparison with Paul's expressions: *Ant.*, XIX. i. 1: (Caligula) thought that as he was a god. . . . XVIII. viii. 1: treated him as one of the gods. XVIII. viii. 2: to erect his statue in the temple of God.

The attempt of Caligula did not succeed; in fact, he died during the commotion which his command had created. He therefore was not Antichrist, but his attempt showed that the spirit of Antichrist was abroad. 'His order caused great alarm among the Jews, who even after his death (A.D. 41) continued to fear lest one of his successors should revive and enforce it.'[1]

According to Bousset, we cannot understand why Antichrist should be connected with Jerusalem. But surely this is adequately explained by the fact that the men who in Jewish writings adumbrated the final Man of Sin had some connection with Temple desecration. Thus, Antiochus the prototype had placed within the Temple courts at Jerusalem an idol-altar; Pompey, the 'insolent one' of the Psalms of Solomon, captured Jerusalem and entered the Holy of Holies. And as we have seen, Caligula's mad attempt was also concerned with the same city and building. This remarkable series would sufficiently account for the view that the final Antichrist would go farther still and would sit in the Temple as a god himself.[2] The reference to the Temple and to Jerusalem runs throughout. Of course, when the temple was destroyed in A.D. 70 various modifications entered the legend.

Bousset maintains that one of the alterations that the Christians made to the Jewish version was to make Antichrist an apostate Jew, and he finds this in Paul's language.

---

[1] *H.D.B.*, i. 12. Abomination of Desolation (Driver).

[2] Cheyne, however, suggests that the reference here (2 Thessalonians ii. 4) and in Mark xiii is to Antichrist's statue sitting or standing in the Temple (*E.B.* i. 22).

In his view 'those who receive not the love of the truth' (ii. 10) are the Jews criticized so strongly in the First Epistle. It is usually held that the restraining element was the Roman Empire (neuter, ii. 6) headed by the emperor (masculine, ii. 7). But if Caligula, an emperor, came so near to being Antichrist himself, it is difficult to think of the head of the Empire as being a 'restrainer' in virtue of his position. These difficulties are well dealt with in the explanation of A. S. Peake, who adds the following valuable comment to Andrews' notes on 1 and 2 Thessalonians (in Peake's *Commentary*):[1]

It is in favour of the view that the mystery of lawlessness, and self-deification of the man of sin, refers to the temper manifested in Caligula, that it is difficult, with all Paul's reason for exasperation with the Jews and lurid anticipations of their impending fate (1 Thessalonians ii. 14–16), to believe that he would expect such an outbreak of lawlessness and deification of a man to spring from a people so passionately monotheistic and devoted to the Law. It is accordingly at least plausible to interpret the passage in the following way: The mystery of lawlessness has already manifested itself in Caligula. At present it is held in check by Claudius, the reigning emperor of Rome. When he is 'taken out of the way', his successor will be the man of sin, carrying to a climax the impious tendencies already revealed by Caligula. The guarded character of the language is much easier to understand if Paul identified the man of sin with the next Roman emperor. There was no such need for cautious language if the Empire played a good part throughout.

We have here something which has a bearing upon the sense of urgency revealed in this correspondence. The previous chapters have been concerned with the Parousia itself, but have given no explanation of the belief in its imminence. This subject will be referred to later, but one reason emerges already. If the spirit of Antichrist was already in operation, as the Caligula affair suggested, then

[1] See also Peake's *Critical Introduction to the New Testament*, p. 15.

the end of all things was at hand, the end of the age was near.

In its Jewish form, the legend declared that the Man of Sin would be destroyed by God Himself, or by Michael, or the Messiah:

1. In the Sibylline Oracles, for example, it is said of God, that He 'shall Beliar consume and all the overbearing men who shall have put faith in him' (iii. 73).

2. Another tradition said that he would be destroyed by Michael. The source of this was probably Daniel xi. 45–xii. 1: 'he shall come to his end, and none shall help him. And at that time shall Michael stand up . . .'

3. Yet another tradition said that Messiah son of David would destroy Antichrist; cf. Isaiah xi. 1–4: 'There shall come forth a shoot out of the stock of Jesse . . . with the breath of his lips shall he slay the wicked.' Several Jewish authorities explain 'the wicked' in this verse as a reference to the Man of Sin. Paul quotes this passage of Isaiah xi in 2 Thessalonians ii and, as Bousset says (p. 225), this reference 'does not seem to be made independently, but to have been handed down to him through the general Jewish tradition'.

The Christians, to whom Jesus was both Lord and Messiah, said that Antichrist would be destroyed at the Parousia. Paul in 2 Thessalonians ii. 8 combines a Messianic passage of the O.T. with theophanic language in the words, 'whom the Lord Jesus shall slay with the breath of his mouth, and bring to nought by the manifestation [Epiphany] of His Parousia'.[1]

---

[1] The following passage from the Christian part of the Ascension of Isaiah is of interest. Beliar is in this case apparently Nero, as he is described as the slayer of his mother. iv. 13, 'and many believers and saints having seen Him for whom they were hoping, who was crucified, Jesus the Lord Christ, and those also who were believers in Him—of these few in those days will be left as His servants, while they flee from desert to desert, awaiting the coming of the Beloved. 14. And after 1,332 days the Lord will come with His angels and with the armies of the Holy Ones from the seventh heaven with the glory of the seventh heaven, and He will drag Beliar into Gehenna and also his armies' (S.P.C.K. ed. 1917).

CHAPTER 22

THE LITTLE APOCALYPSE (B)

As we have seen, Jesus foretold the destruction of Jerusalem and its Temple. Now, in the O.T. it was said that the attack of the nations on Jerusalem would be followed by the coming of the Lord (e.g. Zechariah xiv). Thus it was to be expected that the Parousia should become attached to the words of Jesus about the destruction of the Temple. This is what we find in Mark xiii, where the opening verses, which are historical and which concern the Temple's fate, are followed by the passage usually known as the Little Apocalypse. It is to this that we now return to study it as a production of the early Church.

We shall find here exactly the same features as we have traced in the Thessalonian letters:

A. O.T. passages concerning the Day of the Lord have been applied to Jesus.

B. It is, moreover, another Antichrist document, drawing upon Daniel xi-xii and the Jewish tradition.

A. All agree that some sayings in the Little Apocalypse are genuine words of Jesus, but it is generally maintained that verses 24-7 (in Mark xiii) are extraneous.

24 speaks of portents preceding the Advent, 'The sun shall be darkened, and the moon shall not give her light'. This is a quotation from the familiar Day of the Lord passage, Isaiah xiii-xiv. xiii. 6, 'the Day of the Lord is near'; xiii. 10, 'The sun shall be darkened in his going forth, and the moon shall not cause her light to shine'. As in the case of 1 and 2 Thessalonians, the LXX shows more striking agreement.

The next verse (25) reads: 'And the stars shall be falling from heaven, and the powers that are in the heavens [αἱ δυναμεις των οὐρανων] shall be shaken.' This comes from the description of the Day of the Lord in Isaiah xxxiv. 4 as given in the LXX, not the Hebrew: 'And all the powers of the heavens shall melt . . . and all the stars shall fall.' καὶ τακήσονται πᾶσαι αἱ δυνάμεις τῶν οὐρανῶν . . . καὶ πάντα τὰ ἄστρα πεσεῖται.

26. One new feature in Mark xiii that we did not find in 1 and 2 Thessalonians is the reference to Daniel vii. 13 in 26: 'And then shall they see the Son of man coming in clouds with great power and glory.' Two reasons for this are possible and both may have played a part: (a) Once the Parousia doctrine was formed, the Christians would try to find traces of a similar message in the teaching of Jesus. His words to the High Priest (Mark xiv. 62) taken from Daniel vii. 13 would now be understood in a new sense. We have seen that the words in Daniel originally spoke of an ascent to God, not a descent to the earth, and that Jesus used them in the former sense. When, however, the Parousia doctrine came into being in the early Church, the words would be interpreted in a new light. Accordingly, in the Little Apocalypse the coming of the Son of man with clouds is now taken to refer to the descent of Christ in glory. (It is clear that the Parousia teaching of the Epistles was not derived from Jesus' use of Daniel vii. 13; nowhere in the Epistles is Jesus called Son of man or His Advent described as a coming with clouds. The language of the Epistles reflects O.T. theophanies, not Daniel vii. 13.) (b) Antichrist was recognized by Christian writers in the little horn of Daniel vii (verse 8); this is followed a little later in the chapter by the Son of man coming with clouds (verse 13), which must 'therefore' be later than Antichrist's appearance; cf. Hippolytus, *Christ and Antichrist*, which contains much early material, xx–xxii, xxv–xxvi.

It must be noted that the earlier and more correct meaning of Daniel vii. 13 still lingered in the Church side by side with the new interpretation which referred it to the Parousia, e.g. Cyprian, *Testimonies*, ii. 26.

This is followed by the Gathering of the Elect: 27: 'and shall gather together his elect from the four winds, from the uttermost part of the earth to the uttermost part of heaven'. καὶ ἐπισυνάξει τοὺς ἐκλεκτοὺς ἐκ τῶν τεσσάρων ἀνέμων ἀπ'ἄκρου γῆς ἕως ἄκρου οὐρανοῦ.

The former part of this verse is a quotation from Zechariah ii. 6, where the LXX reads, 'from the four winds of heaven will I gather you'. ἐκ τῶν τεσσάρων ἀνέμων τοῦ οὐρανοῦ συνάξω ὑμᾶς. (The context in Zechariah ii provides another passage which speaks of the coming of God: 'Sing and rejoice, O daughter of Zion; for lo, I come and I will dwell in the midst of thee,' ii. 10.) It is important to notice that the Hebrew of verse 6 is quite different from the LXX, and reads: 'For I have spread you abroad as the four winds of the heaven. Flee from the land of the north, saith the Lord.' This shows that the Little Apocalypse was constructed by readers of the LXX. There is no need to call it a *Jewish*-Christian apocalypse. (The point also has some bearing on Torrey's theory that our Gospels were originally written in Aramaic.)

The latter part of Mark xiii. 27 suggests the influence of Deuteronomy xxx. 4, another passage which speaks of the gathering of the dispersed: '. . . in the uttermost parts of heaven, from thence will the Lord thy God gather thee' (R.V.). LXX: ἀπ'ἄκρου τοῦ οὐρανοῦ ἕως ἄκρου τοῦ οὐρανοῦ, ἐκεῖθεν συνάξει σε Κύριος.

It is incredible that this passage of Mark xiii (24–7)— a patchwork of O.T. testimonies, partly in LXX language —can be the teaching of Jesus. Study of the language confirms the theory, now widely accepted, that we must trace here the hand of the early Church.

B. The influence of Daniel xi-xii and the Antichrist Legend can be traced in this chapter as well as the Day

of the Lord passages already mentioned. xi. 21 marks the
beginning of the section concerning Antiochus, and this
part of Daniel speaks of four matters which we have
recognized in 2 Thessalonians ii—apostasy, Antichrist,
profaning of the Temple, and divine deliverance. These
appear also in Mark xiii (for Antichrist see below). In
addition, the Daniel passage uses the striking phrase,
'abomination of desolation' (xi. 31), and speaks of wars
(xi. 40–2), rumours (ἀκοαί, xi. 44), and a time of
unprecedented tribulation (xii. 1). These also all reappear
in Mark xiii, in some cases with identical phraseology:
abomination of desolation (14), wars and rumours
(ἀκοαί) of wars (7), tribulation (19) 'such as there hath
not been the like [θλῖψις οἵα οὐ γέγονεν] from the
beginning of the creation which God created until now';
cf. Daniel xii. 1: 'There shall be a time of trouble, such
as never was [LXX, θλῖψις οἵα οὐ γέγονεν] since
there was a nation even to that same time.'

It has been plausibly argued[1] that Mark xiii. 14 interprets 'the abomination of desolation' as Antichrist himself; the masculine participle coupled with a neuter noun
is not a grammatical blunder, but is intentional.

Other features, too, apparently came from the Antichrist tradition as the Jews had developed it. Thus, as
Bousset has shown,[2] the flight of the faithful was a part of
the tradition in its purely Jewish form. It has been
maintained earlier (Chapter 9) that Jesus used the
language of flight in reference to the fall of Jerusalem,
Luke xvii. 31, though not flight 'to the mountains'; it
may well be that genuine words of His have been worked
into the Little Apocalypse at this point (Mark xiii. 15–16).
Similarly, the words of Jesus to the daughters of Jerusalem
as He journeyed to Calvary, Luke xxiii. 28–9, may
lie behind Mark xiii. 17. This confirms the view
that genuine words of Jesus have been combined

---

[1] Streeter, *Four Gospels*, p. 492.   [2] *Antichrist Legend*, p. 212 ff.

with apocalyptic material assembled by the early Church.

Matthew's additions to the Little Apocalypse are very instructive and show further O.T. influence.

Thus, in xxiv. 30, 'and then shall all the tribes of the earth mourn', Matthew inserts a Testimony from Zechariah xii. 12:

Matthew: καὶ κόψονται πᾶσαι αἱ φυλαὶ τῆς γῆς.
Zechariah: καὶ κόψεται ἡ γῆ κατὰ φυλὰς φυλάς.
verse 14. πᾶσαι αἱ . . . φυλαί.

Matthew connects this with the words from Daniel vii. 13, which immediately follow. (It is interesting to find these two quotations together again in Revelation i. 7. Revelation has not taken them from Matthew, as the phrase 'they which pierced him' in Revelation i. 7 shows; this is found in Zechariah xii, but is absent from Matthew. They occur together again in Justin; they probably appeared together in an early Testimony book.) Matthew makes more O.T. references than any other Evangelist, and several of his additions to Mark (both in the Little Apocalypse and in the Passion narrative) are of this kind.

In Matthew xxiv. 30–1 two more additions which comparison with Mark xiii reveals are '*the sign*' of the Son of man and the '*great trumpet*'. These are of great interest and should be considered together, as they both have to do with the gathering of the elect.

In the O.T. and also in later Jewish writings two things are associated with the gathering of the dispersed: the trumpet and the ensign (or standard). The following prayer still appears in the Jewish Daily Prayer Book:

Sound the *great trumpet* for our freedom; lift up the *ensign* to gather our exiles, and gather us from the four corners of the earth. Blessed art thou, O Lord, who gatherest the banished ones of thy people Israel.[1]

Again, in the additional New Year Service:

'Our God and God of our fathers, sound the great trumpet for our freedom, lift up the ensign to gather our exiles; bring our scattered ones among the nations near unto thee, and gather our dispersed from the ends of the earth' (pp. 253–4).

Earlier in the same service Isaiah xxvii. 13 is quoted in full, where the 'great trumpet' occurs (this is the only *great* trumpet in the O.T.); and Isaiah xi. 12 is quoted dealing with the ensign.

Now, the LXX in Isaiah xi. 12 has, for 'ensign', σημεῖον, the word which Matthew has introduced into xxiv. 30 and which is wrongly translated 'sign'. In xxiv. 31 he has added the great trumpet from Isaiah xxvii. 13 (LXX, τῇ σάλπιγγι τῇ μεγάλῃ; Matthew, μετὰ σάλπιγγος μεγάλης).

These two are found together several times in the O.T. Isaiah xviii. 3: 'All ye inhabitants of the world, and ye dwellers on the earth, when an ensign [נֵס] is lifted up on the mountains see ye, and when the trumpet is blown, hear ye.' The LXX has σημεῖον and σάλπιγξ, as in Jeremiah li. 27 (LXX, xxviii. 27). The standard and the trumpet are again together in Jeremiah iv. 21 (Hebrew).

Matthew's word, σημεῖον, means not only 'sign'; it is also the Biblical Greek for 'ensign' or 'standard' and should be so translated here. These two additions he has made in 30–1 are the familiar ensign and trumpet associated with the gathering of the elect, the very matter being dealt with at that point of the Little Apocalypse.

If we trace the word for standard, נֵס, through the

O.T., we shall find that the LXX often translates it by σημειον or some cognate word. In addition to the above citations; Numbers xxi. 8–9: Moses sets the brazen serpent on a standard or pole, ἐπὶ σημείου.

In Isaiah xxxiii. 23, where נֵס means the flag of a ship, LXX has οὐκ ἀρεῖ σημεῖον. Also Jeremiah li. 12 (LXX, xxviii. 12). נֵס is translated σημείωσις in Psalm lx. 4; σύσσημον in Isaiah v. 26, xlix. 22, lxii. 10; and σημαῖα in Isaiah xxx. 17.

Σημεῖον is not only Biblical Greek for 'standard'; it is also a good classical word in that sense and is so used by Euripides, Herodotus, and Xenophon (Liddell and Scott, s.v.).

There is therefore no need to follow Torrey in his suggestion that σημεῖον in Matthew xxiv. 30 is את (accusative) misread as אות in the Semitic original which he hypothecates.

Jerome was nearer the mark with the second of his two suggestions:

> *Signum hic, aut crucis intelligamus, ut videant Judaei quem compunxerunt; aut vexillum victoriae triumphantis.*

cf. Milton, *Paradise Lost*, Bk. vi, 774 *ff.*:

> Then unexpected joy surpris'd,
> When the great ensign of Messiah blaz'd
> Aloft, by Angels borne, his sign in Heaven.

Luke xxi is probably a paraphrase of Mark xiii. Luke evidently understood the prophecy to refer to the fall of Jerusalem, an event which had taken place since the publication of Mark's Gospel and before the final writing of his own. Instead of the abomination of desolation, he substitutes the armies surrounding Jerusalem (20).

Further, instead of the tribulation being followed immediately by the Parousia, an indefinite interim period is introduced: 'and Jerusalem shall be trodden down of

the Gentiles, until the times of the Gentiles shall be fulfilled'. (24): ἔσται πατουμένη ὑπὸ ἐθνῶν. This may
be a reminiscence of Zechariah xii, which deals with the
Siege of Jerusalem in verse 2 and continues: 'I will make
Jerusalem λίθον καταπατατούμενον πᾶσι τοῖς ἔθνεσι'
(3, LXX). This does not correspond with the Hebrew
(the Hebrew word is a *hapax legomenon*), but the LXX
might be held to suggest a period during which Jerusalem
would be trampled down until the time of the ultimate
victory described so vividly in Zechariah xiv. This is just
the kind of adjustment which is familiar in apocalyptic
writings, revision in the light of subsequent events.

It is possible that the apocalyptic passage, Isaiah xxiv.
17, lies behind Luke xxi. 34–5:

Isaiah: παγὶς ἐφ'ὑμᾶς τοὺς ἐνοικοῦντας ἐπὶ τῆς γῆς.

Luke: . . . ὡς παγὶς ἐπεισελεύσεται γὰρ ἐπὶ πάντας τοὺς
καθημένους ἐπὶ πρόσωπον πάσης τῆς γῆς.

If Luke xxi is a paraphrase of Mark xiii, it is freer than
Luke's usual practice; and it has been alternatively
suggested that Luke is here following a different source.[1]

---

[1] Dr. V. Taylor thinks that a non-Marcan basis (which did not, however,
appear in Proto-Luke) has received Marcan additions. This is similar to
the view of Dr. T. W. Manson in *Mission and Message of Jesus*, pp. 615 ff.
He suggests that Mark and Luke offer two versions of a Palestinian document
which was in existence about A.D. 40. For our present purpose it is worth
noting that in the opinion of Taylor and Manson Luke xxi. 26b-27 has been
inserted from Mark xiii and did not stand in the non-Marcan source in
its original form.

CHAPTER 23

THE NOTE OF IMMINENCE

THE foregoing chapters help to explain why the early Church, in working out its beliefs concerning the last things, came to regard the Parousia as near. The theophanic passages of the Day of the Lord would not have been sufficient in themselves to indicate a time, but when they were connected with the Antichrist tradition the sense of imminence was inevitable.

We have seen that Jesus 'definitely looked forward to a future in time and in this earth in which His followers would have to live and work',[1] and that there is no good evidence to show that the Apostles in the very earliest days after Pentecost lived in momentary expectation of the Parousia and the end of the age. We do find, however, this spirit of vivid expectancy in 1 and 2 Thessalonians, and one reason for this has already been suggested—the adoption of the Antichrist legend. The signs of the times seemed to indicate that the mystery of iniquity was already active (as Paul says in 2 Thessalonians ii. 7), and this in the light of Daniel xi–xii, etc., was taken to show that the end of the age was near. Later in the century it was still the apostasy which was regarded as a sure sign of the last days:

Little children, it is the last hour: and as ye heard that antichrist cometh, even now have there arisen many antichrists; whereby we know that it is the last hour (1 John ii. 18).

But there were several other factors which no doubt contributed to the conviction that the end of all things was at hand.

[1] R. N. Flew, *Jesus and His Church*, p. 121.

N

Some of the Testimonies themselves spoke of the Advent's speedy approach. (The fact that they were originally written centuries before would not prevent this deduction; they were torn from their original period as they were from their context); cf. Hebrews x. 37:

> 'For yet a very little while,
> He that cometh shall come, and shall not tarry.'
> (LXX of Isaiah xxvi. 20 and Habakkuk ii. 3.)

Another factor to be considered is that many Jews at the time of Jesus' ministry were looking for the speedy arrival of the Messianic Age which was to be inaugurated with a catastrophic judgement. The preaching of John the Baptist is to be thus interpreted; while several passages speak of those who were looking for the consolation of Israel (Luke ii. 25, 38; cf. Mark xv. 43). Now, Jesus taught that the long-expected Kingdom of God had dawned, though in a very different manner from that popularly expected. We have already noted such passages as Luke xi. 20 and x. 24. In spite of this declaration that the age of fulfilment had come, it is easy to understand that some followers of Jesus could not believe that His ministry, death, and Resurrection were any more than the prelude to more dramatic events. They had looked for so much: the overthrow and destruction of evil, the establishment of a righteous kingdom, a new order. What they had already witnessed surely could not be the whole story of the 'divine intervention'. And so the spirit of expectancy would be carried over into the Christian Church. Instead of seeing that Jesus had transmuted their hopes, they projected them into the future.

It was hard for them to see what is plain to us, that a new era in human history had dawned. Later Paul developed his great conception that God's purpose to sum up all things in Christ is now being fulfilled through the reconciling ministry of the Church. It is fortunate that we have the letters of Paul in which we can trace the emergence of this nobler view.

A small point which has some bearing upon the general background of ancient thought is that conceptions of an 'end of the world' were not lacking among pagans. Stoics held that the universe was periodically destroyed by fire and a new beginning made. Epicureans held that the world was inevitably wearing out and would pass away to give place to another formed by another concourse of atoms. It was a prevailing pagan belief that the world was deteriorating. First came the age of gold, but we are living in the last age of iron (Hesiod, *Works and Days*); the powers of nature are failing, creatures and harvests are smaller and feebler than they used to be (cf. Lucretius, Bk. V); we are living in one of the periods in which the world is left to itself; it is like a ship which finally begins to flounder until God takes the helm (Plato, *Politicus* myth). We should not attribute much to this pagan view, except that Gentile Christians would tend to carry these conceptions into their Christianity. Cf. Philo: 'As generation follows generation the powers and qualities of body and soul which men receive are feebler.'[1]

More important is the consideration that Jesus foretold the fall of Jerusalem within a generation (cf. Luke xi. 50, 'required of this generation'; the injunctions to the disciples, Luke xvii. 31–2, etc., also imply that it would be during their lifetime). The early Christians would obviously study this question in the light of O.T. prophecy, and they would find that a siege of Jerusalem is there associated with the end of the age and the great Day of God. In Zechariah xiv the gathering of nations to Jerusalem and the taking of the city is immediately followed by the coming of the Lord and his standing upon the Mount of Olives, and then the age of peace and victory. So in Zechariah xii the siege (2–3) is followed by divine

[1] *Op. Mund.*, 141 (Loeb Ed., I, 113).

intervention and the new age; cf. also Joel iii, Isaiah xxix. In Daniel xii the tribulation of Israel is followed by deliverance in a similar way.

Mark xiii as it now stands is in general agreement with this programme and suggests that the fall of the Temple and the attack on Judea with its fearful tribulation would be immediately followed by the Parousia, and all these events would be fulfilled within the generation of Jesus' contemporaries (cf. 2, 4, 14, 24–6, 30).

It is probable too that the words of Jesus in Mark ix. 1 were misunderstood. While He plainly asserted in His teaching the arrival of the Kingdom of God, His words suggest that the Kingdom had come in an incipient way and that a fuller coming of the Kingdom would follow His death (Luke xii. 49–50; Mark ix. 1; cf. Chapter 12). We have found the historical fulfilment of these prophetic words in the events of Pentecost. But it would not be at all strange if the early Christians misunderstood them. We have seen how Matthew later altered them introducing the Parousia (xvi. 28).

On more than one occasion Jesus had to rebuke the disciples for their dullness and to ask if they were without understanding. His words about the leaven of the Pharisees were taken to refer to bread, and while He was referring to a spiritual peril they were thinking about forgotten provisions. Similarly, when Jesus spoke of the opposition the disciples would meet in their work in the future in contrast with the conditions of their previous mission, and used language about a sword that was obviously symbolic, they understood Him to be speaking about literal weapons and evidently discovered two in the upper room (Luke xxii. 38): 'and they said, Lord, behold, here are two swords. And he said unto them, It is enough'[1] —meaning, 'Enough of the subject, you do not understand.' Even then, they apparently took the swords unknown to

[1] Ἱκανον εστιν.

their Master, and one of them was used in the Garden of Gethsemane in a way that was entirely against His wishes.

It is not surprising therefore if this saying of Jesus in Mark ix. 1 was taken to imply that some of the apostolic band would never die.[1]

Summing up, we may say that the indication of some outstanding crisis within a generation, the Antichrist legend and the Caligula affair, and the reference to the lifetime of the Apostles, would all converge to produce a spirit of great excitement and expectancy about the middle of the first century. This is exactly what we find in the Thessalonian correspondence.

[1] This logion probably lies behind John xxi. 22, which speaks of a tradition that John would never die, and hints that the words on which it was based were misunderstood.

CHAPTER 24

THE REIGN OF CHRIST

THE Day of the Lord in the O.T. was the prelude to His reign of peace, and this conception had its influence on Christian thoughts concerning the future (Psalm lxxxii. 8; Zechariah xiv, etc.). It is well known that the golden era of the Kingdom was sometimes thought of as the reign of God without any mention of the Messiah, and sometimes it was thought of as the reign of the Son of David.

We have seen reason to believe that Jesus re-interpreted both the Kingdom and the Messiah, finding the secret of His kingship not in material splendour or coercion, but in service and love, and regarding the Cross as the true way of victory. This is one of the thoughts which the Church never lost, and one which binds the Gospels and the Epistles into a unity.

This conception is wonderfully illustrated in the Book of *Revelation* in the picture of the slain Lamb in the midst of the throne (v), whose sacrifice inspires the new song:[1]

Worthy art Thou . . . for thou wast slain, and didst purchase unto God with Thy blood men of every tribe and tongue and

---

[1] 'But the Lamb has triumphed not in right of conquest alone, but in virtue of insight. That indeed is clear from His choice of this path to victory. For while others have sought to reach their goal by force and violence and aggression, He has gone beneath their superficial view and grasped the deep paradox that victory comes through suffering, submission, and self-surrender. And therefore,

> He was oppressed, yet He humbled Himself,
> And opened not His mouth,
> As a lamb that is led to the slaughter,
> And as a sheep before its shearers is dumb.

And thus He is able to divine the future because He has discovered the principle which controls it' (A. S. Peake, *Revelation of John*, p. 267; cf. the whole passage, 264–8).

people and nation, and madest them to be unto our God a kingdom and priests; and they reign upon the earth (9–10).

But unfortunately the rest of the book is not sustained at this sublime level. In xix Christ is described as a warrior descending from the opened heavens to fight His enemies; after vanquishing them, He reigns upon the earth for a thousand years with the risen martyrs. At the end of this period the Last Judgement takes place and heaven and earth flee away to be replaced by a new universe. In this way the O.T. Messianic prophecies are literally fulfilled. This doctrine of a *Millennium* is only found here in the N.T. (in a book which had a great struggle ever to win a place in the canon). Nevertheless it was strongly represented in patristic writings.

The conception of a temporary kingdom on the present earth arose in Judaism as a compromise between two conflicting views: (*a*) According to one, the present earth will be the site of an everlasting Messianic kingdom. (*b*) According to the other, the present universe will be destroyed and a new creation will provide the scene of the eternal kingdom. This view is represented in 2 Peter iii:

But the day of the Lord will come as a thief; in the which the heavens shall pass away with a great noise, and the elements shall be dissolved with fervent heat, and the earth and the works that are therein shall be burned up. . . . But, according to His promise, we look for new heavens and a new earth, wherein dwelleth righteousness (10–13).

The temporary kingdom was a compromise between these two conceptions; it was true that the eternal kingdom would have its being in a new heaven and earth, but there would nevertheless be a temporary kingdom on the present earth before its destruction.[1] Periods of varying

[1] The Apocalypse of Weeks, in the Book of Enoch, provides one of the earliest instances.

length were suggested by different authorities. Some said 400 years (e.g. the late first century A.D. 2 Esdras vii. 28), and this figure was reached, as stated in the Talmud, by combining Psalm xc. 15 with Genesis xv. 13—the children of Israel were afflicted 400 years in Egypt and they were to be blessed 'according to the days wherein thou hast afflicted us, and the years wherein we have seen evil'.[1]

But in Revelation the temporary kingdom is to last a thousand years, possibly the seventh in a week of millennial 'days' beginning with the creation as in the Epistle of Barnabas, where it is said that since a day is as a thousand years—

in six days, that is, in six thousand years, shall all things be accomplished. And what is that He saith, 'And He rested on the seventh day'? He meaneth this, that when His Son shall come, and abolish the season of the wicked one, and judge the ungodly; and shall change the sun, and the moon, and the stars; then He shall gloriously rest on that seventh day.

Further on the writer speaks of 'the eighth day, that is, the beginning of the other world' (xv).

Some have attempted to find the idea of a millennium in Paul, but it is doubtful if he held the conception at any time. The most likely passage in this connection is 1 Corinthians xv. 23–6.

(23) . . . they that are Christ's, at his coming. (24) Then cometh the end, when he shall deliver up the kingdom to God, even the Father; when he shall have abolished all rule

---

[1] According to the Rabbis, the temporary kingdom occurs before the great 'renewing' and belongs to 'the present age', not 'the age to come'; cf. Talmud (Bab.), Sanhed. 97*b*: 'A Hebrew scroll found in Roman archives said 4,231 years after the creation the world will be orphaned (i.e. in great distress). As to the years following, some of them will be spent in the war of the great sea monsters, and some in the War of Gog and Magog, and the remaining period will be the Messianic era, whilst the Holy One, blessed be He, will renew his world only after 7,000 years.

'R. Abba, the son of Raba, said: The statement was after 5,000 years.'

and all authority and power. (25) For he must reign, till he hath put all enemies under his feet. (26) The last enemy that shall be abolished is death.

It has been maintained that the reign spoken of in 25 begins with the Parousia and is the kingdom delivered up to God the Father as stated in 24. The sequence of events is therefore (*a*) the Parousia and the resurrection of them that are Christ's, (*b*) the millennial reign on earth, (*c*) the end, when the kingdom is delivered up to the Father. This would agree with the scheme adopted in Revelation xix-xx.

However, closer examination of Paul's language in the light of other passages in his letters shows that the kingdom referred to in 1 Corinthians xv. 24-5 is the same as Christ's present session at the right hand of God, and the delivering up of this kingdom follows the Parousia. In Paul's view, the rule of Christ began with His exaltation as Lord, His victorious struggle against evil powers is in great part already achieved (cf. Colossians ii. 15); the repeated use of Psalm cx emphasizes the fact that already dominion is His (Ephesians i. 20 *ff.*, Colossians iii. 1).

The point of verse 25 is as follows: The Apostle wishes to justify his statement that Christ will finally deliver up His kingdom to the Father; he is anticipating the objection that this implies an ending to Christ's rule. And so he refers to the well-known testimony, Psalm cx. 1, and virtually underlines the word 'until'; it is necessary for Him to reign, in fulfilment of the scripture, until and only until God has put all His enemies under His feet. When death is abolished by the final resurrection, the last of these enemies will have been destroyed, the limit of the reign will be reached, and consequently the kingdom must be delivered up to the Father. This point is followed by a similar treatment of Psalm viii in 27-8. Thus in Paul's teaching the Parousia does not inaugurate, but ends the reign of Christ, or rather leads to its absorption in the complete kingdom of God.

Nor is there any evidence that the Apostle believed that the present universe would be destroyed. To judge by Romans viii, he rather returns to the view found in parts of the O.T. (e.g. Isaiah xi) that the universe would be renewed, transformed, and delivered from all imperfection. Had he expected the destruction of the present earth and its replacement by an entirely new one, he would surely not have spoken of the whole creation groaning and travailing and eagerly anticipating its approaching liberation. To him creation was not decaying and nearly dead; it was earnestly expecting deliverance from bondage. According to this presentation, God will so transform the present universe that it will become a fitting home for the saints in the resurrection body. The coming glory includes both the deliverance of the creation and the redemption of the body (Romans viii. 18–23).

The millennium of Revelation xx is the only mention of a temporary kingdom in the N.T., and it is the clearest instance of Christ's future reign. It appears that the more prevalent view in the first century was of an eternal reign which would follow the Parousia and the Judgement.

As hinted earlier, the O.T. Theophanies were connected, not only with judgement, but also with the eternal reign of God. Further, the early Christians, in searching the scriptures, would find descriptions of the Messiah reigning in peace and prosperity. These appeared to be as yet unfulfilled, and the doctrine of the Second Advent made it possible to connect them with that event; those prophecies which still awaited fulfilment would be accomplished at the Parousia and after. Since Jesus was both Lord and Christ, there was no difference between 'the Lord' reigning on the earth and 'the Messiah' fulfilling his regal office. Thus in Cyprian's Testimony Book, the section we have mentioned earlier, 'That Jesus Christ shall come as a Judge', is immediately followed by another entitled 'That He will reign as a King for ever'. This includes testimonies concerning the Messiah (Zechariah ix; Psalm ii, etc.) and others concerning God (Psalm xxii. 27–8, '. . . for the kingdom is the Lord's; and he shall rule over all nations'; Psalm xxiv. 7–10, etc.).

In this way an answer was provided to the objection that Jesus could not be the Messiah because He had not fulfilled the O.T. predictions about a glorious king. Judging by the accounts which have come down to us of disputes with the Jews, this objection was one which *they* developed. 'Jesus', they said, 'was not a glorious figure, He was crucified in ignominy and shame; therefore He was not the Messiah.' The Christians replied in two ways:

(*a*) They said first of all that the O.T. foretold the sufferings of the Messiah, and here they made much of such passages as Isaiah liii and Psalm xxii as well as applying every bit of wood in the O.T. to the Cross.[1]

(*b*) But they went on to point out that there were *two Advents*: one in lowliness, which had already taken place, and a second in glorious majesty, which was to come. At the second Advent all the outstanding predictions about a glorious king would be fulfilled.[2]

Mention was made at the beginning of the chapter to the disparity in the Book of Revelation between the vision of the slain Lamb on the throne and the later literal reign in Jerusalem. If we examine the writings of those Fathers who believed most firmly in a millennium we find a similar remarkable fact. While they point out in the usual fashion the two Advents, the first in humiliation, the second in glory, they also introduce the idea that Christ

[1] Some of the 'prophecies' of the Cross are remarkable, e.g. Deuteronomy xxviii. 66 (LXX), 'thy life shall be hanging before thine eyes'. This actually means 'shall be in suspense', but the words are repeatedly referred to the Crucifixion; Irenaeus, Cyprian, Tertullian, Athanasius.

[2] cf. Justin, *Dialogue with Trypho*, xxxii. l-lii; Tert., *Adv. Marcion*, iii. 7, etc.

is reigning now, He is now on the right hand of God and He reigns 'from the tree'. There is thus an uneasy compromise between two conflicting views. Side by side with the view of a literal kingdom on earth to be set up at the Parousia, there is the conception of a spiritual kingdom now in operation, whose centre and symbol is the Cross—the thought which lived on from the teaching of Jesus and of which Christianity never lost sight.

It thus appears that they had not really made up their minds on the question: Has the reign of Christ begun or not? Was it inaugurated by the Cross and Resurrection or is it to begin with the Parousia? Is it a kingdom of love and attraction, or one of miracle and coercion? They halt between two opinions, and the genuine teaching of Jesus on the subject lived on in uneasy juxtaposition with the crude literalism of the millennarians. Two instances may be quoted: Justin, who is most insistent on the 'thousand years in Jerusalem', nevertheless writes: 'The Spirit of prophecy . . . intimated that Christ, after He had been crucified, should reign.' Then follows a long quotation from Psalm xcvi, ending with the words, 'The Lord hath reigned from the tree' (1 *Apol.* xli). Tertullian (in *Answer to the Jews*, xiv) deals with the objection that Christ was not a figure of glory by insisting on the two Advents; all that was missing in the first would be supplied in the second.

And thus to the present moment they [i.e. the Jews] affirm that their Christ is not come, because He is not come in majesty; while they are ignorant of the fact that He was first to come in humility, etc.

But a few sentences later he finds the fulfilment of Psalm ii, with its picture of universal dominion and of a king whose inheritance reaches to the ends of the earth, in—

the Son of God who has already illuminated the whole world with the rays of His Gospel. . . . For at the present day nations are invoking Christ which used not to know Him; and peoples at the present day are fleeing in a body to the Christ of whom in days gone by they were ignorant. You cannot contend that that is future which you see taking place...[1]

[1] In some parts of the N.T. (apart from Revelation) there is an inconsistency which is somewhat similar. Some of the writers speak at times as though some great divine inbreaking is imminent, the end of all things is at hand. Yet they also speak as men who stand already within the New Age. In Hebrews, for example, there are passages which imply that a great 'shaking' is to take place at any time, and the long-expected divine order will come. But there are other passages which say just as plainly that the New Age has already begun; even now we have come to the New Jerusalem; the New Covenant which was to function in the Messianic Age is already in operation in the Christian dispensation (viii). The writer sees that there is a line of demarcation between the Two Ages, but cannot decide on which side of the line he (or she) stands.

Thus in the N.T. there is a vivid realization that the Kingdom has come in Christ, the days of fulfilment have already dawned; but side by side with this, there is a feeling in some parts that Christians are living in an interlude, a mere prologue.

There is, of course, a sense in which a tension between present and future is necessary to Christianity, but this is different from indecision concerning spiritual principles. The note of hope is vital to Christianity, which can never regard the present world and life in the body as final. The Christian must always look forward—both to the time when the will of God will be done perfectly on earth as in heaven, and to the time in his personal experience when he will know as he has been known and when he will see face to face. But though we see not yet all things subjected to Him, we see Jesus crowned.

CHAPTER 25

PAULINE AND JOHANNINE TEACHING

THE idea of development in Paul's thought has some-times been exaggerated and sometimes denied altogether. But if his letters are read in chronological order it is difficult to avoid the impression that his thought under-went important modifications, especially in eschatology, as the years passed and as his spirit deepened. There was at least a change of emphasis. (It is perhaps suggestive that the word *Parousia* is used six times of the Advent of Christ in the brief Thessalonian letters and occurs only once again in that sense in all the remaining letters, I Corinthians xv. 23.)

In his earliest letters, the Parousia is regarded as near and bizarre apocalyptic details are prominent. In Romans, however, a longer interval before the Parousia is implied; the process of Gentile evangelization is to con-tinue, and all Israel is finally to be saved (xi. 25–7). Though in xiii. 10 we still have the language of urgency, the process outlined in ix-xi surely called for considerable time: as the Jews' falling away meant Gentile enrichment, so their conversion will mean 'life from the dead', xi. 11 *ff*.

Bousset made the interesting suggestion that the idea expressed in the words 'all Israel shall be saved' was derived from the Antichrist legend.[1] He shows that those fleeing to the mountains in the Little Apocalypse were originally the faithful Jews flying from Antichrist. Further, the return of the lost tribes was early grafted on the Antichrist legend; this explains the 144,000 sealed from the twelve tribes in Revelation vii. The Christian version of the legend, as revealed in the Fathers, retained

[1] cf. *Antichrist Legend*, pp. 215, etc.

this point that there would be faithful Jews at the time of Antichrist and in some writers it was connected with the work of Elijah; cf. Augustine, *City of God*, xx. 30: 'Elijah shall come, the Jews shall believe, Antichrist shall persecute, Christ shall judge.' Bousset writes: 'Most significant is it that we can now understand how Paul (Romans xi. 26) came to speak of a conversion of Israel in the last days.' But whether or not Bousset is right in tracing here the influence of the Antichrist legend, it is clear that the Apostle is speaking, not of a mere detail in a brief apocalyptic programme, but of a great spiritual event with far-reaching effects.

Yet though Romans ix-xi represents a stage beyond 1 and 2 Thessalonians it is not Paul's final position. He still believes that there is a place for Israel *qua* Israel in the divine purpose.

The final stage is found in Ephesians. The Pastoral letters are not quoted here, since they are generally held to be non-Pauline, though containing Pauline elements. Ephesians is the climax and coping-stone of his thought, and though it too is held by some authorities to come from Pauline circles rather than the Apostle himself, the arguments against its genuineness are not conclusive and its wealth of thought seems to demand a Paul for its author.[1] In this great Epistle or treatise, the emphasis is on the Church and its reconciling ministry. It is the purpose of God to sum up all things in Christ, and in this cosmic process the Church is His instrument. Even now the barrier between Jew and Gentile has been broken down, and finally harmony in the whole universe is to be achieved. It is through the Church, the body of Christ, that God's eternal purpose is to be realized and His manifold wisdom made known. No mention is made of the Second Advent at all, but some future consummation is

[1] E. F. Scott (Moffatt Commentary) argues strongly for the conservative view.

hinted at in the phrase 'the day of redemption' (iv. 30). A distinctive task for Israel in the future is not now envisaged as part of the divine plan; the eternal purpose is rather the creation from Jews and Gentiles alike of the new community, making of the twain one new man.

It is not suggested that Paul ever relinquished his belief in the Parousia, but it ceased to occupy the centre of his interest. He came to see more in those parts of the divine purpose which had already received their fulfilment in Christ. It was not simply that his thought deepened, but in his missionary labours he saw 'God in action' and the deeper message came, not through detached reasoning, but through seeing with his own eyes the deed of God in the building up of a world-community in Christ. It is significant that the development in his thought took place during the fourteen years or so of his missionary labours, not in the similar period which preceded this task. In his case fuller insight came not through solitude and study but through strenuous service in which he witnessed the Gospel in action.

It was also his understanding of the Cross which enabled Paul to rise above the imperfect message with which he began. In 1 Corinthians i he admits that to men the Crucifixion appeared to be weakness and foolishness. The Jews were seeking some display of divine power, some unmistakable divine intervention; and in reply Paul points to the Cross, maintaining that there in the revelation of divine love was the power and wisdom of God. Here we have the heart of the Gospel and the true corrective of the apocalypticism with which the Church itself was in danger of being obsessed in those early days. This message, too, is in line with what we found in the teaching of Jesus.

This development in Paul's thought is not the result of a brilliant and original mind inventing new conceptions. It is rather the emergence of an element present all along, but which finally won its way to the central place, shedding cruder thoughts which at first hid its full meaning. Paul's final message is in harmony with the teaching of His Lord. (Is not Ephesians implicit in the sayings about building a new temple made without hands, the little flock, etc.?)

It is easy to understand that some who had been looking for a display of power and a catastrophic judgement were frankly disappointed with the first advent. We remember the querulous inquiry of John the Baptist, 'Art thou he that should come or look we for another?'—the early Christians did not look for 'another' but they looked for this same Jesus to come back and fulfil the main part of His task in a more realistic spirit. They were too near to the life of Jesus to grasp its significance or to foresee its results. And so, instead of abandoning their earlier expectations, many merely projected them into the future. As we have seen, the Church all along had the true answer to these difficulties in the teaching of a present spiritual kingdom centring in the Cross, the teaching which goes back to Jesus Himself. It is instructive to see how in Paul's writings this fundamental message gradually comes to the fore while fervid apocalypticism recedes. The Parousia is retained partly because of its association with the Last Judgement, and partly because it provides a denouement to mark the victorious consummation. In individual life this consummation is found in eternal life beyond the grave and in being with Christ. In the life of mankind it is found in some glorious climax when God shall be all in all. Finality has not yet been reached but even now Christ is enthroned far above all rule and authority (Ephesians i. 20–1).[1]

---

[1] It is possible that Luke remained at the stage represented by Romans xi, in which there is a place for Israel as such after the period of Gentile evangelization. In Luke xxi, Jerusalem is to be trampled down 'until the times of the Gentiles be fulfilled'. This may imply that Israel's fortunes will then turn. At all events, the language is reminiscent of Romans xi; 'until the

In the *Fourth Gospel* there is a clear understanding that a New Age has dawned in human history with the coming of Jesus, and transmuted eschatology finds itself thoroughly at home in these pages. John[1] leads us to find the decisive divine event not in the future coming of Christ, which is barely mentioned (xiv. 3, xxi. 22), but in His first coming. Guided by the prologue, we shall not speak of 'divine intervention' so much as the culmination of a long development in the Incarnation, subsequent history being the outworking of this central fact of the human story. Here we have the present spiritual kingdom and the salvation of the world through the attraction of the Cross:

xviii. 36: My kingdom is not of this world.

xii. 24: Except a grain of wheat fall into the earth and die, it abideth by itself alone; but if it die, it beareth much fruit.

32: And I, if I be lifted up from the earth, will draw all men unto Myself (cf. iii. 14 *ff.*)

The glory of Christ is not something which is to follow in the future as a contrast to His sufferings; His sacrifice is His glorification:

When therefore Judas was gone out, Jesus saith, Now[2] is the Son of man glorified, and God is glorified in him, and God shall glorify him in himself, and straightway shall he glorify him (xiii. 31–32).

[1] 'John' is used (as in the case of Matthew and the First Gospel) as an abbreviation for 'writer of the Fourth Gospel'.
[2] The word 'now' thus roughly corresponds to the 'from now' in the reply to Caiaphas (Matthew xxvi. 64; Luke xxii. 69; cf. Chapter 6).

---

fulness of the Gentiles be come in' (25); then 'all Israel shall be saved' (26).

A tradition of this kind persisted, and the repentance of the Jews was regarded as a sign of the approaching Advent (see e.g. Apocalypse of Peter: M. R. James, *Apocryphal New Testament*, p. 511). This scheme is possibly reflected in Acts iii. 19–21, where it has been put into Peter's speech, and where again the repentance of the Jews is linked with the return of Christ. Here too there is an 'until', and certain 'times' in the divine plan must be awaited.

The Passion and its sequel are included in one complex whole as the climax of His glorification.

By the time when John was written, about the end of the first century, the Parousia, the Resurrection, and the Judgement held a firm place in the Christian tradition,[1] and they are clearly accepted in the Johannine presentation (xiv. 3, xxi. 22, v. 28–9, vi. 39 *ff*., xii. 48), but they occupy a minor position. John certainly has an 'eschatology' in the sense that every one with any beliefs at all concerning the great issues of immortality and the close of human history is an eschatologist, but 'apocalyptic' (which is a particular form of eschatology) is not represented in these pages. Apocalyptic finds its centre in the future; its main concern is with some great divine interposition that shall bring the evil and intolerable present to a sudden close. The Book of Revelation has this attitude; it is concerned with 'things which must shortly come to pass' (i. l). But the Fourth Gospel does not find its centre here; nor is it an ellipse with the two Advents as its foci. Its theme is the One whose glory has already dawned on the world, who is even now the life and light of men. God's great help and deliverance for men is not something to be hoped for; it is offered now in Christ, and those who receive Him have eternal life as a present possession. The irruption of the divine order is inaugurated, not by the Parousia, but by the Incarnation. Through the Cross, Christ will draw all men unto Himself. He died to gather into one the children of God that are scattered abroad (xi. 52), including other sheep 'who are not of this fold' (x. 16). His finality is not static, for the Spirit will continually take of the things of Christ unfolding new truth from this inexhaustible source as men are able to bear.

---

[1] The words concerning Christ as judge of 'quick and dead' (1 Peter iv. 5; Acts x. 42; 2 Timothy iv. 1) appear to reflect a time when the Christian message was hardening into fixed terms; cf. the Creeds.

John in all probability knew the Gospels of Mark and Luke,[1] and it is significant that, while in their pages the Last Discourse of Jesus with His disciples takes the form of the apocalyptic utterances of Mark xiii and Luke xxi, in John the Last Discourse is of a very different character. It is true that the Parousia is mentioned in xiv. 3,[2] as we have seen, but the main thought is of a coming of a very different kind:

If a man love me, he will keep my word, and my Father will love him, and we will come unto him, and make our abode with him (xiv. 23).

More prominent still is the coming of the Holy Spirit, who at times seems to be Jesus Himself coming in a new way.

One feature of the Gospel which runs throughout is the message that what men seek, often in distant places and times, is present before them in Jesus. The woman of Samaria looks for the Messiah in the future, but Jesus replies: 'I that speak unto thee am He.' The paralytic mourns the absence of friends to dip him in the pool, but Jesus says: 'Arise, take up thy bed, and walk.' The disciples discuss hypothetical supplies of bread which might satisfy the multitude, but Jesus proceeds to feed them; and when later they look back to the bread supplied

---

[1] cf. W. F. Howard, *The Fourth Gospel*, pp. 144 *ff*.; but see his later *Christianity According to St. John*, p. 17.

[2] The remaining references to Christ's coming to His disciples in this discourse, and their relation to the promise of the Paraclete, are still being debated. The meaning of xiv. 18 is brought out by the verses which follow. A manifestation to the disciples and not to the world (19, 22) could hardly apply to a return in visible glory concerning which it was believed that 'every eye should see Him'; and 23, which further develops the promise, excludes such an interpretation. xiv. 28 and xvi. 16 *ff*. appear to refer to the Resurrection; cf. xvi. 16, 'again a little while and ye shall see Me', 22, 'And ye therefore now have sorrow; but I will see you again, and your heart shall rejoice', with xx. 20, 'The disciples therefore were glad when they saw the Lord'. Further, 'that day' (23–6) is connected with the new way of prayer which Christ's glorification would make possible.

through Moses in the wilderness, Jesus declares: 'I am the Bread of Life.' Martha looks forward to the resurrection at the last day for re-union with her brother, but Jesus replies: 'I am the Resurrection and the Life.' So when Thomas is perplexed about 'the way', Jesus says: 'I am the Way.'[1] He is Himself the answer to every question and the satisfaction of every need.

We have seen that in the N.T. generally the old prophecies of a divine manifestation were referred to the future coming of Christ, while a few of them (like Isaiah xxxv and xl) were referred to His first coming. This latter conception is in line with John's thought, for to him the life of Jesus was an epiphany:

And the Word became flesh and dwelt among us, and we beheld his glory, . . .

No man hath seen God at any time; the only begotten Son, which is in the bosom of the Father, he hath declared him (i. 14, 18).

(This thought is even clearer if we accept the variant reading rendered by Moffatt: 'the divine One, the only Son.')

Led by this Gospel, we shall find the fulfilment of the old prayer for God to come with delivering power, not in some future crisis, but in Him 'who for us men and for our salvation came down from heaven and was incarnate by the Holy Ghost of the Virgin Mary and was made man'.

Lord shew us the Father, and it sufficeth us.
He that hath seen Me hath seen the Father.

[1] iv. 25–6, v. 7–8, vi. 7 *ff.*, vi. 31–5, xi. 23–5, xiv. 5–6.

Part Four

The Parousia in Jewish Writings of the Christian Era

CHAPTER 26

GENERAL CONSIDERATIONS

In some ways, this section may be regarded as a work of supererogation, for nothing adduced from later Jewish writings can alter the facts on which Parts One to Three have been based, and such works as 2 Esdras and 2 Baruch, coming as they do from the latter part of the first Christian century, are hardly relevant to our main inquiry, which was to find the origin of the Christian doctrine of the Parousia.

We have found a satisfactory answer to our original question and we have emphasized the fact that prior to the time of our Lord the general expectation was of a human Messiah who should be born on the earth. We saw too that the single exception to this view was to be found in the Similitudes of Enoch, but that the conception was basically different from that of the N.T., and the contention that Jesus accepted their teaching was dismissed, not merely as unproved, but as disproved. Further, we found no good evidence to support the pre-Christian date of the Similitudes.

Some reference, however, should be made to Jewish teaching of the Christian era, for if we find there the doctrine of a transcendent Messiah who is to descend in clouds—or this conception and that of a human king set forth as alternatives—the question of the origin of this

Jewish form of the doctrine will arise. Moreover, a doubt might be suggested to our minds by the following consideration: If the idea of a glorious Messianic descent proves to be prominent and frequent in this later literature, it would possibly provide grounds for assuming an earlier tradition, even though no pre-Christian literary evidence can be found. On the other hand, if such an idea is absent or rare, this will confirm our main argument. It would therefore be wise to round off the main contention by a brief account of the evidence.

There is no doubt about the fact that the prevailing thought throughout Jewish literature, whether B.C. or A.D., is of a Messiah who is born on earth. Justin Martyr's *Dialogue with Trypho the Jew* shows that in the second century the Jewish expectation was of a Son of David Messiah. Though Justin was a Christian, the beliefs he ascribes to the Jew are on the whole a reliable picture of the doctrines of that period. In xlix Trypho says: 'We all expect that Christ will be a man of men.' In viii he says: 'But Christ—if he has indeed been born, and exists anywhere—is unknown, and does not even know himself, and has no power until Elijah comes to anoint him, and make him manifest to all.' This marks no advance upon the view of Josephus, who knows nothing of any Messiah except the human king. The Jewish Prayer Book now in use shows that similar ideas still prevail:

'Give then glory, O Lord, unto Thy people, praise to them that fear Thee, hope to them that seek thee, and free speech to them that wait for Thee, joy to Thy land, gladness to Thy city, a flourishing horn unto David Thy servant, and a clear shining light unto the son of Jesse, Thine anointed, speedily in our days' (Service for New Year, Singer, p. 239).

Orthodox Judaism to-day does not countenance such a conception as a Messiah descending from the clouds.

The evidence shows that the Similitudes of Enoch did

not have any important influence on Jewish thought. It was the Christian Church which preserved and took over such writings as Enoch, 2 Esdras, 2 Baruch, etc., and the peculiar view of the Similitudes cannot be traced in later Jewish writings. As Charles wrote in *E.B.*, 224*b*:

It will be observed that the Messianic doctrine in this section [i.e. Enoch xxxvii-lxxi] is unique, not only as regards the other sections of Enoch, but also in Jewish literature as a whole.

It is important to notice that since many of the Jewish apocalypses have been preserved by the Christian Church we must be prepared for Christian interpolations in them. Some of these are obvious, e.g. the name of Jesus in 2 Esdras, but not all can be identified with certainty. As Harnack maintained, 'The Christians in receiving these Jewish apocalypses did not leave them intact, but adapted them with greater or lesser Christian additions (see Ezra, Enoch, Ascension of Isaiah)'; and again: 'Christians altered the text of the LXX in a Christian direction, just as they revised the Jewish apocalypses.'[1]

Another point is that in some ways Jewish thought has come under Christian influence. (The influence of one religion upon another may take the form of borrowing or the stimulation of a rival conception.)

This is especially the case with eschatology, and attention may be called to the article in the *Jewish Encyclopaedia* on 'Apocalyptic Literature (Neo-Hebraic)', where it is said: 'In the course of its development the Christian apocalyptic drew freely from later Jewish sources, which, on the other hand, were often influenced directly or indirectly by the apocalyptic of the Church.'[2] If, there-

[1] *History of Dogma*, I. 101, 114.

[2] That Jewish eschatology was influenced by Christian was also the opinion of Dr. Charles, who in the course of his commentary on Enoch wrote: 'No Jewish book except 2 Esdras teaches indubitably the doctrine of a general resurrection; and this may be due to Christian influence, as 2 Esdras cannot be earlier than A.D. 80.'

fore, in certain Jewish writings produced after the development of the Christian Parousia doctrine we find traces of a similar conception, and Christian interpolation is ruled out, the most likely explanation will be that they are due to Christian influence.

There may be a somewhat similar phenomenon in the emergence of the idea of a suffering Messiah in Judaism. Nothing of the kind can be traced before the rise of Christianity, but afterwards there are rare and occasional hints of this kind. It is probable that this development is the outcome of contacts with the Christian Church, which drew attention to O.T. passages apparently pointing in this direction. See *E.B.*, 3,063; also Bousset: 'The notion of a suffering and dying Messiah would seem to have been suggested by disputation with the Christians.'[1]

Whether something of a like nature took place in regard to the Parousia can only be decided by considering the literary evidence.

[1] *Antichrist Legend*, p. 103.

CHAPTER 27

APOCALYPTIC LITERATURE

2 *Baruch*

THE Syriac Apocalypse of Baruch, usually known as 2 Baruch, is dated A.D. 90. Some regard it as a unity, and others as a composite work with elements falling in the period A.D. 50–90. Only two verses have any bearing on the question of the Parousia:

xxix. 3: The Messiah will then begin to be revealed.

Something will be said concerning the word 'revealed' under 2 Esdras, but the point need not detain us now since, according to Charles, the true reading should probably be 'the principate of the Messiah will be revealed' as in xxxix. 7.

xxx. 1: 'And it will come to pass after these things, when the time of the advent of the Messiah is fulfilled, and he will return in glory, then all who have fallen asleep in hope of him shall rise again.'

It is difficult to regard this as a Jewish saying. The word 'return' suggests that the Messiah has been on the earth previously. I can only regard the passage as a Christian interpolation—not an uncommon feature of these apocalypses, as we have already seen.

Charles, however, in his commentary on the book (1896) writes:

'When the time of the advent of the Messiah is fulfilled,' etc. This can have only one meaning, and this is that, at the close of His reign, the Messiah will return in glory to heaven. The word translated advent is [here he gives the Syriac], which in turn was an ordinary rendering of παρουσία. Now παρουσία can mean, not only 'coming' or 'advent', but also 'presence' (cf. 2 Corinthians x. 10; 2 Maccabees xv. 21; and probably 2 Corinthians vii. 6–7; 2 Thessalonians ii. 9). Hence we should render: 'When the time of the presence of the Messiah is fulfilled.'

'Return in glory.' These words imply that the Messiah pre-existed in heaven before His advent. He returns whither He had come. This is also the teaching of Enoch xlvi. 1–2, xlviii. 3, lxii. 7, 2 Esdras xii. 32, xiii. 26 (?), xiv. 9. This seems also to be the legitimate interpretation of Psa. Sol. xviii. 6.

In 2 Esdras vii. 29–30, the Messiah and the righteous die at the close of the Messianic kingdom.

'Then all who have fallen asleep in hope of Him shall rise again.' The resurrection follows immediately on the return of the Messiah into heaven; on his death in 2 Esdras vii. 29–30. The words 'of him' cannot be original. The text was probably 'those who have fallen asleep in hope'; cf. LXX of Psalms xvi. 9. The corruption could have arisen easily in the Syriac. . . .

This interpretation is a very difficult one. The idea that the resurrection takes place when the Messiah goes away is most unlikely. The phraseology too has to be altered on this view, as the clause 'all who have fallen asleep in hope of Him shall rise again' is Christian language. It seems more natural to regard the passage as referring to a descent of the Messiah followed by the resurrection of those who died 'in hope of Him'. It must then be a Christian interpolation. Dalman says that xxix. 3 and xxx. 1 must both be struck out as glosses (*Words of Jesus*, p. 270; see also 296).

2 Esdras

This moving and tragic apocalypse was produced by the travail of Jerusalem's fall in A.D. 70, and the various parts of it are dated roughly in the 30 years which followed. Box gives 100–135 as the time of the final redaction.

The apocalypse is strictly found in iii-xiv of the Second

Book of Esdras; i-ii and xv-xvi are Christian and contain nothing relevant to our present inquiry. Consideration is usually restricted to iii-xiv.[1]

Box gives the following dates in his edition and commentary, *The Ezra-Apocalypse:*

iii-x: The Salathiel Apocalypse, A.D. 100; interspersed in these same chapters is the Ezra Apocalypse, which he dates before 70.

xi-xii: The Eagle Vision belongs to the period 69–96.

xiii: The Man from the Sea; before 70.

xiv: An Ezra piece dated after 70.

He also ascribes certain passages to the Redactor, and these include the important passage, vii. 26–44.

Our main concern is with the Messianic teaching of the book. In iii-x the Messiah is only to be found in vii. 28 *ff.* This context speaks of a temporary Messianic kingdom lasting 400 years; at the end of this period Messiah dies.

For my Son the Messiah shall be revealed, together with those who are with him, and shall rejoice the survivors 400 years. And it shall be, after these years, that my Son the Messiah shall die [the Latin has *filius meus Jesus*] and all in whom there is human breath. Then shall the world be turned into the primeval silence seven days, like as at the first beginnings; so that no man is left. And it shall be after seven days that the age which is not yet awake shall be roused, and that which is corruptible shall perish. And the earth shall restore those that sleep in her, and the dust those that are at rest therein. . . . And the Most High shall be revealed upon the throne of judgement; and then cometh the end (28–33).

In the Eagle Vision, xi-xii, the Messiah is the familiar Lion of David; but xii. 31–2 needs mention, as it implies his pre-existence:

This is the Messiah whom the Most High hath kept unto the end of the days who shall spring from the seed of David and shall come and speak unto them.

[1] See Oesterley, *Introduction to Books of the Apocrypha*, 1935, pp. 142 *ff.*

In xiii the Man from the Sea is obviously the Messiah, and his pre-existence is assumed; cf. xiii. 25:

Whereas thou didst see a man coming up from the heart of the sea: this is he whom the Most High is keeping many ages [*conservat multis temporibus*] and through whom he will deliver his creation.

Also xiii. 32:

And it shall be when these things shall come to pass, and the signs shall happen which I showed thee before, then shall my Son be revealed whom thou didst see as a man ascending.

In xiv, the 'Ezra piece', the heavenly pre-existence of the Messiah is implied in the words:

For thou [i.e. Ezra] shalt be taken up from among men and henceforth thou shalt remain with my Son, and with such as are like thee, until the times be ended (verse 9).

In Box's view, the pre-existent Messiah is confined to xiii, xiv, and the Redactor, the Redactor being responsible for the insertions in vii and xii. 32. Oesterley, however, takes a different view regarding vii. 26 *ff.* as an integral part of iii-x.

Some authorities find a Parousia strangely enough in the Man who arises from the sea and flies with the clouds of heaven (xiii). There is, however, a difference between descending from heaven and arising from the sea.

The words are either literal or figurative. If literal, then it is certainly not an advent from heaven in glory. If figurative, the meaning is that the Messiah emerges into the situation, whence is not stated.

It is probable, as several have maintained, that the writer is here using mythical material which he does not understand. It is possible that a sun-god lies behind the figure of the Man and that details from the O.T. have been added (e.g. Daniel ii. 45). Following a suggestion of

Gressmann's,[1] it may be said that there are signs of the Egyptian sun-god; as the sun arises from the eastern waters of the Nile and climbs up into heaven, sending forth great heat, so the Man arises from the waters, flies with the clouds, sends a fiery stream from his mouth. The mountains Bakhu and Manu in Egyptian lore marked the points at which the sun rose and set, and thus the sun at times appeared to be resting on the mountain peak— some such description as this may be connected with the mountain in the Esdras vision.

Whether this be the source, or one of the sources, or not, the Jewish writer has his own interpretation of the imagery; thus to him the sea is a symbol of mystery and concealment:

> Just as one can neither seek out nor know what is in the deep of the sea, even so can no one upon earth see my Son but in the time of his day (xiii. 52).

The mode of Messiah's coming is nowhere described in 2 Esdras as a glorious descent from the sky with angelic retinue. Those who approach the book with N.T. conceptions in their minds may read a Parousia in such a word as '*revealed*', which is used of the Man from the Sea, xiii. 32, and also in vii. 28. (Both passages have been quoted in full above.)

(*a*) Such words as 'appear' and 'revealed' can be used of a human Messiah, a son of David. According to one tradition, he would be unknown until Elijah made him manifest; he would be on earth, but would remain incognito until the time came for him to be revealed. Similar language was used to express the thought that when a certain stage of history was reached the time would be ripe for Messiah's appearance, viz. his birth as shoot of David or his public manifestation.

---

[1] *Der Messias*, 1929, p. 407.

cf. b San. 38a:[1]

Judah and Hezekiah, the sons of R. Hiyya . . . began by saying, The son of David cannot *appear* ere the two ruling houses in Israel shall have come to an end, viz. the Exilarchate in Babylon and the Patriarchate in Palestine, for it is written etc. . . .

Similarly, b Sukkah 52a:

Our Rabbis taught, The Holy One, blessed be He, will say to the Messiah, the Son of David (May he *reveal* himself speedily in our days!), 'Ask of me anything, and I will give it to thee. . . .'

The word 'reveal' is used of Gog and Magog (2 Baruch lxx. 7.):

Then the Most High will reveal those peoples whom He has prepared before and they shall come and make war with the leaders that shall then be left

and of Antichrist (2 Thessalonians ii. 8).

(*b*) But it appears that in 2 Esdras we have not merely an emergence from earthly concealment; cf. vii. 28, xii. 31–2, xiii. 25, xiv. 9, all quoted in full earlier.

'Those who are with him' in vii. 28 is explained by vi. 26, which evidently refers to Elijah and Enoch, often regarded as Messiah's forerunners:

And the men who have been taken up, who have not tasted death from their birth, shall appear. Then shall the heart of the inhabitants of the world be changed, and be converted to a different spirit (cf. Malachi iv. 6, the two witnesses of Revelation xi. etc.).[2]

---

[1] 'b San.' means, of course, the tractate 'Sanhedrin' in the Babylonian Talmud, just as 'j' refers to the Jerusalem Talmud. The folio numbers of the 1520–3 edition, Venice, are still used (98a, etc.).

The quotations from the Babylonian Talmud are here taken from the Soncino Press edition.

[2] Charles writes: 'Here [i.e. vii. 28] we have in germ the idea of a first resurrection of the saints to the temporary Messianic kingdom' (*Eschatology*, 2nd ed., 1913, p. 341).

The implication is that Messiah is reserved in heaven and this is distinct from earthly concealment. But even this does not warrant us in concluding that therefore he must make his appearance on earth by descending in glory; this is nowhere stated and we have no right to read it between the lines. The following considerations show that even a pre-existent Messiah could take up his work on earth without a Parousia as its prelude.

Elijah, we remember, was also reserved in heaven according to general belief; but some of Jesus' contemporaries regarded Him as the returned Elijah (Luke ix. 8: 'it was said by some that Elijah had appeared'); and the early Christians looked upon John the Baptist in this way. In their view, he had been reserved in heaven for centuries and had reappeared on the earth, but no Parousia was involved. A pre-existent Messiah, therefore, does not by any means involve an advent of the Parousia type.

It is true that Enoch xxxvii. *ff.* and 2 Esdras both regard the Messiah as pre-existent, but there are marked differences in the two conceptions. In Enoch Messiah appears with God for the judgement; in 2 Esdras Messiah does not judge—the judgement takes place 400 years later than his appearance and is most emphatically reserved for God. In v. 56–vi. 6, a passage of real eloquence, the question is asked, 'Show thy servant by whom thou wilt visit thy creation', and the reply closes with the words, '. . . through me alone and none other were they created; as also the End shall come through me alone and none other'. This passage is evidently a polemic and the writer may have had the Similitudes of Enoch in mind as well as the Christians. As Box puts it:[1]

The polemic is directed against views which were held by early Christians, but which were probably not confined to

[1] *Apocrypha and Pseudepigrapha*, II, 574.

Christian circles. At the same time it is possible that what the apocalyptic writer has in mind here is the Christian doctrine of the return of Christ in glory to judge the world.

The Assumption of Moses speaks of Moses as pre-existent but no one ever suggested that his earthly life began with a descent from the sky. 'Accordingly He designed and devised me and He prepared me before the foundation of the world, that I should be the mediator of His covenant' (i. 14). Mention may be made of the doctrine of the pre-existence of souls, if further proof is needed that this does not necessarily imply that earthly life will begin with a descent in glory; cf. Slavonic Enoch xxiii. 5: 'For all souls are prepared to eternity, before the formation of the world.'

2 Esdras xii. 31–2 confirms the view that the pre-existent Messiah was to enter upon his earthly task by arising from the Davidic family:

'This is the Messiah whom the Most High hath kept unto the end of the days, who shall spring from the seed of David and shall come and speak unto them.'

Sibylline Oracles

These oracles contain both Jewish and Christian elements and we cannot always distinguish them with certainty. The relevant passages come from Books iii and v.[1]

v. 414

There came from the wide heavenly spaces a blessed man, holding in his hands a sceptre which God put in his grasp, and he brought all into subjection (ἦλθε γὰρ οὐρανίων νώτων ἀνὴρ μακαρίτης . . .).

The date of this is given as the reign of Hadrian (A.D. 117–138). There are Christian elements in Book v, but

[1] cf. Lanchester in Charles's *Apocrypha and Pseudepigrapha*, II. 368 *ff.*

P

this passage is probably Jewish. Even so it may be nothing more than the exalted language used concerning kings in the Greek and Roman periods ('Hofstil'), and which became attached to the Jewish Messianic teaching. See Bousset,[1] who aptly compares Cicero's words concerning Pompey:

'*omnes nunc in iis locis Pompejum sicut aliquem non ex hac urbe missum, sed de caelo delapsum intuentur.*'[2]

iii. 652

And then from the sun God will send a king.

This may mean from the east, or it may be another example of 'Hofstil'. But, as it should probably be dated B.C., it has already been dealt with in Chapter 2.

v. 108–10

And then a king sent from God against him shall destroy all the mighty kings and the best of men. And so shall the judgement come from the Immortal upon men.

The date of this is *c.* A.D. 120–130. The words 'sent from God' do not refer to a Parousia; they are applied e.g. to John the Baptist in John i. 6.

v. 256–9 is obviously Christian:

Then there shall come from the sky a certain exalted man, whose hands they nailed upon the fruitful tree, etc. . . .

There is a Hebrew Elijah Apocalypse, written A.D. 261, which describes wars and attacks upon Israel. Then (according to the account given in the *Jewish Encyclopaedia* under 'Apocalyptic Literature') the Messiah whose name is Winon[3] appears from heaven accompanied by hosts of

---

[1] *Die Religion des Judentums* (ed. H. Gressmann, 1926), p. 226.

[2] See also the references given in the footnote on p. 21, *supra*.

[3] One name given to the Messiah in the Talmud is Yinnon. This was derived from Psalms lxxii. 17, where the קרי has שְׁמוֹ יִנּוֹן.

angels and engages in a series of battles. The Messianic kingdom lasts forty years. Antichrist is prominent and the work resembles the Apocalypse of the N.T., by which it may have been influenced.

A German translation of this Elijah Apocalypse may be found in Wünsche's *Aus Israels Lehrhallen: Kleine Midraschim*. Several times it is said that 'Messiah comes' and various dates for his coming are given, but nowhere is it said that he comes 'from heaven' as stated in the *Jewish Encyclopaedia*. The five volumes of Wünsche's work give a useful collection of Jewish apocalypses of the Christian era, but in none of them is there any mention of Messiah descending in visible glory. The Midrasch Wajoscha, Book of Zerubbabel, Midrasch Daniel, Mysteries of Simeon ben Jokkai, Prayer of Simeon ben Jokkai, Signs of the Messiah, and Messias-Haggada are among the relevant tractates included. All these have a great deal in common and obviously spring from the same tradition. They usually mention the tribulations which are to befall the Jews in the last times and refer to two Messiahs, the first being the son of Joseph who is slain by Armilus the man of sin, and the second the son of David who slays Armilus and reigns in glory.

In the Book of Zerubbabel, Messiah is said to have been born in the days of David and to be in seclusion at Rome, where he is bound until the time of the end. In the time of crisis he openly reveals himself and comes to Jerusalem. In the Mysteries of Simeon, the Messiah is not acknowledged by the Jews on his appearance. They reject him (Isaiah liii. 3 is quoted) and maintain that there is no other Messiah than the son of Joseph, who has already been killed. He hides himself from them, and when he comes later from his seclusion they recognize him as their leader. Daniel vii. 13 is quoted here, and in a few other places in this collection of apocalypses, but it is clear that the words imply merely the splendour and majesty of the

p*

Messiah. The point will arise again in the next chapter that when Jewish writers quote this passage of Daniel they do not envisage a descent from heaven.

Another recension of the Signs of the Messiah, different from that followed by Wünsche, may be found in Volume 52 of *Revue des études juives* (1906), where Marmorstein gives the Hebrew original and a translation into French. Here it is said that God will bring the Messiah, son of David, from His prison. 'He will come forth from prison as a king and will ride on the clouds, as it is written, Behold, He came with clouds. . . .'[1]

---

[1] The *Ascension of Isaiah* does not need to be dealt with here, as the Parousia is only mentioned in the part known to be Christian. The Jewish part (the Martyrdom of Isaiah) has nothing concerning a Messiah.

The *Apocalypse of Abraham*, *c.* A.D. 100, a Jewish book with Christian interpolations, may be mentioned on account of iii. 1: 'And then I will sound the trumpet out of the air, and will send mine Elect One, having in him all my power, one measure; and this one shall summon my despised people from the nations, and I will burn with fire those who have insulted them and who have ruled among them in this Age.' The word 'send' does not necessarily imply a Parousia, and according to Box (S.P.C.K. ed., 1917) the Messiah in this work is a divinely endowed man who is sent by God at the appointed time. He refers to Galatians iv. 4, John xvii. 3, in connection with the word 'sent'.

CHAPTER 28

RABBINIC WRITINGS

ONE or two references in rabbinic writings are some-times alleged to refer to Messiah's descent from the sky:

b San. 98a

R. Alexandri said: R. Joshua b. Levi pointed out a contra-diction. It is written, in its time (will the Messiah come), whilst it is also written, I (the Lord) will hasten it. (Isaiah lx. 22 for both)—If they are worthy, I will hasten it: if not (he will come) at the due time.

R. Alexandri said: R. Joshua opposed two verses: it is written, And behold, one like the son of man came with the clouds of heaven; whilst (elsewhere) it is written, (behold, thy king cometh unto thee) lowly, and riding upon an ass!—If they are meritorious, (he will come) with the clouds of heaven; if not, lowly and riding upon an ass.

Joshua's date is about A.D. 250.

At first sight this passage appears to imply that in one case, 'if they are meritorious', the Messiah will descend from heaven, and in the other, 'if not', he will be an earthly king.

In that case it might even be suggested that the Chris-tian demonstration that in the O.T. there were two distinct strands of Messianic teaching—one concerning a figure of glory and another of suffering—had driven the Jews to the view that the two sets of prophecies were alternative; they were not successive in their operation, as the Christians alleged, but the condition of the people would determine which of the two would be fulfilled.

But this interpretation can hardly be sustained. Though Daniel vii. 13 is here regarded as a reference to the Messiah, it should be taken as symbolic as in all rabbinic references to it. The meaning of this passage may be that in one case he will be a figure of lowliness, and in the other a figure of glory.

Rashi,[1] however, in his comment on the Sanhedrin passage, referred to the 'clouds' as symbolizing the speedy coming of the Messiah in contradistinction to the slow pace, symbolized by the 'ass'. This interpretation is supported by the earlier part of the passage quoted, in which the words 'I will hasten it' are contrasted with 'in its time'.

Daniel vii. 13 is often referred to the Messiah by the rabbis, but the coming with clouds is regarded as symbolic by all Hebrew commentators. This is in agreement with the view of orthodox Judaism to-day. R. Saadia (early tenth century) took the clouds to indicate 'the great magnificence and power which God shall give unto the Messiah'.

In the Midrash on Psalm xxi. 7, R. Samuel ben Nachman joins Daniel vii. 13 with Jeremiah xxx. 21 (which reads, 'And I will cause him to draw near, and he shall approach unto Me'). He adds: 'Behold in what manner? The angels shall bring him into the midst of them.' This suggests that the clouds are symbolic of angels and that the coming is not an advent to the earth, but rather Messiah's approach to God. An approach to God is, of course, what the passage originally described.

'Anani', or cloud-man, as a Messianic title is connected with this use of Daniel vii. 13. In the Midrash Tanchuma it is said that Anani, who appears last in the Davidic line in 1 Chronicles iii. 24, is the Messiah:

Who is Anani? This is 'king Messiah', as it is said: I saw in night visions and behold with the clouds of (Anani) heaven, etc.

cf. *b San. 96b*, where the Messiah is called 'Bar-Nafle'. A footnote mentions υἱὸς νεφέλων as a possible derivation, but R. Nachman takes the word as denoting 'Son of the fallen', with reference to Amos ix. 11, '*ha-nofeleth*'. In that case Bar-Nafle is connected with the

---

[1] I owe this point to Rabbi Isidore Epstein.

Hebrew נפל (fall) rather than the Greek νεφέλη (cloud).[1]

Another passage from the Talmud may be included:

b San. 38b

. . . How explain Till thrones are placed? One (throne) was for Himself and one for David. Even as it has been taught: one was for Himself and one for David: this is R. Akiba's view. R. Jose protested to him; Akiba, how long wilt thou profane the Shechinah? Rather, one (throne) for justice, and the other for mercy. Did he accept (this answer) from him or not? Come and hear! For it has been taught: one is for justice and the other for charity; this is R. Akiba's view. Said R. Eleazar b. Azariah to him: Akiba, what hast thou to do with Aggada? . . . But one was a throne, the other a footstool: a throne for a seat and a footstool in support of His feet.

This is apparently the source of the view that R. Akiba identified the human figure of Daniel vii. 13 with the Messiah. But it will be noticed that 13 is not under discussion, but the thrones of 9. We know that in the struggle with Rome in the second century A.D. Akiba recognized Bar Cochba as Messiah.

The results of this chapter are entirely negative and of the previous chapter nearly so. No survey of this kind can claim to be exhaustive and fresh records are still coming to light, while those already discovered are not all accessible; but the evidence shows that references to a Messianic descent are very rare indeed, and occur in apocalyptic writings in which on other grounds Christian influence is suspected. This confirms the previous contention that the Parousia is a Christian doctrine.

[1] A quotation from the Zohar may perhaps be mentioned here, *Tol'doth*: 'Some blessings have been fulfilled in this world, and the rest will be fulfilled on the advent of the Messiah, when Israel will be one nation on earth and one people of the Holy One, blessed be He. . . . And they will exercise dominion both on high and here below, as it is written, "And, behold, there came with the clouds of heaven one like unto a Son of man" (Daniel vii. 13), alluding to the Messiah, concerning whom it is also written: "and in the days of those kings shall the God of heaven set up a Kingdom" (Daniel ii. 44).'

EPILOGUE

THE firm hold which the Second Advent has had upon Christian thought is partly due, as suggested earlier, to the need felt for a denouement of some kind to human history. If the doctrine was not a part of Jesus' message and arose in the way indicated, the question arises: What then is to be the future destiny of the human race?

The question is perhaps one for constructive theology rather than Biblical exegesis. Our inquiry, a search for origins, has been mainly historical; but it may be pointed out that such passages as John xii. 32, the Epistle to the Ephesians, the Parables of the Mustard Seed and the Leaven, encourage us to look for a world-wide triumph of the Gospel. We noted earlier the old pagan view of a world that was wearing out and becoming effete, and it must be admitted that this pessimistic outlook has often invaded Christian thought. But Clement of Alexandria struck the authentic Christian note when he said that Jesus turned sunset into sunrise. The Gospel came with a message of hope to a decaying world and assured men that the Dayspring from on high had visited them.[1]

It is sometimes said that belief in progress is a modern, post-Darwinian idea; but the following quotation is not taken from the *Origin of Species* but from Origen, the Christian Father:

If, as Celsus says, all did as I do, then the barbarians also would receive the Divine Word and become the most moral and gentle of men. All other religions would cease from the earth and Christianity alone would be supreme, which indeed is destined one day to have the supremacy, since the divine truth is continually bringing more souls under its sway (*Contra Celsum*, viii. 68).

[1] cf. John Foster, 'Eschatology and the Hope of a New World, *Expository Times*, Vol. liv, pp. 10 ff., October, 1942.

As the late Dr. Temple reminded us,[1] we are still living in the days of the early Church. Yet already sufficient has happened to confirm the Christian belief that God's purpose is to sum up all things in Christ. The emergence of a world Church through the modern missionary movement, as evidenced, for example, in the Tambaram Conference of 1938, has shown that Christ appeals to every colour and nation. He alone can unite the world into a living fellowship. He alone can provide the framework of a world civilization. The infant Christ did not disdain the gifts of the Magi, and just as the N.T. appropriates the Stoic conception of the 'conscience' and makes use of Platonic elements, so the Kingdom of Christ can assimilate and use all that is good and true in every culture.

Evolution does not mean the advance of every species. It calls attention to a selective process; new types emerge which shoot forward and oust the others. This long process shows that some mutations are rewarded, others disastrous. In man the genetic process of selection gives place to a cultural one, and biology yields to history, and the principle of selection is continued in a new way. Running through the whole process, certain broad trends can be traced. Victory does not always belong to the swift and the strong, or even to the cunning; but co-operation and mutual help have greater survival value than brute force. One may even claim support from biology for the view that the meek will inherit the earth:

The geological record is full of cases where the development of enormous horns and spines (sometimes in the male sex only) has been the prelude to extinction. It seems probable that in

[1] 'The earth will in all probability be habitable for myriads of years yet. If Christianity is the final religion, the Church is still in its infancy. Two thousand years are as two days. The appeal to the "primitive Church" is misleading; we are the primitive Church' ('The Church', in *Foundations* (ed. Streeter), p. 340).

some of these cases the species literally sank under the weight of its own armaments (J. B. S. Haldane).[1]

This law operates in human history; empires which copy the methods of the tyrannosaurus end in the same place—the museum. Tiglath Pileser and his imposing empire are to-day a mere memory; but the words of his humble contemporary, Amos the herd-man, still resound in the world. And the empire of the thorn-crowned Nazarene is the most enduring of all.

But even if the Gospel does triumph and the meek inherit the earth, we are told that life will be impossible beyond a certain point, and that the human race will be extinguished either by fire or frost. This, however, assumes that the universe is a self-contained system and takes no account of the continuing activity of God—such activity as is implied in the words: 'My Father worketh even until now, and I work.' The idea that the universe is a self-enclosed whole and that the mere passage of time brings out certain latent possibilities is absurd. Upon this world there is the pressure and penetration of a higher world. To a Christian, the conception of a world isolated from God is a figment of the imagination; for He upholds all things by the word of His power.

Moreover, man has been endued with such enormous powers that he can control the forces of Nature. This control is continually increasing and no one can set any limits to its possible advance. There was a time when life was confined to the sea. To an angelic observer, it would have seemed impossible that forms of life could ever maintain themselves on the dry land—yet this has happened. So to-day it seems unlikely that man's power can extend beyond the earth; but if millions of years lie before the race, who knows what developments may occur?

Man alone, according to Julian Huxley,[2] has the power

[1] *Causes of Evolution*, p. 120.   [2] *The Uniqueness of Man*.

of further advance; all other creatures have reached the limit of their particular lines of development. Man has the responsibility of the increasing control over Nature which is coming into his hands. Or, as the Bible puts it: 'Thou madest him to have dominion over the works of Thy hands' (Psalm viii). Man may ultimately be able to renew and wind up the universe. Already there is a sense in which he transcends it, for as a thinking reed he has the advantage of the powers which crush him. 'There is surely a piece of Divinity in us, something that was before the Elements, and owes no homage unto the Sun.'[1]

It may be that God will renew His creation, as the apocalyptists desired, not through His direct power, but through the mind of man. A great geneticist has written: 'There is no theoretical limit to man's material progress but the subjection to complete conscious control of every atom and every quantum of radiation in the universe.'[2] (If anything remotely resembling this ever takes place, the jibes about man's insignificance because of his diminutive size will be shown in their true worth.)

It may be said that this is purely a question of the improvement of scientific knowledge. But recent events have shown that man's increasing powers turn to worse than dust and ashes, unless there is the guidance of moral and spiritual ideals. 'The perfection of an evolving world can only come with the perfection of man.'[3] It is only in Christ that man can find true leadership and power. It is in Him that cosmic reconciliation will be achieved (Ephesians). It may be that finally the veil between this world and the next will be removed, and that Romans viii will have a grander fulfilment than any imagined by its writer:[4]

---

[1] Sir Thos. Browne, *Religio Medici*.
[2] J. B. S. Haldane, *The Inequality of Man* (p. 144 in Pelican ed.).
[3] C. Ryder Smith, *The Christian Experience*, p. 286.
[4] cf. C. Ryder Smith, *op. cit.*, pp. 284–90.

Even the creation waits with eager longing for the sons of God to be revealed . . . the hope being that creation as well as man would one day be freed from its thraldom to decay and gain the glorious freedom of God's children.[1]

[1] Romans viii. 19, 21 (Moffatt). It should be noted that the tentative suggestions made in this Epilogue do not necessarily follow from the main body of the work; it would be possible to accept the earlier argument and to envisage quite a different picture for the future course of history. Even if the doctrine of the Parousia did come from O.T. conceptions, it does not follow by any means that there is therefore no place for it in Christian thought; it may still be the case that belief in some 'Day of the Lord' is quite sound. We may hold that the time will come when, through the power of the Gospel, 'the knowledge of the Lord will cover the earth'; or we may dismiss such a hope as 'Utopian' and regard the earth as a battle-ground of good and evil, a fit training-ground for immortal spirits. But whichever view we prefer, we may still believe that, in a way we cannot fully conceive, 'history will be consummated by some supreme manifestation of the presence and power of Christ.' Something of this kind is quite compatible with the suggestions made here.

The great truths which the Advent doctrine has preserved through the centuries (the final victory of Christ, the fact of judgment, the certainty of re-union) still remain even if we have to express them in new ways.

TEXTUAL INDEX

GENERAL INDEX

Printed in Great Britain by
The Camelot Press Ltd., London and Southampton